How to Comply
with Sarbanes-Oxley Section 404

How to Comply with Sarbanes-Oxley Section 404

Assessing the Effectiveness of Internal Control

Michael Ramos

WILEY

John Wiley & Sons, Inc.

Published by John Wiley & Sons, Inc., Hoboken, New Jersey.
Published simultaneously in Canada

For general information on our other products and services, or technical support, please contact our Customer Care Department within the United States at 800-762-2974, outside the United States at 317-572-3993 or fax 317-572-4002.

Wiley also publishes its books in a variety of electronic formats. Some content that appears in print may not be available in electronic books.

For more information about Wiley products, visit our Web site at *www.wiley.com.*

Library of Congress Cataloging-in-Publication Data:

Ramos, Michael J.
  How to comply with Sarbanes-Oxley section 404 : assessing the effectiveness of internal control / Michael J. Ramos.
    p. cm.
  ISBN 0-471-65366-7 (CLOTH)
  1. Corporations—Accounting—Corrupt practices—United States. 2. Corporations—Accounting—Law and legislation—United States. 3. Disclosure of information—Law and legislation—United States. I. Title.
HF5686.C7 R348 2004
657'.95—dc22

                                        2003021211

Printed in the United States of America

10 9 8 7 6 5 4 3 2 1

About the Author

Michael Ramos was an auditor with KPMG. Since 1991 he has worked primarily as an author, corporate trainer, and consultant, specializing in emerging accounting and auditing matters. This is his eighth book.

Contents

Contents

Preface

I was a teenager when I first heard the phrase "the journey is the reward," which made sense because I'm basically a process-oriented person. Results are just a by-product of the journey. As I'm writing this I have a cup of coffee on my desk, and it occurs to me that the quality of the coffee is directly related to the process used to select the coffee beans, roast and grind them, and combine them with hot water. Measurable goals are important, but I try not to focus too much on output because so much of that is out of my control. As a writer, I can't guarantee that I'll write a book that will sell thousands of copies. All I can do is create a process that has a lot of integrity and that gives me every opportunity to write a good book. As for sales . . . well, I definitely have little say in that, but I do know that a prerequisite for good sales is a well-written book.

Increasingly, it seems we live in a society that emphasizes results, the first corollary to the adage "the ends justifies the means." Process doesn't matter, only results. It seems as though my notions of a quality process are a bit quaint in today's business society.

And then came Sarbanes-Oxley.

Sarbanes-Oxley is about process. For the last 70 or so years, the protection of the investing public focused primarily on the reporting of results. Provide the public with fair, transparent financial results, give them the information necessary to understand those results, and that was all they needed to make fully informed decisions. Sarbanes-Oxley changed that and said that the reporting of results alone is not sufficient. In addition to financial results, entities now have to analyze and evaluate the quality of the *processes* and controls used to report these results.

This new requirement on evaluating an entity's processes and controls is a significant shift in thinking. The practical implications of complying with this requirement are staggering, and it will be several years before we fully understand what these are. Evaluating a process is much different from analyzing a result. Process analysis is ambiguous, subjective, and nonlinear, and our repertoire of tools and techniques for performing such an evaluation is relatively limited. Expertise from a wide range of disciplines will be required to implement fully the requirements of Sarbanes-Oxley. Information technology, risk management, securities law, organizational development, and business process analysis—professionals from all of these areas have valuable contributions to make in the evaluation of internal control. In writing this book, I have drawn from all of these disciplines.

I am a CPA, an auditor by training, though it has been several years since I actively participated in an audit engagement. Auditors, too, bring a valuable perspective to the evaluation and reporting on internal control effectiveness. After all, the internal control evaluation and report focuses exclusively on financial reporting, which is the auditor's area of expertise. Management's report will be audited by the entity's independent auditors, and so the evaluation process used by management must dovetail with the expectations and requirements of the outside auditors. Many of the concepts, testing techniques, and reporting requirements of the new rules are drawn from the auditing literature. In writing this book, I wanted to use my knowledge of auditing to describe a process for internal control evaluation that was comprehensive and well structured. I also hope that the book reflects some of the qualities that I believe have served me well in my professional career—thoroughness, curiosity, and analytical integrity.

When I started writing this book, in April 2003, the final SEC rules on internal control reporting had not yet been published. Even today, as I finish the final revisions, critical standards from the PCAOB regarding the independent auditor's responsibilities for auditing internal control remain to be published in final form. Those of us who are involved in this area of the financial reporting process face a significant amount of uncertainty as we try to fulfill our responsibilities.

In a sense, this book is a work in progress, version 1.0, if you will. Over the ensuing months and years, the body of knowledge relating to the evaluation and reporting of internal control will expand rapidly. I anticipate the need to make continuous revisions as my own experience and knowledge about the topic continue to evolve.

Clearly, this edition of the book will not be the definitive work on the subject of internal control evaluation and control. At the time it was written, there was just too much uncertainty and lack of experience in the subject matter. My goal in writing this book was simply to gather as much information about the subject as possible, to sort through it, and then to apply my professional knowledge and skill in a way that organized it in a logical, easily accessible fashion.

Many people have questions about how to implement the requirements of the Sarbanes-Oxley Section 404 requirements. All I hoped to do was to think through these questions as thoroughly as possible and to share what I discovered with as many of you as possible.

MICHAEL RAMOS

September 2003

Acknowledgments

TECHNICAL ADVISORY BOARD

This book was written with the assistance of a technical advisory board. Board members have provided financial support, input, and feedback during the lengthy development of these materials. I am deeply indebted to the board members and their firms for their generous support, encouragement, and patience.

The members of the technical advisory board are:

L. Douglas Bennett
Partner, Director of Accounting
and Auditing
BKD, LLP

Gregory A. Coursen
Partner, Director of
Professional Standards
Plante & Moran, PLLC

Jeff Brown
Partner
Moss Adams, LLP

Krista M. Kaland
Partner, Director of Assurance Services
Clifton Gunderson LLP

John Compton
Partner
Cherry Bekaert & Holland, LLP

Michael C. Knowles
Partner
Frank, Rimerman & Co.

Bill Drimel
Assistant Director of Audit
and Accounting
Clifton Gunderson LLP

Travis Webb
Partner
BKD, LLP

OTHER ACKNOWLEDGMENTS

I am also grateful for several other individuals who have contributed technical advice and other support toward the development of these materials. These individuals are: Greg Ramos, Andy Blair, and David Schacter from Sherman and Howard LLC; Theresa Garcia of Trust, Leadership and Growth; Jennifer Wilson and her team at Convergence Coaching; the editors at *Compliance Week*; Bryan Polster,

Brian Kreischer and Randy Von Feldt of Frank, Rimerman; Richard MacAlmon of MarbleLogic; Rama Wong of Rama Design; Cindy Vindasius.

Finally, I would like to thank John DeRemigis for his enthusiasm for this project and the staff at Wiley, particularly Judy Howarth and Jennifer Hanley for their diligence and commitment to the book.

Chapter 1

The Engagement Approach

Chapter Summary

Overview of the Securities and Exchange Commission (SEC) rules requiring
- Management's assessment of the effectiveness of the entity's internal control over financial reporting,
- Independent auditors' audit of management's report on internal control, and
- Management's required quarterly reporting on the effectiveness of the entity's disclosure controls and procedures

Summary of the relevant auditing standards relating to internal control.

Description of a structured approach for the evaluation of an entity's internal control.

Suggestions for outside consultants on structuring an engagement to assist management in evaluating the effectiveness of internal control and preparing for an independent auditor's audit of management's internal control report.

MANAGEMENT'S REQUIRED ASSESSMENT OF THE ENTITY'S INTERNAL CONTROL

The Sarbanes-Oxley Act of 2002 made significant changes to many aspects of the financial reporting process. One of those changes is a requirement that management provide a report, both quarterly and annually, on the effectiveness of certain aspects of the entity's internal control over financial reporting. This chapter summarizes these reporting requirements. Chapter 8 provides more detailed guidance and examples.

Definition of Internal Control

For the purposes of complying with the internal control reporting requirements of the Sarbanes-Oxley Act, the SEC rules provide the working definition of the term *internal control over financial reporting*. Rule 13a-15 (f) defines internal control over financial reporting as follows:

> The term internal control over financial reporting is defined as a process designed by, or under the supervision of, the issuer's principal executive and principal financial officers, or persons performing similar functions, and effected by the issuer's board of directors, management and other personnel, to provide reasonable assurance regarding the reliability of financial reporting and the preparation of financial statements for

external purposes in accordance with generally accepted accounting principles and includes those policies and procedures that:

(1) Pertain to the maintenance of records that in reasonable detail accurately and fairly reflect the transactions and dispositions of the assets of the issuer;

(2) Provide reasonable assurance that transactions are recorded as necessary to permit preparation of financial statements in accordance with generally accepted accounting principles, and that receipts and expenditures of the issuer are being made only in accordance with authorizations of management and directors of the issuer; and

(3) Provide reasonable assurance regarding prevention or timely detection of unauthorized acquisition, use or disposition of the issuer's assets that could have a material effect on the financial statements.

When considering the SEC's definition, you should note the following:

- The term *internal control* is a broad concept that extends to all areas of the management of an enterprise. The SEC definition narrows the scope of an entity's consideration of internal control to the preparation of the financial statements—hence the use of the term "internal control *over financial reporting.*"
- The SEC intends their definition to be consistent with the definition of internal controls that pertain to financial reporting objectives that was provided in the Committee of Sponsoring Organizations of the Treadway Commission (COSO) Report. (See Chapter 2 for a detailed discussion of the COSO Report.)
- The rule makes explicit reference to the use or disposition of the entity's assets—that is, the safeguarding of assets.

This book, unless otherwise indicated, uses the term *internal control* to mean the same thing as "internal control over financial reporting," as defined by the SEC rules.

Annual Reporting

Section 404 of the Sarbanes-Oxley Act requires chief executive officers (CEOs) and chief financial officers (CFOs) to evaluate and report on the effectiveness of the entity's internal control over financial reporting. This report is contained in the company's Form 10K, which is filed annually with the SEC. The SEC has adopted rules for its registrants that effectively implement the requirements of the Sarbanes-Oxley Act, Section 404.

Under the SEC rules, the company's 10K must include[1]

(A) *Management's Annual Report on Internal Control Over Financial Reporting.* Provide a report on the company's internal control over financial reporting that contains:

(1) A statement of management's responsibilities for establishing and maintaining adequate internal control over financial reporting,

(2) A statement identifying the framework used by management to evaluate the effectiveness of the company's internal control over financial reporting

(3) Management's assessment of the effectiveness of the company's internal control over financial reporting as of the end of the most recent fiscal year, including a statement as to whether or not internal control over financial reporting is effective. This discussion must include disclosure of any material weakness in the company's internal control over financial reporting identified by management. Management is not permitted to conclude that the registrant's internal control over financial reporting is effective if there are one or more material weaknesses in the company's internal control over financial reporting, and

(4) A statement that the registered public accounting firm that audited the financial statements included in the annual report has issued an attestation report on management's assessment of the registrant's internal control over financial reporting

(B) *Attestation Report of the Registered Public Accounting Firm.* Provide the registered public accounting firm's attestation report on management's assessment of the company's internal control over financial reporting

(C) *Changes in Internal Control Over Financial Reporting.* Disclose any change in the company's internal control over financial reporting that has materially affected, or is reasonably likely to materially affect the company's internal control over financial reporting.

The company's annual report filed with the SEC also should include management's fourth-quarter report on the effectiveness of the entity's disclosure controls and procedures, as described in the next section.

Effective Dates. The requirement to disclose material changes in the entity's internal control (item (c) above) became effective on August 14, 2003. The effective date for the other provisions of the rules described above—that is, management's report on the effectiveness of internal control and the related auditor attestation—become effective at different times, depending on the filing status of the company.

- *Accelerated filer.* A company that is an accelerated filer as of the end of its first fiscal year ending on or after June 15, 2004, must begin to comply with the internal control reporting and attestation requirements in its annual report for that fiscal year.[2]
- *Nonaccelerated filer.* Smaller companies, foreign private issuers, and other nonaccelerated filers are required to comply with the full requirements of the new rules for their first fiscal year ending on or after April 15, 2005.

Quarterly Reporting

Section 302 of the Sarbanes-Oxley Act requires quarterly reporting on the effectiveness of an entity's "disclosure controls and procedures." Item 307 of SEC

Regulation S-K implements this requirement for the company's quarterly Form 10Q filings by requiring management to

> Disclose the conclusions of the company's principal executive and principal financial officers, or persons performing similar functions, regarding the effectiveness of the company's disclosure controls and procedures as of the end of the period covered by the report, based on the evaluation of these controls and procedures.

In addition to reporting on disclosure controls, the company's quarterly reports also must disclose material changes in the entity's internal control over financial reporting.

Note that for these quarterly filings

- Management is *not* required to evaluate or report on internal control over financial reporting. That evaluation is required on an *annual basis only*.
- The company's independent auditors are *not* required to attest to managements evaluation of disclosure controls.

Disclosure Controls and Procedures. With these rules, the SEC introduces a new term, *disclosure controls and procedures*, which is different from *internal controls over financial reporting* defined earlier. SEC Rule 13a-15(e) defines disclosure controls and procedures as those that are

> Designed to ensure that information required to be disclosed by the issuer in the reports that it files or submits under the Act is
>
> - Recorded
> - Processed,
> - Summarized, and
> - Reported
>
> within the time periods specified in the Commission's rules and forms. Disclosure controls and procedures include, without limitation, controls and procedures designed to ensure that *information required to be disclosed* by an issuer in the reports that it files or submits under the Act is *accumulated and communicated* to the issuer's management, including its principal executive and principal financial officers, or persons performing similar functions, as appropriate to allow timely decisions regarding required disclosure.

Thus, "disclosure controls and procedures" would encompass the controls over all material financial and nonfinancial information in Exchange Act reports. Information that would fall under this definition that would *not* be part of an entity's internal control over financial reporting might include the signing of a significant contract, changes in a strategic relationship, management compensation, or legal proceedings. Chapter 2 of this book provides additional guidance on disclosure controls and procedures and the effect these might have on management's assessment of the effectiveness of internal control.

The Disclosure Committee. In relation to its rule requiring an assessment of disclosure controls and procedures, the SEC also advised all public companies to create a disclosure committee to oversee the process by which disclosures are created and reviewed, including the

- Review of 10Q, 10K, and other SEC filings; earnings releases; and other public information for the appropriateness of disclosure
- Determination of what constitutes a significant transaction or event that requires disclosure
- Determination and identification of significant deficiencies and material weaknesses in the design or operating effectiveness of disclosure controls and procedures
- Assessment of CEO and CFO awareness of material information that could affect disclosure

The existence and effective operation of an entity's disclosure committee can have a significant effect on the nature and scope of your work to evaluate the effectiveness of the entity's internal control. For example:

- The effective functioning of a disclosure committee may be viewed as an element that strengthens the entity's control environment.
- The work of the disclosure committee may create documentation that engagement teams can use to reduce the scope of their work.

Management Certifications

In addition to providing a report on the effectiveness of its disclosure controls and internal control over financial reporting, the company's principal executive officer and principal financial officer are required to sign two certifications, which are included as exhibits to the entity's 10Q and 10K. These two certifications are required by the following sections of the Sarbanes-Oxley Act:

- Section 302, which requires a certification to accompany each quarterly and annual report filed with the SEC
- Section 906, which added a new Section 1350 to Title 18 of the United States Code, and which contains a certification requirement subject to specific federal criminal provisions. This certification is separate and distinct from the Section 302 certification requirement.

Exhibit 1.1 provides the text of the Section 302 certification. This text is provided in SEC Rule 13a-14(a) and should be used exactly as set forth in the rule.

Exhibit 1.1 Section 302 Certification, SEC Rule 13a-14(a)/15d-14(a)

I, [identify the certifying individual], certify that:

1. I have reviewed this [specify report] of [identify registrant];
2. Based on my knowledge, this report does not contain any untrue statement of a material fact or omit to state a material fact necessary to make the statements made, in light of the circumstances under which such statements were made, not misleading with respect to the period covered by this report;
3. Based on my knowledge, the financial statements, and other financial information included in this report, fairly present in all material respects the financial condition, results of operations and cash flows of the registrant as of, and for, the periods presented in this report;
4. The registrant's other certifying officer(s) and I are responsible for establishing and maintaining disclosure controls and procedures (as defined in Exchange Act Rules 13a-15(e) and 15d-15(e)) and internal control over financial reporting (as defined in Exchange Act Rules 13a-15(f) and 15d-15(f)) for the registrant and have:
   (a) Designed such disclosure controls and procedures, or caused such disclosure controls and procedures to be designed under our supervision, to ensure that material information relating to the registrant, including its consolidated subsidiaries, is made known to us by others within those entities, particularly during the period in which this report is being prepared;
   (b) Designed such internal control over financial reporting, or caused such internal control over financial reporting to be designed under our supervision, to provide reasonable assurance regarding the reliability of financial reporting and the preparation of financial statements for external purposes in accordance with generally accepted accounting principles;
   (c) Evaluated the effectiveness of the registrant's disclosure controls and procedures and presented in this report our conclusions about the effectiveness of the disclosure controls and procedures, as of the end of the period covered by this report based on such evaluation; and
   (d) Disclosed in this report any change in the registrant's internal control over financial reporting that occurred during the registrant's most recent fiscal quarter (the registrant's fourth fiscal quarter in the case of an annual report) that has materially affected, or is reasonably likely to materially affect, the registrant's internal control over financial reporting; and
5. The registrant's other certifying officer(s) and I have disclosed, based on our most recent evaluation of internal control over financial reporting, to the registrant's auditors and the audit committee of the registrant's board of directors (or persons performing the equivalent functions):
   (a) All significant deficiencies and material weaknesses in the design or operation of internal control over financial reporting which are reasonably likely to adversely affect the registrant's ability to record, process, summarize and report financial information; and
   (b) Any fraud, whether or not material, that involves management or other employees who have a significant role in the registrant's internal control over financial reporting.

Exhibit 1.2 provides an example of the Section 906 certification. Note that some certifying officers may choose to include a "knowledge qualification," as indicated by the optional language in italics. Officers who choose to include this language should do so only after consulting with their SEC counsel. Unlike the Section 302 certification, which requires a separate certification for both the CEO and CFO, the company can provide only one 906 certification, which is then signed by both individuals.

Subcertification. A great deal of the information included in financial statements and other reports filed with the SEC originates in areas of the company that are outside the direct control of the CEO and CFO. Because of the significance of information prepared by others, it is becoming common for the CEO and CFO to request those individuals who are directly responsible for this information to certify it. This process is known as *subcertification*, and it usually requires the individuals to provide a written affidavit to the CEO and CFO that will allow them to sign their certifications in good faith.

Items that may be the subject of subcertification affidavits include:

- Adequacy of specific disclosures in the financial statements or other reports filed with the SEC, such as *Management's Disclosure and Analysis* included in the entity's 10Q or 10K.
- Accuracy of specific account balances.
- Compliance with company policies and procedures, including the company's code of conduct.
- Adequacy of the design and/or operating effectiveness of departmental internal controls and disclosure controls.
- Accuracy of reported financial results of the department, subsidiary, or business segment.

THE INDEPENDENT AUDITOR'S REPORTING RESPONSIBILITIES

Exhibit 1.3 describes the relationship between the various rule-making bodies, companies, and their auditors regarding the reporting on internal control. As

Exhibit 1.2 Section 906 Certification, 18 U.S.C. Section 1350

In connection with the [annual/quarterly] report of [name of registrant] (the "Company") on Form (10K/10Q] for the period ended _____ (the "Report"), the undersigned in the capacities listed below, hereby certify, pursuant to 18 U.S.C. ss. 1350, as adopted pursuant to Section 906 of the Sarbanes-Oxley Act of 2002, that *to my knowledge*

(i) The Report fully complies with the requirements of Section 12(a) or 15(d) of the Securities Exchange Act of 1934; and

(ii) The information contained in the Report fairly presents, in all material respects, the financial condition and results of operations of the Company.

Exhibit 1.3   Relationship of the Rules, Regulations, and Standards

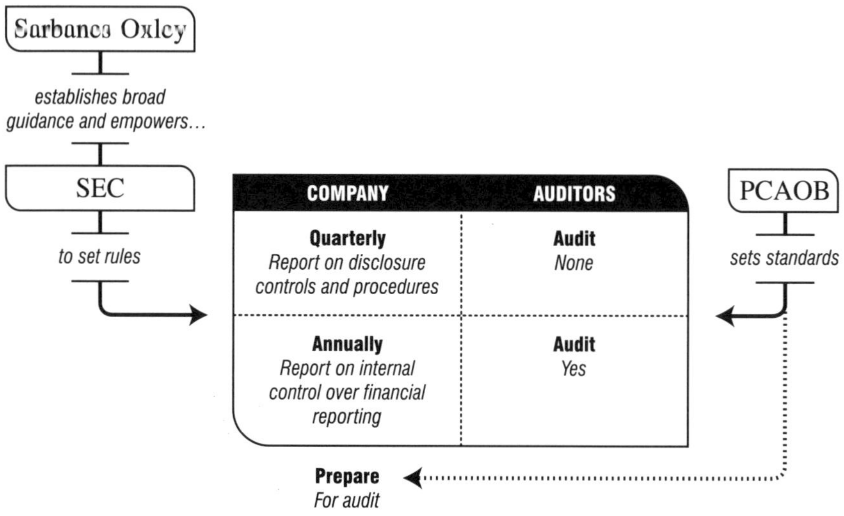

described previously, Sections 302 and 404 of the Sarbanes-Oxley Act require management of public companies to report on the effectiveness of the entity's internal control on an annual basis. The company's independent auditors are required to audit this report. The SEC is responsible for setting rules to implement the Sarbanes-Oxley Act requirements. Those rules include guidance for reporting by the CEO and CFO on the entity's internal control over financial reporting and disclosure controls, but they do not provide any guidance or set standards for the independent auditors. The Public Company Accounting Oversight Board (PCAOB) sets the auditing standards, which will have a direct affect on auditors and how they plan and perform their engagements.

In addition, the auditing standards will have an *indirect effect* on the company as it prepares for the audit of their internal control report. Just as in a financial statement audit, the company should be able to support its conclusions about internal control and provide documentation that is sufficient for the auditor to perform an audit. Thus, in preparing for the audit of its internal control report, it is vital for management, and those who assist them, to have a good understanding of what the independent auditors will require.

The Auditing Standard

Note to users: At the time this book was written, the PCAOB had just released a draft of a proposed auditing standard relating to the independent auditors audit of management's report on internal controls. The following overview is based on this *proposed* standard.

It is expected that this standard will become final by the time the first edition of this book is published. To more fully understand the independent auditor's requirements and how they affect your management's assessment process, you should obtain and read the final standard once it becomes available. The standard will be posted on the PCAOB Web site at *www.pcaobus.org*.

The PCAOB standard directly applies only to independent auditors and *not* to entities that perform their own, internal assessment of internal control. However, in providing guidance to auditors on what is required in an internal control audit, the standard will have a significant, *indirect* effect on the work performed by the entity. Once the final standard becomes available, you should obtain and read a copy of it with an eye toward careful consideration of the following issues.

Overall Objective of the Auditor's Engagement

The auditor's objective in an audit of internal control is to express an opinion about management's assessment of the effectiveness of the company's internal control over financial reporting. This objective implies a two-step process:

1. Management must perform its own assessment and conclude on the effectiveness of the entity's internal controls.
2. The auditors will perform their own assessment and form an independent opinion as to whether management's assessment of the effectiveness of internal control is fairly stated.

Thus, internal control is assessed twice, first by management and then by the independent auditors. That the auditors will be auditing internal control—and in some cases, reperforming some of the tests performed by the entity—does not relieve management of its obligation to document, test and report on internal control.

To form his or her opinion, the auditor will

- Evaluate the reliability of the process used by management to assess the entity's internal control
- Review and rely on the results of *some* of the tests performed by management, internal auditors, and others during their assessment process
- Perform his or her own tests

Evaluation of Management's Assessment Process

The proposed standard provides guidance on the *required* elements of management's process for assessing the effectiveness of internal control. The absence of one or more of those required elements may result in a modification to the standard audit report. For this reason, it is critical that your process comply with all requirements established by the new standard.

The *proposed* audit standard states that the auditor should determine whether management's assessment process has addressed the following elements:

- Determining which controls should be tested, including controls over relevant assertions related to all significant accounts and disclosures in the financial statements. Generally, such controls include:
  - Controls over initiating, recording, processing, and reporting significant accounts and disclosures and related assertions embodied in the financial statements.
  - Controls over the selection and application of accounting policies that are in conformity with generally accepted accounting principles.
  - Antifraud programs and controls.
  - Controls, including information technology general controls, on which other controls are dependent.
  - Controls over significant nonroutine and nonsystematic transactions, such as accounts involving judgments and estimates.
  - Controls over the period-end financial reporting process, including controls over procedures used to enter transaction totals into the general ledger; to initiate, record, and process journal entries in the general ledger; and to record recurring and nonrecurring adjustments to the financial statements(for example, consolidating adjustments, report combinations, and reclassifications).
- Evaluating the likelihood that failure of the control could result in a misstatement and the degree to which other controls, if effective, achieve the same control objectives
- Determining the locations or business units to include in the evaluation for a company with multiple locations or business units
- Evaluating the design effectiveness of controls
- Evaluating the operating effectiveness of controls based on procedures sufficient to assess their operating effectiveness. To evaluate the effectiveness of the company's internal control over financial reporting, management must have evaluated controls over all relevant assertions related to all significant accounts and disclosures.
- Determining the deficiencies in internal control over financial reporting that are of such a magnitude and likelihood of occurrence that they constitute significant deficiencies or material weaknesses
- Communicating findings to the auditor and to others, if applicable
- Evaluating whether findings are reasonable and support management's assessment

This book provides detailed guidance to help you comply with each of these required elements of management's assessment process. Appendix 1B summarizes these requirements and provides a cross reference to the chapters in this book where you can find the related guidance.

Documentation

The proposed standard to provides guidance on the nature and extent of the documentation required by the entity to support its assessment of internal control effectiveness. The standard also states that inadequate documentation may be a deficiency in internal control, which could be a material weakness.

The overall requirement for documentation is that it should provide "reasonable support" for management's conclusion. In order to attain this threshold, the documentation should include

- The design of controls over relevant assertions related to all significant accounts and disclosures in the financial statements. The documentation should include the five components of internal control over financial reporting described in the COSO integrated framework (discussed in Chapter 2)
- Information about how significant transactions are initiated, recorded, processed and reported
- Enough information about the flow of transactions to identify where material misstatements due to error or fraud could occur
- Controls designed to prevent or detect fraud, including who performs the controls and the related segregation of duties
- Controls over the period-end financial reporting process
- Controls over safeguarding of assets
- The results of management's testing and evaluation

Scope of Testwork

The proposed standard also provides guidance on the nature, timing and extent of the auditor's procedures for a number of situations, including

- Extent of testing of multiple locations, business segments or subsidiaries
- Required tests when the entity uses a service organization to process transactions
- Updated testwork required when the original testing was performed at an interim date in advance of the reporting date

To the extent that the PCAOB audit standard affects management's assessment of internal control, further guidance on these matters is provided in subsequent chapters of this book.

Use of Work of Internal Auditors and Others

The proposed auditing standard provides extensive guidance on the extent to which the independent auditors may rely on the work performed by management (including work performed by internal auditors and others) in their internal control audit. The standard defines three categories of controls and the extent to which the independent auditor may rely on the work of others to reach a conclusion.

1. *No reliance*. For some areas the auditor is prohibited from using the results of management's tests. These areas include
   - Controls that are part of the control environment
   - Controls over the period-end financial reporting process
   - Controls that have a pervasive effect on the financial statements

   That the independent auditors can not rely on the results of management's tests in this area does not relieve management of its responsibilities to perform these tests. That is, tests directed toward these control areas will be performed twice, once by management and again by the independent auditors.
2. *Limited reliance*. The auditor's use of the results of procedures performed by management should be limited in the following areas:
   - Controls over significant nonroutine and nonsystematic transactions
   - Controls over significant accounts, processes, or disclosures where the auditor has assessed the risk of failure of the controls to operate effectively as high.
3. *Full reliance*. Auditors are allowed to use the results of management's tests in all other areas, such as controls over routine processing of significant accounts and disclosures.

The degree to which the auditor can rely on the tests performed by management and others also is affected by the *competence* and *objectivity* of the individuals who perform the tests. In general, the independent auditor will evaluate competence using factors such as education and professional experience of the individuals who performed the work, the work program and procedures, and the quality of the documentation. Objectivity generally relates to the organizational status of the engagement work teams and whether that status was appropriate to allow the team to have full access to top management; and whether the individuals performing the work can maintain their objectivity about the areas in which the work was performed.

Determination of Material Weakness

The SEC reporting rules require entity management to disclose material weaknesses in internal control. Engagements to assess the effectiveness of internal control should be planned and performed in a way that will detect material misstatements. Thus, it is critical that you have a working definition of the term. The proposed audit standard provides the following definitions:

- An *internal control deficiency* exists when the design or operation of a control does not allow management or employees, in the normal course of performing their assigned functions, to prevent or detect misstatements on a timely basis.
- A *significant deficiency* is an internal control deficiency that adversely affects the entity's ability to initiate, record, process, or report external financial data reliably in accordance with generally accepted accounting principles. A significant deficiency could be a single deficiency or a combination of deficiencies, that results in more than a remote likelihood that a misstatement of the annual or interim financial statements that is more than inconsequential in amount will not be prevented or detected.
- A *material weakness* is a significant deficiency that, by itself, or in combination with other significant deficiencies, results in more than a remote likelihood that a material misstatement of the annual or interim financial statements will not be prevented or detected.

The definition of material weakness provided in the *proposed* auditing standard is different from the traditional definition included in the auditing literature. The proposed standard states that "more than a remote likelihood" is the threshold for determining whether a deficiency is significant. Under previous guidance, the threshold was "a relatively low risk."

At this early point in the standards setting and implementation process, it is unclear as to what effect, if any, this change in definition will have on the identification and reporting of material weaknesses. Some auditors are of the opinion that "more than a remote likelihood" is a lower threshold than "relatively low risk." If that is the case, than the adoption of the new auditing standard (if the definition in the proposed standard is retained in the final version) will result in a greater number of internal control deficiencies being classified as material weaknesses. For this reason, as described in more detail in Chapter 3, it is critical that management reach a consensus on this matter with the entity's independent auditors.

Chapter 8 provides additional guidance on determining the relative magnitude of internal control deficiencies.

Auditor Independence

As described in more detail in Chapter 3, the internal control reporting requirements described in the Sarbanes-Oxley act raise significant questions about the type and extent of assistance independent auditors may provide their clients relating to the assessment of internal control. The proposed auditing standard provides some guidance on this issue.

SEC Rule 2-01 provides the primary guidance on auditor independence issues. That rule establishes certain underlying principles for auditor independence, including

- The auditor must not act in the capacity of management.
- The auditor cannot audit his or her own work.

The proposed auditing standard reaffirms those underlying principles and goes on to require management to be actively involved, in a substantive and extensive matter, in any internal control related services that the independent auditor provides to the entity. Additionally, the audit committee must pre-approve all internal control-related services performed for the entity by its independent auditors. Under the proposed standard, the audit committee would be prohibited from pre-approving internal control-related services as category, but rather would be required to specifically pre-approve each specific engagement.

A STRUCTURED, COMPREHENSIVE APPROACH FOR EVALUATING INTERNAL CONTROL

Engagement Objective

This book provides guidance to help entity management

- Assess the effectiveness of the entity's internal control, and
- Facilitate the efficient audit of the entity's internal control by the independent auditors

A Structured Approach

There is no one way to structure an engagement to achieve the above objectives. Exhibit 1.4 summarizes the approach followed in this book.

Exhibit 1.4 Process for Evaluating Effectiveness of Internal Control

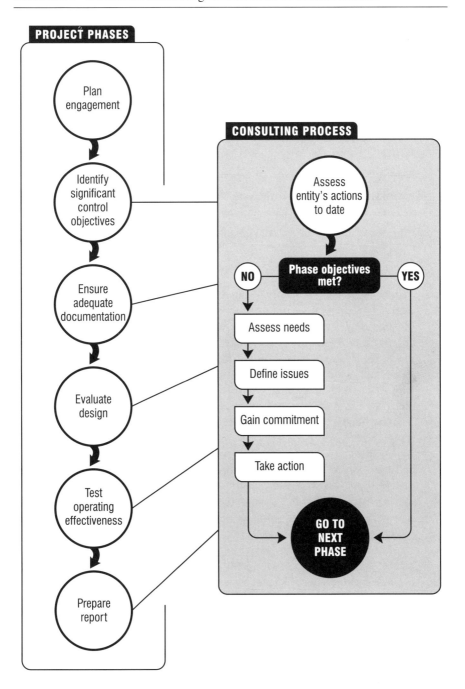

Distinct Phases and Their Objectives. The left-hand side of Exhibit 1.5 describes *what* should be done to issue and support management's report about the effectiveness of the entity's internal controls. The diagram depicts six sequential steps, which start with planning and end with reporting. The objective of each of these steps is as follows:

- *Engagement planning.* The primary objectives of the engagement planning phase are to
  - Assess information needs and identify sources of information required to effectively perform the assessment of internal control.
  - Determine the overall scope of the engagement.
  - Establish the terms of the working relationship both within the project team and between the project team and the project owner.
  - Coordinate the efforts with the independent auditors.
- *Assess internal control effectiveness.* This phase represents the bulk of the engagement and can be broken down into four separate components.
  1. *Identify significant controls.*[3] Management's assessment is based on the effectiveness of internal control *taken as a whole*, not on the effectiveness of individual components of control or individual controls. This holistic approach to assessing effectiveness recognizes the interdependence of the control components. Implicit in this approach is the notion that some individual controls are more significant to the overall operating effectiveness of internal than other controls. For example, the effectiveness of an entity's control environment or computer general controls is a prerequisite for the effective operation of an individual control procedure for a specific transaction.

     Additionally, the terms "internal control over financial reporting" and "disclosure controls and procedures" both incorporate the notion of materiality. For example, the attestation standards state that evaluating the effectiveness of the design of a specific control is concerned with whether the control is suitably designed to prevent or detect *material* misstatements.

     For these reasons, the first step in evaluating the effectiveness of internal control *taken as a whole* is to identify significant individual controls, both at the entity and the business process level. Your assessment of internal control effectiveness will focus on these significant controls.
  2. *Ensure adequate documentation of significant controls.* The documentation of a control is an important design element of the internal control system. For example, it is difficult for control procedures to be reliable consistently if there is no formal means for communicating the requirements of the procedure. For this reason, management should review the entity's documentation of significant controls to ensure that it is adequate.

3. *Evaluate the design effectiveness of significant controls.* To evaluate the design of controls requires that procedures be performed to determine whether the control is suitable to prevent or detect material misstatements. The nature of the procedures performed will vary according to the circumstances.
4. *Evaluate the operating effectiveness of significant controls.* Tests of operating effectiveness are concerned with
   - How the control was applied
   - The consistency with which it was applied
   - By whom it was applied
- *Report.* The process ends when the CEO and CFO prepare their report on the effectiveness of the entity's internal control.

Subsequent chapters in this book provide more detailed guidance on each of these phases in the process.

A Consultative Approach to Achieving Project Objectives. The right side of Exhibit 1.4 describes a separate process that is repeated continuously for each of the steps required to evaluate the effectiveness of internal control. As you undertake your engagement, you should consider that the entity may have already taken steps to evaluate the effectiveness of its internal control. For example, the company may have accumulated evidence to support its assessment of internal control in conjunction with

- The quarterly disclosure control reporting requirements
- Internal control–related work performed by internal auditors and others
- Internal control reporting required by other regulations, such as the Federal Deposit Insurance Corporation Improvement Act (FDICIA), which applies to financial institutions

Thus, each step in the evaluation process begins with obtaining an understanding of the actions already taken by the entity to achieve the engagement objectives. If those steps are adequate and achieve the objective, then no further work is necessary. If those steps are not adequate, then you are in a position to assess the entity's needs, recommend solutions, gain commitment, and then implement them.

For example, suppose that as part of its quarterly reporting on internal control, ABC has formed a disclosure committee to oversee that process. Part of the committee's responsibilities is to identify significant disclosure control policies and procedures. However, ABC has not taken any steps to identify significant controls over financial reporting. In that situation, the first step in the evaluation process would be to review the work of the disclosure committee related to significant disclosure controls and to assist in the identification of significant internal controls over financial reporting.

CONSIDERATIONS FOR OUTSIDE CONSULTANTS

Some entities may lack the resources or expertise necessary to conduct a thorough, comprehensive assessment of their internal control. In order to comply with the SEC reporting requirements, these entities may engage outside consultants to provide them the necessary assistance. This section provides guidance to consultants who have been engaged in such a capacity. Although the section is written for external consultants, employees and internal project leaders involved with the assessment process may find some of the guidance that follows to be useful.

Pre-Engagement Considerations

Before you begin your engagement to help management assess the effectiveness of internal control, you will need to gather information and come to a mutual understanding with the client on whether you will be engaged to perform the work, and if so, how the engagement will be structured. In this pre-engagement phase, your objectives are to

- Obtain a commitment from the client to move forward with the project.
- Understand the client's expectations for the conduct and results of the project.

Most likely, you will be required to meet with the prospective client in order to achieve these goals. Following are some suggestions for how to prepare for and conduct such a meeting.

Preparing to Meet the Prospective Client

Obtain a Basic Understanding of the Client. Your first step in preparing for a meeting prior to entering into the engagement should be to obtain a basic understanding of the prospective client. This understanding should be sufficient to enable you to

- Ask insightful questions about the entity and its operations.
- Understand the implications of answers that are provided.
- Identify the most significant issues that will affect engagement performance.

This preliminary understanding of the client should *not* be detailed enough for you to plan the engagement. Understanding the client at that level of detail will be the first phase of the engagement itself.

To obtain this understanding you may wish to

- Read the entity's most recent 10K to gain an understanding of its most significant business processes and the scope and complexity of its operations. Chapter 3 provides suggestions for what to look for when reading an entity's 10K.

- Review information posted on the company's Web site, particularly in its investor relations section.

- Make inquiries of the entity's independent auditors, especially if you have an existing relationship with them or they were responsible for introducing you to the prospective client.

Identify Assumptions and Goals. Before meeting with the prospective client, it may be helpful for you to identify any assumptions you have about your proposed work together with the goals of your meeting. By articulating these assumptions and goals, you will be better able to quickly reach a mutual understanding of the nature of the work and the results that can be expected.

When preparing for the meeting, consider exploring answers to the following questions:

- What assumptions are you making about the prospective engagement? For example:
  - Management's understanding of the process that will be followed by the independent auditors during their audit of the internal control report
  - Management's understanding of the depth and quality of documentation required to support their assessment of internal control effectiveness
  - The entity's existing process for evaluating the effectiveness of internal control
  - The resources the entity has to commit to the project
  - The role, if any, that the independent auditors will play in the assessment of internal control
- What are you basing your assumptions on? For example:
  - Conversations with the prospective client
  - Discussions with the prospective client's independent auditors
  - Information contained in public filings or the entity's own Web site
- What assumptions would it be appropriate for you to share with the prospective client if the opportunity arose?
- Under what assumptions is your client operating? For example:
  - Your and your firm's knowledge and expertise
  - The amount of work required to assess the effectiveness of internal control and prepare for an audit of that assessment
  - The urgency of the project
- What is the prospective client's goal for the interaction? For example, the prospective client may be considering several options for how they will conduct their assessment and who they will involve, and their goal for the meeting may be to assess your and your firm's qualifications.

Identify Key Players. Prior to meeting with the prospective client, you should consider who should be involved in the meeting. From the prospective client, you will want to be sure that the meeting includes the client's internal project leader and, if someone else, the person(s) who will make the decisions about whether to retain the services of you and your firm.

From your firm, in addition to yourself, you also should include individuals with expertise that are particularly relevant to the prospective client's situation. For example, if your prospective client's business processes are heavily technology dependent, you should include an individual with information technology (IT) auditing experience in your meeting. Prospective clients that operate in industries with highly specialized business practices and needs will expect you and your firm to demonstrate a depth of expertise in those specialized practices.

Meeting with the Prospective Client

Your initial meeting(s) with a prospective client can be broken down into two phases:

1. Information gathering, in which your primary role is to ask questions, listen, and gather information
2. A second phase in which you describe your overall approach to the engagement as a means to help them decide whether to retain your services

During this meeting it is important to refrain from offering solutions, even if those solutions seem obvious. You need to thoroughly assess needs and understand the situation and the client before you offer a solution. To offer a solution prematurely is to risk proposing the wrong solution or the solution to a different problem.

Gather Information

Assess Client Understanding. The prospective client's understanding of their own needs can vary widely. On one end of the spectrum, the client may have already performed a significant amount of work to assess its internal controls, and as a result of that work, designated you and your firm to oversee the remainder of the process. At the other end of the spectrum, the prospective client may have made very little progress. You should seek to determine where the prospective client falls along that spectrum of understanding.

Assess Current Situation. During your meeting with the client, you should obtain information about the current situation. For example, you may wish to make inquiries about

- Whether the prospective client has established a project team that has the overall responsibility for conducting the assessment of internal control. If so, then it would be helpful to know
  - The members of the project team
  - The progress the team has made to date
  - The role, if any, that the independent auditors will play in management's evaluation process.
- Any known or suspected issues identified to date, including
  - Scope of work
  - Lack of adequate documentation
  - Means for assessing effectiveness
  - Identified or suspected control deficiencies
  - Other reporting issues
- How the prospective client will measure the success of the project

Your Role on the Project Team. It is important for you to clarify the prospective client's expectations regarding your role in assisting them in the project. They may be looking for someone to lead the project team and take full responsibility for performing the work necessary for management to make an assessment of the effectiveness of internal control. Or they may simply wish to engage you to help in certain limited matters, such as performing tests of the operating effectiveness of specific controls. You should clarify your responsibilities and ensure that the working relationship (e.g., to whom you will report or the authority you have to make decisions) is aligned with that level of responsibility.

Additionally, you should try to determine the prospective client's understanding of *how you will add value* to the project. There are several ways in which you can add value, including

- *Technical expertise.* You can provide technical expertise in a number of areas, including internal control design, the design and evaluation of tests of internal controls, and the documentation and support required by the independent auditors to perform their attestation of the entity's report on internal control.
- *Problem solving.* The prospective client may look to you to provide solutions when problems are identified. For example, if internal control deficiencies arise, you may be asked to design new controls to address the deficiency.
- *Business strategy.* As you gain an understanding of the entity's internal control, you may find opportunities for improvement that fall outside of financial reporting and disclosure. The prospective client may expect you to identify these areas for improvement to internal control that will help the entity achieve operational goals and strategies.
- *Project administration.* The prospective client may expect you to take the lead in conducting the project, relying on you to take the initiative to form an effective

project team, work within the time and budget constraints, provide regular project status reports to management, and coordinate the project with the independent auditors

For each of your information-gathering objectives you should develop a questioning strategy for your meeting with the prospective client. Appendix 1C to this chapter is a list of example questions you may consider when implementing such a strategy.

Describe an Overall Approach to the Engagement

Once you gain an understanding of the client's situation and their expectations, the meeting will invariably shift to you and how you will approach the engagement. This is natural, since the prospective client will want to alleviate some of the uncertainty they have about how the engagement will be performed. Again, it should not be necessary for you to provide a detailed plan for engagement performance—you have not gathered enough information at this point to provide such a plan in any meaningful way.

However, it is appropriate for you to discuss your overall approach to the engagement. In describing that approach, you should emphasize the following:

- *The project will be done in phases.* Depending on the needs of the client, the engagement will start with planning; proceed through an assessment of the documentation, design, and operating effectiveness of significant controls; include a provision for remedial action, if any; and conclude with the preparation of the report.

  This phased approach allows the client to maintain control of the project, how it proceeds, and whether you will continue in the role that was originally envisioned. At the conclusion of each phase, you will present the work product, and the client will determine whether and how to proceed to the next phase. Presenting your engagement in this fashion will alleviate a great deal of the uncertainty the prospective client has about the project.
- *The work builds on what the prospective client has already done.* Each phase of the project begins by understanding the steps the entity has already taken to achieve the objective of the work. Needs are evaluated and only the work that is necessary to achieve the stated objective is proposed. Work is not started until there is agreement on the scope of the work, the procedures that will be performed, and the deliverables and their timing. You will communicate with the independent auditors during each phase to ensure that the approach and resulting work product will meet their needs.

Clarifying the Work Arrangement

Once you have been engaged by management to help in their assessment of internal control, then your agreement should be documented in an engagement letter or contract. A written agreement between you and your client is the best way to make sure that the two parties have an understanding of the services you will provide.

For consulting services, a common structure to written agreements is one that includes

- The main agreement, which describes the general nature of the work and other matters such as fees, the limitations of the work, ownership of any resulting intellectual property, confidentiality, and so on
- An exhibit to the agreement, which describes the work and the related deliverables in more detail. As described above, your work will be done in phases, with the client having the control to decide whether and when to move on to the next phase. As you and the client reach an agreement as to the nature and scope of each phase of the agreement, you would prepare an additional appendix to your engagement letter to document this agreement.

Main Agreement. The main agreement remains unchanged; as you and the client agree to additional phases in the process, you would draft and have the client sign additional appendixes.

Your firm most likely has a standard engagement letter that can serve as the basis for your main agreement. In modifying this standard letter for an engagement to help in the assessment of the effectiveness of internal control, consider the following:

- *Description of services.* The main agreement should refer to the attachment for a complete description of services.
- *Clarify responsibilities.* The CEO and CFO are responsible for establishing and maintaining adequate internal controls and procedures for financial reporting and for assessing the effectiveness of the company's internal controls. Working under the direction of the company's senior management, your responsibility is to assist them in making their assessment.
- *Guarantees and limitations.* Your agreement should clearly state that you do not guarantee any results (e.g., that the independent auditors will issue a "clean opinion" on management's report on internal control). You also should consider any limitations on what the client can expect from your work. For example, your engagement is not designed to detect occurrences of fraud.
- *Open-ended phrases.* Be careful not to give the impression that the scope of your work is open-ended and includes whatever is necessary to "get the job done." Phrases such as "other such services as necessary" should be avoided.
- *Separate engagement letters from proposals.* If you prepare a written proposal for a prospective client, it is generally good practice to *not* include an engagement letter or contract as an attachment. You do not want to give the client the impression that your engagement included all the services that you might have mentioned in a proposal or other marketing collateral.

- *Ownership of work product.* Typically, in a consulting engagement, the work product becomes property of the client. In some instances, you may wish to retain the ownership or right to future use of certain by-products of your engagement, for example, training materials or process methodologies. In either case, be sure to clearly delineate ownership rights in your engagement letter.

Description of Services Exhibit. In general, you should consider including the following in your exhibit describing the services you will perform at each phase of the engagement.

- *Description of services/objective.* A brief description of the services to be performed and their objective; for example, "assist in the identification of significant internal controls, which will serve as the basis for testing and evaluating the entity's internal control over financial reporting and disclosure controls"
- *Process.* A summary of the process you will use to deliver the services
- *Deliverables.* A description of what you will produce as a result of the work
- *Fees.* Fees are not part of the main agreement but are determined separately for each phase of the work. Thus, the fees should be included in the exhibit
- *Schedule and timing.* When the product will be delivered and, if appropriate, the timing of significant milestones
- *Assumptions.* Summarize the assumptions upon which the agreement is based, for example, that the client will be providing certain resources.

APPENDIX 1A

Action Plan: Structuring the Engagement

The following action plan is intended to help you implement the suggestions contained in this chapter for structuring an engagement to assess the effectiveness of internal control.

1. Understand Rules and Standards

Become familiar with the relevant rules and standards pertaining to the assessment of internal control. For example:

- Consider the summary guidance on the following matters presented in this chapter:
  - SEC annual and quarterly reporting requirements
  - PCAOB internal control auditing standard
- Read the final SEC rules related to management's reports on internal control, including the related commentary.

• Read the final PCAOB auditing standard relating to internal control reporting.

2. Choose an Approach

Develop a structured, comprehensive approach for assessing and reporting on the effectiveness of internal control. Possible action steps include

• Become familiar with the engagement approach described in this chapter.
• Modify approach as necessary to meet the needs of the entity, expectations of management, qualifications of potential team members, and so on.

Additional considerations for outside consultants:

3. Assess Prospective Clients

Identify and gather information about prospective clients.

4. Meet Prospects

Meet with prospective clients and

• Gather information about client's needs.
• Assess their current situation.
• Clarify client's expectations about your role on the engagement team.

5. Reach Understanding

Obtain a written understanding of your work arrangement with the client.

APPENDIX 1B

Requirements for Management's Assessment Process: Cross Reference to Guidance

---

As indicated in this chapter, the proposed PCAOB auditing standard related to the audit of internal control requires the independent auditor to evaluate management's process for assessing the effectiveness of the company's internal control. The standard then describes certain elements that should be present in management's process.

Exhibit 1.5 summarizes those required elements and provides a cross-reference to the chapters in this book where you can find guidance to help you comply with these requirements.

Exhibit 1.5

PCAOB Audit Standard Requirement	Applicable Guidance
Determine which controls should be tested.	Chapter 4
Controls over initiating, recording, processing, and reporting significant accounts and disclosures and related assertions	Chapter 7
Controls over the selection and application of accounting policies	Chapters 4 and 6
Antifraud programs and controls	Chapters 4 and 6
Controls on which other controls are dependent.	Chapters 4and 6
Controls over significant nonroutine and nonsystematic transactions, such as accounts involving judgments and estimates	Chapters 4 and 6
Controls over the period-end financial reporting process	Chapters 4 and 6
Evaluate the likelihood that failure of controls could result in a misstatement.	Chapter 8
Determine the locations or business units to include in the evaluation for a company with multiple locations or business units.	Chapter 3
Evaluate the design effectiveness of controls.	Chapters 6 and 7
Evaluate the operating effectiveness of controls.	Chapters 6 and 7
Determine whether the deficiencies in internal control constitute significant deficiencies or material weaknesses.	Chapter 8
Communicate findings to the auditor and to others, if applicable.	Chapter 8
Evaluate whether findings are reasonable and support management's assessment.	Chapter 8

APPENDIX 1C

Pre-Engagement Questioning Strategy and Example Questions

SUGGESTIONS FOR ASKING EFFECTIVE QUESTION

During your initial meetings with a prospective client, prior to the engagement, you will need to gather information to assess their overall needs. The following are some example questions you might ask the prospective client to assess the current situation and the client. Here are some tips for questioning strategies:

- Questions about the situation are designed to uncover certain facts (e.g., the existence of any known internal control deficiencies), but you should not limit yourself to a mere fact-finding mission. You should ask questions that help you understand client perceptions and expectations.
- Questions that begin with "why" can put the prospective client on the defensive. "What" questions usually are more effective. For example, the question "Why hasn't the entity formed a disclosure committee?" could be rephrased to "What has prevented you from forming a disclosure committee?"
- Talk about outcomes ("What do you hope to accomplish?") rather than problems. People would rather talk about their goals and what they are trying to achieve, which goes beyond solving the current problem.
- Questions that focus on the prospective client should be directed toward understanding what is important to them. The answers to these questions will help you to deliver services that have value for the client.

EXAMPLE QUESTIONS[4]

Assess Current Situation

- What actions have you taken to date to begin assessing the effectiveness of the entity's internal control?
- If you have formed a project team or disclosure committee
  - What are their responsibilities?
  - To whom do they report?
  - Who is part of the team or committee?
  - What has been the nature of the work to date, and what, if any, conclusions have they reached?
- What are the known and suspected but undetermined issues with respect to
  - The nature and scope of the evaluation process
  - The design and operating effectiveness of internal controls
- How did you come to identify known or suspected issues, for example, from communications received from independent auditors, as a result of an internal evaluation of internal controls and so on?
- What is your timetable for completing the project?
- What results would you like to achieve as a result of your assessment of internal controls?
  - Other than reporting compliance, what other benefits will the project provide the company?
- (For external consultants) What is preventing you from performing the work entirely with in-house resources?

Understand What the Client Values

- What is important to you about this project?
- What concerns you about this project? Consider
  - Any uncertainties surrounding the process for making the assessment of internal controls
  - Any uncertainties related to the outcome of the assessment and the possible identification of internal control deficiencies
- If you had to name one (priority, outcome, objective, concern) for the project, what would it be?
- How will you know that the project has been successful?

Notes

1. See Regulation S-K, Item 308 (17 CFR §229.308).
2. "Accelerated filer" is defined in Exchange Act Rule 12b-2. Generally, companies with a market capitalization of $75 million or more are considered accelerated filers.
3. As described more completely in Chapter 2, internal controls should be considered within the context of an entity's overall risk management strategy. In order to identify and understand an entity's significant controls, it is important to understand the significant risks facing the entity. You may wish to identify and assess these risks as a separate engagement step. However, the approach described in this book considers this risk assessment to be a component of this process step, the identification of significant controls. See Chapter 4 for additional details.
4. These questions were adapted from *The Consultative Approach*, by Virginia LaGrossa and Suzanne Saxe, published by Jossey-Bass/Pfeiffer, 1998.

Chapter 2

Internal Control Criteria

Chapter Summary

Describe the COSO internal control integrated framework, which will most likely be the criteria used by entities to assess the effectiveness of their internal control.

Summarize the value chain business activities approach for analyzing activity-level controls.

Provide additional guidance on internal control considerations related to an entity's use of information technology, including

- The generally accepted information technology control objectives contained in the COBIT (Control Objectives for Information and related Technology) report
- The consideration of controls when an entity uses an outside service organization to process certain transactions

THE NEED FOR CONTROL CRITERIA

A set of criteria is a standard against which a judgment can be made. As described in Chapter 1 of this book, choosing an appropriate control criteria is a precondition to performing an assessment of the effectiveness of an entity's internal control. In the United States, the internal control integrated framework published by the Committee of Sponsoring Organizations of the Treadway Commission (COSO) is the most commonly used criteria to assess the effectiveness of internal control. Therefore, a significant portion of this chapter will be devoted to discussing the COSO framework.

Increasingly, information technology (IT) has become ingrained into entities' business processes and controls. The consideration of IT-related controls must be integrated with the entity's overall assessment of its internal control—it is no longer acceptable to treat IT controls separate and distinct from other elements of internal control. The COBIT framework, published by the Information Systems Audit and Control Association (ISACA), provides a generally accepted set of IT-related control objectives. This chapter also will describe this guidance, which may be integrated into the COSO framework.

Your understanding of the criteria used to assess the effectiveness of the entity's internal control is a cornerstone for developing an effective engagement approach.

THE COSO INTERNAL CONTROL INTEGRATED FRAMEWORK

In 1985, the Committee of Sponsoring Organizations of the Treadway Commission (COSO) was formed to sponsor the National Commission on Fraudulent Financial Reporting, whose charge was to study and report on the factors that can lead to fraudulent financial reporting. Since this initial undertaking, COSO has expanded its mission to improving the quality of financial reporting. A significant part of this mission is aimed at developing guidance on internal control. In 1992, COSO published *Internal Control—Integrated Framework*, which established a framework for internal control and provided evaluation tools that business and other entities could use to evaluate their control systems.[1]

Key Characteristics of the COSO Framework

The COSO internal control framework describes five components of internal control: the control environment, risk assessment, control procedures, information and communication, and monitoring. Before providing a detailed description of each of these five components, it is important to "step back" and provide a discussion of the important characteristics of the COSO approach to internal control.

A Holistic, Integrated View. The COSO framework contains five components of internal control, and one of the most important characteristics of the framework is understanding how these components relate to each other. COSO envisions these individual components as being tightly integrated with each other in a nonlinear fashion. Each component has a relationship with and can influence the functioning of every other component.

For example, the assignment of authority and responsibility is an important element of an entity's control environment. Suppose that management decides to delegate the authority and responsibility for establishing marketing and sales programs to its marketing department. The COSO guidance related to the control environment component states that the decision to assign authority and responsibility should be to consider

- Policies describing appropriate business practices
- Knowledge and experience of key personnel
- Resources provided for carrying out duties

However, the control environment component of internal control does not exist in a vacuum. The decision to delegate authority will affect other components to varying degrees. In our example, if the company assigned responsibility for marketing and sales programs to the marketing department, that decision would also affect

- *Risk assessment*. The marketing department would want to determine which of their activities affect the entity's accounting and Securities and Exchange Commission (SEC)-required disclosures, establish objectives for those activities, and identify the risks to achieving those objectives. For example, marketing and sales terms affect the timing of revenue recognition for financial statement purposes. The marketing department will want to assess the risk that its marketing and sales activities are not properly accounted for.

- *Control procedures.* For example, the marketing department may wish to establish standard sales agreements in order to reduce the risk that individual salespeople would enter into inappropriate transactions.

- *Information and communication.* For example, communication channels would need to be opened between the marketing department and the accounting department to ensure that the terms of all marketing programs were known to the accounting personnel so that all the relevant accounting implications (e.g., revenue recognition) were properly considered.

- *Monitoring.* For example, senior management would have to establish a method for monitoring the activities of the marketing department to make sure that its initiatives were consistent with the entity's overall business objectives.

Thus, when evaluating the effectiveness of internal control, we look at it as an *integrated whole.* Weak controls in one area can be offset by stronger controls in another area.

BY WAY OF ANALOGY

Consider your experience when you go to the movies. There may be several things you look for in a good movie: writing, directing, acting, music, cinematography. These elements are not related in a linear fashion but in a more complicated, nonlinear way. They play off each other and come together to form an integrated whole. When we walk out of the theater, we judge the entire experience. We may point to individual elements that were particularly enjoyable, but it is how all of the elements come together that serves as the basis for our determination of the quality of the film.

That "coming together" is an important characteristic of how we judge internal control.

A Process. COSO defines *internal control* as a process. When you evaluate internal control, you should remember that you are evaluating a process, not an outcome. Certainly, there is a connection between the two. An effective process is more likely to lead to a desired outcome. The existence of undesirable outcomes may indicate that the process itself was flawed. However, that direct connection may not always hold true. It is possible that an internal control failure can be rightly attributed to something other than a flawed process.

A Business Objective–Driven Approach. The COSO framework views internal control as "built in" to an entity's overall business processes, as opposed to a separate "built-on" component that attaches itself to the company's real business. Building in internal control requires that management

Exhibit 2.1 Limitations of Internal Control

Internal control provides reasonable but not absolute assurance that an entity will achieve its financial reporting objectives. Even an effective internal control system can experience a failure due to the following:

- *Human error.* The people who implement internal controls may make poor decisions that can lead to control failures. People also can make a simple error or a mistake.
- *Management override.* Even in a well-controlled entity, managers may be able to override internal controls for illegitimate purposes.
- *Collusion.* Two or more individuals may collude to circumvent what otherwise would be effective controls.

1. Establish business objectives. For our purposes, those objectives relate to financial reporting.
2. Identify the risks to achieving those objectives.
3. Determine how to manage the identified risks. The establishment of internal controls is just one of several options.
4. Where appropriate, establish control objectives as a way to manage certain risks. Individual controls are then designed and implemented to meet the stated control objectives.

Internal controls have no intrinsic value—they are not valuable in and of themselves. Controls have value only to the degree in which they allow the entity to achieve its objectives. The effectiveness of internal control is judged according to how well it enables an entity to achieve stated objectives.

Flexible, Adaptable, No "One-Size-Fits-All" Approach. The COSO framework is not a rigid, prescriptive approach to internal controls. It recognizes that different entities will make different choices about how to control their businesses. Management will make cost–benefit judgments and choose trade-offs. The result: Internal control is not a "one-size-fits-all" proposition.

Moreover, circumstances change at the entity, and so its internal control must be designed in a way to adapt and remain effective in a dynamic environment. In fact, one of the primary objectives of the monitoring component of internal control is to assess the quality of the system's performance over time, recognizing that circumstances will change.

Reasonable Assurance. COSO recognizes the limitations of internal control. (See Exhibit 2.1.) No matter how well designed or operated, internal control can provide only reasonable assurance that objectives will be met. Reasonable assurance is a high threshold, but it stops short of absolute assurance. The presence of an internal

control failure does not, in and of itself, mean that a system is ineffective. The COSO report states that "even an effective internal control system can experience failure."

The People Factor. COSO recognizes that internal control is effected by people. Documentation of controls is important, but documentation is not all there is to internal control. The effectiveness of internal control depends on the people responsible for carrying out individual control elements—from the chief executive officer (CEO) and board of directors, all the way to rank and file employees charged with performing control-related tasks.

Thus, the design of internal control must take into account the human element and must make allowances for human nature. For example, people are greatly influenced by the actions taken by an entity's senior management—more so than they are by what these individuals say. Therefore, the relative strength of an entity's control environment depends in large part on the actions of the entity's leadership. Or consider that the ability of individuals to carry out their responsibilities depends on how well they understand what is required. This need for understanding requires that the entity's internal controls have an effective communication and training element.

Five Components of Internal Control

The COSO framework describes five interrelated components of internal control.

1. *Control environment.* Senior management must set an appropriate "tone at the top" that positively influences the control consciousness of entity personnel. The control environment is the foundation for all other components of internal controls and provides discipline and structure.
2. *Risk assessment.* The entity must be aware of and deal with the risks it faces. It must set objectives, integrated throughout all value-chain activities, so that the organization is operating in concert. Once these objectives are set, the entity must then identify the risks to achieving those objectives, analyze and develop ways to manage them.
3. *Control activities.* Control policies and procedures must be established and executed to help ensure the actions identified by management as necessary to address risks are effectively carried out.
4. *Information and communications.* Surrounding the control activities are information and communication systems, including the accounting system. These systems enable the entity's people to capture and exchange the information needed to conduct, manage, and control its operations.
5. *Monitoring.* The entire control process must be monitored, and modifications made as necessary. In this way, the system can react dynamically, changing as conditions warrant.

Exhibit 2.2 depicts these five elements of internal control and their inter-relationship.

Additionally, controls may affect the entity either pervasively, on an entity-wide basis, or specifically, on an individual activity, account, or class of transactions basis.

The Control Environment. The control environment sets the tone of the entity. It influences the control consciousness of the people within the organization and is the foundation for all other components of internal control.

The following describes the factors highlighted in the COSO report that contribute to an effective control environment.

Exhibit 2.2 COSO Internal Control Components

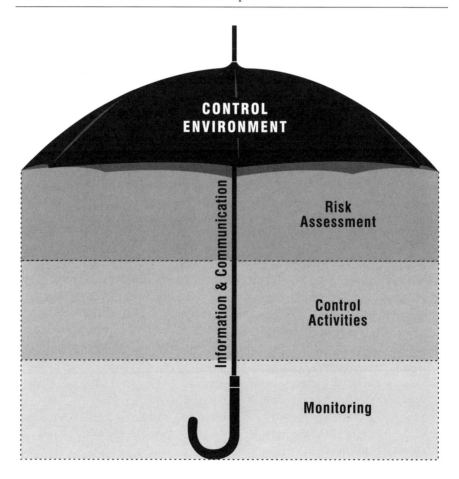

Integrity and Ethical Values. The effectiveness of internal control cannot rise above the integrity and ethical values of the senior management. Integrity and ethical values are essential elements of the control environment because they affect the design, administration, and monitoring of other internal control components.

Management may *tell you* a great deal about their integrity and ethical values. They may even commit their *words* to a *written document.* Responses to inquiries and written policies are good, but the COSO report makes it clear that the effectiveness of an entity's control environment depends primarily on management's *actions* and how these actions affect the entity on a day-to-day basis.

In order for management's integrity and ethical values to have a positive impact on the entity, the following must exist.

- The business owner and management must personally have high ethical and behavioral standards.
- These standards must be communicated to company personnel. In a small business, this communication is often informal.
- The standards must be reinforced.

Through its actions, management can demonstrate its ethical values in a number of ways, including

- *Dealing with signs of problems.* Consider how management deals with signs that problems exist, particularly when the cost of identifying and solving the problem could be high. For example, suppose that senior management became aware of a possible environmental contamination on their premises. How would they react? Would they try to hide it, deny its existence, or act evasively if asked about it? Or would they actively seek advice on how to best handle the situation?
- *Removal or reduction of incentives and temptations.* Individuals may engage in dishonest, illegal, or unethical acts simply because the owner-manager gives them strong incentives or temptations to do so. Removing or reducing these incentives and temptations can go a long way toward diminishing undesirable behavior.

  The emphasis on results, particularly in the short term, fosters an environment in which the price of failure becomes very high. *Incentives* for engaging in fraudulent or questionable financial reporting practices include
  - Pressure to meet unrealistic performance targets, particularly for short-term results
  - High performance-dependent rewards
  - Upper and lower cutoffs on bonus plans
- *Temptations* for employees to engage in improper practices include
  - Nonexistent or ineffective controls, such as poor segregation of duties in sensitive areas, that offer temptations to steal or conceal questionable financial reporting practices

- Senior management that is unaware of actions taken by employees
- Penalties for improper behavior that are insignificant or unpublicized and thus lose their value as deterrents

• *Management intervention.* There are certain situations in which it is appropriate for management to intervene and overrule prescribed policies or procedures for legitimate purposes. For example, management intervention usually is necessary to deal with nonrecurring and nonstandard transactions or events that otherwise might be handled by the accounting system. The COSO report recommends that management provide guidance on the situations and frequency with which intervention of established controls is appropriate. Occurrences of management intervention should be documented and explained.

Commitment to Competence. Competence should relate to the knowledge and skills necessary to accomplish tasks that define an individual's job. Commitment to competence includes management's consideration of the competence levels for particular jobs and how those levels translate into requisite skills and knowledge.

Management's Philosophy and Operating Style. Management's philosophy and operating style encompass a broad range of characteristics. Such characteristics may include

- Senior management's approach to taking and monitoring business risks
- Attitudes and actions toward financial reporting and tax matters
- Emphasis on meeting budget, profit, and other financial and operating goals

Management's philosophy and operating style have a significant influence on the control environment, regardless of the consideration given to the other control environment factors.

Organizational Structure. An entity's organizational structure provides the framework within which its activities for achieving entity-wide objectives are planned, executed, controlled, and monitored.

Significant aspects of establishing an organizational structure include considering key areas of authority and responsibility and appropriate lines of reporting. What is considered "appropriate" will vary according to the size, complexity, and needs of the business. Small business entities usually have fairly simple organizational structures. A highly structured organization with formal reporting lines and responsibilities may be appropriate for large entities, but for a small business, this type of structure may impede the necessary flow of information.

Assignment of Authority and Responsibility. The assignment of authority and responsibility includes

- The establishment of reporting relationships and authorization procedures
- The degree to which individuals and groups are encouraged to use initiative in addressing issues and solving problems

- The establishment of limits of authority
- Policies describing appropriate business practices
- Resources provided for carrying out duties

Alignment of authority and accountability often is designed to encourage individual initiatives, within limits. Delegation of authority means surrendering central control of certain business decisions to lower echelons, to the people who are closest to everyday business transactions.

A critical challenge is to delegate only to the extent required to achieve objectives. This requires ensuring that risk acceptance is based on sound practices for identifying and minimizing risk, including sizing risks and weighing potential losses versus gains in arriving at good business decisions.

Another challenge is ensuring that all personnel understand the entity's objectives. It is essential that each individual knows how his or her actions interrelate and contribute to achievement of the objectives.

The control environment is greatly influenced by the extent to which individuals recognize that they will be held accountable. This holds true all the way to the CEO, who should be accountable to the board of directors, and who has the ultimate responsibility for all activities within the organization, including the internal control system.

Human Resource Policies and Practices. Human resource policies and practices affect an entity's ability to employ sufficient competent personnel to accomplish its goals and objectives. Human resource policies and practices include an entity's policies and procedures for hiring, orienting, training, evaluating, counseling, promoting, compensating, and taking remedial action. In some entities, the policies may not be formalized but they should nevertheless exist and be communicated. For example, in a smaller entity a senior manager may verbally make explicit his or her expectations about the type of person to be hired to fill a particular job, and may even be active in the hiring process. Formal documentation is not always necessary for a policy to be in place and operating effectively.

Standards for hiring the most qualified individuals, with emphasis on educational background, prior work experience, past accomplishments, and evidence of integrity and ethical behavior, demonstrate an entity's commitment to competent and trustworthy people. Hiring practices that include formal, in-depth employment interviews and informative and insightful presentations on the company's history, culture, and operating style send a message that the company is committed to its people.

Personnel policies that communicate prospective roles and responsibilities and that provide training opportunities indicate expected levels of performance and behavior. Rotation of personnel and promotions driven by periodic performance appraisals demonstrate the entity's commitment to advancement of qualified personnel to higher levels of responsibility. Competitive compensation programs that include bonus incentives serve to motivate and reinforce outstanding performance. Disciplinary actions send a message that violations of expected behavior will not be tolerated.

Information Technology Considerations. As described later in this chapter, the Information Technology Governance Institute (ITGI) and the Information Systems Audit and Control Association (ISACA) have published *IT Control Objectives for Sarbanes-Oxley*, which provides extensive guidance on how IT controls should be considered within the context of management's assessment of internal control effectiveness. That document highlights the following important considerations related to an entity's control environment and information technology.

- IT often is mistakenly regarded as a separate organization of the business and thus a separate control environment.
- IT is complex, not only with regard to its technical components but also as to how those components integrate into the company's overall system of internal control.
- IT can introduce additional or increased risks that require new or enhanced control activities to mitigate successfully.
- IT requires specialized skills that may be in short supply.
- IT may require reliance on third parties where significant prcesses or IT components are outsourced.
- The ownership of IT controls may be unclear.

Risk Assessment

As indicated previously, the COSO framework considers internal controls within the context of an entity's stated objectives and the risks of achieving those objectives. Exhibit 2.3 describes this risk assessment process. Note that steps 1 through 4 are part of the risk assessment control component, while steps 5 and 6 are considered to be elements of an entity's control activities. Again, what is important is not which control component an individual element "belongs to" but how it relates to internal control taken as a whole.

Objective Setting. The COSO framework considers objective setting (and therefore the risk assessment process) at both the entity level and the business process activity level. Setting objectives allows management to identify *critical success factors*, which are the key things that must go right if goals are to be achieved.

COSO defines objectives in three broad categories: operations, compliance with laws and regulations, and financial reporting. In relation to reporting on the effectiveness of internal control as described in this book, the objectives that you

Exhibit 2.3 Risk Assessment

STEP 1

Goals	Key Questions	Examples
Set objective	What are we trying to achieve?	Produce reliable financial statements

STEP 2

Goals	Key Questions	Examples
Identify risks to achieving those objectives	What could happen that would affect our objectives?	A natural disaster could destroy computer systems and data

STEP 3

Goals	Key Questions	Examples
Assess risk	What are consequences of risk? What is likelihood event will occur?	Consequences are severe; likelihood is slight

STEP 4

Goals	Key Questions	Examples
Manage risk	In light of the assessment, what is the most cost-effective way to manage the risk?	Insure against loss. Develop business recovery plan. Self-insure.

CONTROL ACTIVITIES

STEP 5

Goals	Key Questions	Examples
Define control objective	For risks to managed through internal control, what are the control objectives?	Implement recovery plan that reduces the impact of a natural disaster

STEP 6

Goals	Key Questions	Examples
Design control	How should control be designed to prevent or detect identified risk?	Design recovery plan. Implement plan. Test on a regular basis.

are concerned with are the financial reporting objectives, which COSO defines as addressing

> The preparation of reliable published financial statements, including interim and condensed financial statements and selected financial data derived from such statements, such as earnings releases, reported publicly.

The term *reliably* means that the financial statements are *fairly presented* in conformity with Generally Accepted Accounting Principles (GAAP). In discussing what it means for a "fair presentation" the COSO report cites Statement on Auditing Standards No. 69, *The Meaning of "Presents Fairly in Conformity with Generally Accepted Accounting Principles" in the Independent Auditor's Report*, which defines "fair presentation" as considering whether

- The accounting principles selected and applied have general acceptance.
- The accounting principles are appropriate in the circumstances.
- The financial statements, including the related notes, are informative of matters that may affect their use, understanding, and interpretation of matters that may affect their use, understanding, and interpretation.
- The information presented in the financial statements is classified and summarized in a reasonable manner, that is, neither too detailed nor too condensed.
- The financial statements reflect the underlying transactions and events in a manner that presents the financial position, results of operations, and cash flows stated within a range of acceptable limits, that is, limits that are reasonable and practical to attain in financial statements.

The concept of materiality is inherent in these judgments related to "presents fairly."

At the activity level, the people who must take action to achieve the objective must have a good, working understanding of what is required of them. It also is important for management to set priorities for activity level objectives, recognizing that some objectives are more important than others.

Identify Risks. The COSO report notes that there are many ways in which management can identify risks and that these risks can arise from both internal and external causes. The COSO framework does not endorse any one particular risk identification process but acknowledges that many can be effective as long as the process is comprehensive and considers all factors that may contribute to or increase risks. Factors to consider include

- Past experiences of failure to meet objectives
- Quality of personnel
- Changes affecting the entity such as competition, regulations, personnel, etc.
- Existence of geographically distributed, particularly foreign, activities

- The significance of an activity to the entity
- The complexity of an activity

At the activity level, management should focus its risk identification efforts on major business units or activities.

Assess and Manage Risks. A commonly acknowledged process for risk analysis includes assessing

- The consequences of the risk (i.e., asking the question "What would happen if . . . ?")
- The likelihood of the identified risk occurring (i.e., asking the question "What are the chances that . . . ?")

Once risks are assessed, management is in a better position to decide on an appropriate way to manage the risk. Risk management techniques include

- Risk avoidance, for example, by choosing to *not* undertake the activity that gives rise to the risk
- Risk transfer, for example, by purchasing insurance or using financial instruments in a hedging strategy
- Risk mitigation, for example, by designing and implementing internal control policies and procedures
- Risk acceptance

Manage Change. The business and operating environment of an entity changes over time, and change can result in previously well-functioning internal controls becoming less effective. The COSO framework acknowledges that change management should be a part of an entity's regular risk-assessment process, but it goes on to identify those conditions that should be the subject of special consideration within the entity's risk assessment process. These conditions are

- *Changes in the operating environment.* Changes in the regulatory or operating environment can result in changes in competitive pressures and significantly different risks.
- *New personnel.* New personnel may have a different focus on or understanding of internal control. When people change jobs or leave the company, management should consider the control activities they performed and who will perform them going forward. Steps should be taken to ensure that new personnel understand their tasks.
- *New or revamped information systems.* Significant and rapid changes in information systems can change the risk relating to internal control. When these systems are changed, management should assess how the changes will impact

control activities. Are the existing activities appropriate or even possible with the new systems? Personnel should be adequately trained when information systems are changed or replaced.

- *Rapid growth.* Significant and rapid expansion of operations can strain controls and increase the risk of a breakdown in controls. Management should consider whether accounting and information systems are adequate to handle increases in volume.
- *New technology.* Incorporating new technologies into production processes or information systems may change the risk associated with internal control.
- *New lines, products, or activities.* Entering into business areas or transactions with which an entity has little experience may introduce new risks associated with internal control.
- *Restructurings.* Corporate restructurings, which usually are accompanied by staff reductions, can result in inadequate supervision, the lack of necessary segregation of duties, or the deliberate or inadvertent elimination of key control functions.
- *Foreign operations.* The expansion of a company outside of the United States will introduce new and unique risks that management should address.
- *Accounting changes.* Although not mentioned in the COSO report, Statement on Auditing Standards No. 55 (as amended), *Internal Control in a Financial Statement Audit*, includes changes in generally accepted accounting principles as a circumstance that requires special consideration in the entity's risk assessment process.

Control Activities

Control activities involve two elements:

1. *Policy.* A policy establishes what should be done.
2. *Procedure.* The procedures are the actions of people to implement the stated policies.

Key Characteristics of Control Activities. The COSO report's discussion of control activities includes several key points, which will affect any entity's evaluation of the effectiveness of its internal control. Some of these key points reiterate the overall concepts described at the beginning of this chapter and include

- *Link to risk assessment process.* There are many different ways to categorize internal controls (e.g., preventive or detective), and these categories may be useful as a means to organize your understanding of an entity's control activities. However, the category into which a particular control activity falls is not nearly as important as the role it plays in achieving a stated objective.

    As described in Exhibit 2.2, the establishment of control objectives and related control policies and procedures is linked to the entity's risk assessment process. When evaluating the effectiveness of control activities, you will need to consider whether they relate to the risk assessment process and whether they are appropriate to ensure that management's directives are carried out.

- *Entity specific.* Entities differ in many ways, including their stated objectives, the circumstances of their business, and the people responsible for managing and controlling the business. For these reasons, no two entities should be expected to have the same set of control activities.

- *Documentation of policies.* The COSO report recognizes that, many times, policies are communicated orally. Unwritten policies can be effective when
  - The policy is a long-standing and well-understood practice, or
  - In smaller organizations where communications channels involve only limited management layers and close interaction and supervision of personnel

- *Performance of procedures.* More important than the documentation of the policy is the performance of the procedures. To be effective, procedures must be performed, thoughtfully, conscientiously, and consistently. Additionally, control procedures should include a follow-up component in which conditions identified as a result of the procedures are followed up and appropriate action taken.

- *Focus on significant activities.* When evaluating control activities, the evaluator should evaluate all significant business activities.

Types of Control Activities. Having said that the category a control is placed in is not as important as how effective the control is at addressing risk, the COSO report then provides examples of types of control activities. These examples do not suggest any hierarchy, structure, or categorizing scheme. Instead, they are provided merely to illustrate the wide range of control activities.

- *Top-level reviews.* These control activities include reviews of actual performance versus budgets, forecasts, and prior-period performance. They may also involve relating different sets of data (e.g., operating or financial) to one another, together with analyses of the relationships, investigating unusual relationships and taking corrective action. Performance reviews may also include a review of functional or activity performance. Note that the control activity is management's analysis and *follow up* on the matters identified as a result of the review. The control activity is *not* the preparation of a budget or forecast.

- *Information processing.* A variety of controls are performed to check accuracy, completeness, and authorization of transactions. The two broad groupings of information systems control activities are general controls and application controls. General controls commonly include controls over data center operations, system software acquisition and maintenance, and access security. Application controls apply to the processing of individual applications, help ensure that transactions are valid, properly authorized, and completely and accurately processed.

- *Physical controls.* These activities encompass the physical security of assets, including adequate safeguards over access to assets and records such as secured facilities and authorization for access to computer programs and data files and periodic counting and comparison with amounts shown on control records. The extent to which physical controls intended to prevent theft of assets are relevant to the reliability of financial statement preparation depends on the circumstances such as when assets are highly susceptible to misappropriation. For example, these controls would ordinarily not be relevant when any inventory losses would be detected pursuant to periodic physical inspection and recorded in the financial statements. However, if for financial reporting purposes management relies solely on perpetual inventory records, the physical security controls would be relevant to the financial reporting process. As described in Chapter 1, the SEC definition of *internal control* makes explicit reference to assurances on controls related to the authorized use or disposition of the company's assets
- *Segregation of duties.* Assigning different people the responsibilities of authorizing transactions, recording transactions, and maintaining custody of assets is intended to reduce the opportunities to allow any person to be in a position to both perpetrate and conceal errors or irregularities in the normal course of his or her duties. Segregation of duties is often a problem for small business entities.

INFORMATION AND COMMUNICATION

Every entity must identify, capture, and communicate pertinent information in a form and time frame that allows people to carry out their control and other responsibilities. The COSO report provides a rather broad description of the characteristics of an effective information and communication system. For the purposes of assessing the effectiveness of controls related specifically to financial reporting objectives, the most relevant of these characteristics include the following:

- *Consider all information sources.* The information needed to prepare reliable financial reports is not limited to financial information—nonfinancial information also is important. For example, the information needed to determine an allowance for inventory obsolescence includes an assessment of current and future market conditions. Frequently, the assumptions underlying significant accounting estimates rely to some degree or another on nonfinancial information.

    Additionally, the preparation of financial statements requires that information be gathered from both internal and external sources. In the inventory obsolescence example, the information needed to make the estimate is not limited to internally generated information such as the amount of inventory on hand. Preparing the estimate will also require management to consider externally generated information, such as consumer demand and the level of supply for the industry as a whole.

- *Integration with control activities.* The entity's information and communication systems are closely integrated with its control activities. In order for control activities to be effective, the following must be communicated clearly to individuals that perform control functions:
  - Specific control activity-related duties
  - Relevant aspects of the internal control system, how they work, and their role and responsibility in the system
  - How their activities relate to the work of others. This knowledge will help them recognize a problem or determine its cause or corrective action.
  - Expected behavior—what is acceptable and unacceptable
  - The notion that whenever the unexpected occurs, attention should be given not only to the event itself but also to its cause
- Additionally, management should recognize that information received from *external* sources may indicate control weaknesses. For example, external auditors are required to report internal control deficiencies to the audit committee and the board of directors. Regulators report the results of their examinations, which may highlight control weaknesses. Complaints or inquiries from customers, vendors, competitors, or other third parties often point to operating problems. These are just examples of the types of information that originates from outside the entity that may provide feedback about the entity's control activities.
- *Integration with risk assessment and change management process.* As described previously, change management is an integral part of an entity's risk management process, and the COSO report identifies several situations that require "special consideration." Recognize that when the entity undergoes change, its information needs change as well. To be effective, an information system must be flexible and responsive to the constantly evolving needs of the business.
- *The key role played by senior management.* Senior management plays an important role in the effective functioning of an entity's information and communication system. The COSO report recommends that entities establish an open and effective means of communicating information upstream, one of the key elements of which is management's "clear-cut willingness to listen." This recommendation is echoed in the SEC's definition of disclosure controls, which include those controls and procedures "designed to ensure that information required to be disclosed by an issuer in its Exchange Act reports is accumulated and communicated to the issuer's management as appropriate to allow timely decisions regarding required disclosure."
- *Routine and nonroutine information.* An entity's information system is *not* limited to merely capturing the company's recurring, routine transactions and events but also must include a means for identifying, capturing, and communicating information that is outside the normal course of business. For example, an entity may form a variable interest entity (formerly known as a "special purpose entity"), which it considers a one-time event. The formation of such an entity has important accounting ramifications, and the company should have a mechanism

to identify the information needed to properly account for such an event, capture that information, and communicate it to the proper individual so that a decision can be made.

- *Formal and informal.* The COSO framework recognizes that an entity's information and communication system includes *informal* communications, such as conversations with customers, vendors, and other third parties and between and among employees.
- *Timing is important.* It is not enough to capture and communicate information. The communication must be done in a timely manner that allows it to be useful in controlling the entity's activities.

For more detailed guidance on the information and communication needs specifically related to financial reporting, you should consider the guidance contained in the auditing literature.[3]

Information System for Financial Reporting. The information system relevant to financial reporting objectives—which includes the accounting system—consists of the methods and records established to record, process, summarize, and report entity transactions (as well as events and conditions) and to maintain accountability for the related assets and liabilities.

The auditing literature describes the necessary elements of an information system for financial reporting, which include the methods and records that

- Identify and record all valid transactions.
- Describe on a timely basis the transactions in sufficient detail to permit proper classification of transactions for financial reporting.
- Measure the value of transactions in a manner that permits recording of their proper monetary value in the financial statements.
- Determine the time period in which transactions occurred to permit recording of transactions in the proper accounting period.
- Present properly the transactions and related disclosures in the financial statements.

This guidance from the auditing literature is consistent with the SEC's definition of internal described in Chapter 1.

MONITORING

Monitoring is a process that assesses the quality of internal control performance over time. It involves assessing the design and operation of controls on a timely basis and taking necessary corrective actions. Monitoring may be done on both an ongoing basis and as part of a separate evaluation.

Examples of ongoing monitoring activities include the following:

- The regular management and supervisory activities carried out in the normal course of business
- Communications from external parties, which can corroborate internally generated information or indicate problems. For example, customers implicitly corroborate billing data by paying their invoices. Conversely, customer complaints about billings could indicate system deficiencies in the processing of sales transactions.
- External auditors regularly provide recommendations on the way internal controls can be strengthened. Auditors may identify potential weaknesses and make recommendations to management for corrective action.
- Employees may be required to "sign off" to evidence of the performance of critical control functions. The sign-off allows management to monitor the performance of these control functions.

Reporting Deficiencies. Providing information regarding internal control deficiencies to the right people is critical if the internal control system is to continue to function effectively. For this reason, the monitoring component of internal controls should include a mechanism for reporting internal control deficiencies and taking appropriate action. COSO uses the term *deficiency* broadly to mean any condition of an internal control system "worthy of attention." Certainly, all deficiencies that can affect the entity's ability to produce reliable financial information should be identified and reported. However, the COSO report also makes the point that even seemingly simple problems with a relatively simple, obvious solution should be carefully considered because they might have far-reaching implications. Reinforcing a concept introduced in its discussion of information and communication, when errors and deficiencies are identified, their underlying causes should be investigated.

Findings of internal control deficiencies should be reported to the individuals who are in the best position to take action. This includes not only the person responsible for the activity involved, but also to at least one level of management above the directly responsible person.

BUSINESS PROCESS ACTIVITIES

The COSO framework recognizes that controls exist at two different levels within an organization: the entity level and the activity level. For example, employee hiring and training policies affect the control environment at an entity level—they have a pervasive effect on how controls are implemented and performed. A bank reconciliation is a control procedure performed at an activity level, namely, the activity of receiving and disbursing cash. Any evaluation of internal controls must consider all significant controls at both the entity and activity level. In performing this evaluation an important issue to consider is how one defines *activity*.

The auditing literature, which is concerned with internal control over financial reporting, takes a financial statement approach to examining activity-level controls. Under this approach, an evaluator would identify activities such as accounts and classes of transactions that are significant to the financial statements. For example, within an entity the activity-level controls might be assessed as they relate to sales, purchases, cash receipts and disbursements, and so on.

The COSO framework does not take a financial statement approach to analyzing activity-level controls. In both the detailed discussion of the framework and in its example evaluation tools, COSO takes a "business process activity" approach to activity level controls. This approach is based on the value-chain analysis.[2]

The notion behind the value chain is that companies are successful when they provide customers with value. The value chain consists of value activities, which are the physically and technologically distinct activities a company performs. The value activities are building blocks used by the company to create value for its customers. Value activities are of two types: primary activities and support activities.

Primary Activities

The primary activities are those involved in the physical creation of the product, its sale and transfer to the customer, and after-sale service. Exhibit 2.4 describes a "chain" of primary activities.

The order of events in the value chain are read left to right—an entity starts with inputs, it produces a product, ships and sells it, and ultimately must service it. The primary activities in the value chain are described as follows:

- *Inbound logistics*. Activities associated with receiving, storing, and disseminating inputs to the product. These include material handling, warehousing, inventory control, vehicle scheduling, and returns to suppliers.

- *Operations*. Activities associated with transforming inputs into the final product. These include machining, packaging, assembly, equipment maintenance, testing, printing, and facility operations.

- *Outbound logistics*. Activities associated with collecting, storing, and physically distributing the product to buyers. These include finished goods warehousing, material handling, delivery vehicle operation, order processing, and scheduling.

Exhibit 2.4   Value Chain of Primary Activities

| INBOUND LOGISTICS | OPERATIONS | OUTBOUND LOGISTICS | MARKET and SALES | SERVICE |

- *Marketing and sales.* Activities associated with providing a means by which buyers can purchase the produce or service and inducing them to do so. These include advertising, promotion, sales force, quoting, channel selection, channel relations, and pricing.
- *Service.* Activities associated with providing service to enhance or maintain the value of the product in the hands of the buyer. These include installation, repair, training, parts supply, and product adjustment.

Support Activities. In addition to these primary activities, entities also engage in a set of "support" activities. These activities support the primary activities and each other by providing purchased inputs, technology, human resources, and various entity-wide functions such as cost accounting.

These support activities can be added to the company's primary activities to create the overall value chain for the entity, as depicted in Exhibit 2.5.

These support activities are

- *Firm infrastructure.* Activities involved in general management, planning, finance, accounting, legal, government affairs, and quality management.
- *Human resource management.* Activities associated with recruiting, hiring, training, development, and compensation of all types of personnel. Human resource management affects competitive advantage in any company, particularly in service companies, such as certified public accounting (CPA) firms.
- *Technology development.* Activities associated with efforts to improve products, services, and processes. Technology development can take many forms, from basic research and product design, to process equipment design and servicing procedures.
- *Procurement.* Activities involved in the purchase of inputs used throughout the entity's value chain, including both primary and support activities. Procurement typically is spread throughout the company, which tends to obscure its overall magnitude and allows many purchases to go unscrutinized.

Exhibit 2.5   Overall Value Chain

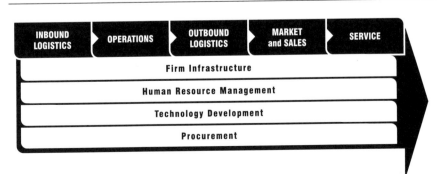

Different Entities Have Different Value Chains. The way in which an entity defines the components of its value chain will vary according to the industry. For example, a financial institution may define its value chain in terms of loan origination and the subsequent packaging and sale of loan pools on the secondary market. Its definitions of *inputs, operations, outputs,* and *service* will reflect that definition of the value chain. Additionally, the relative importance of each primary activity will depend on the industry the client is in. For a wholesale distributor, the acquisition, storage, and distribution of inventory will be significant. For a software company, the marketing and postsale support of its product may be more significant than how the physical product, if any, is stored and distributed.

Some entities may have operations in two related but different industries. For example, a large-production home builder may also have a mortgage company, which allows it to offer financing to the buyers of its homes. The home-building business is quite different from the financial services businesses, and in this situation, you may wish to analyze the two businesses separately by creating two separate value chains.

Appendix 2A provides examples of value-chain analyses for two different businesses.

Understanding the entity's value chain will help you identify the significant business activities for which activity-level controls should be assessed. This value-chain analysis is *not* a replacement for the traditional financial statement approach to identifying the significant activities of an entity that must be controlled or for analyzing those controls. Rather, this book treats the value-chain analysis as a *supplement to* these more traditional approaches. Chapter 4 provides guidance on identifying significant controls using a blended approach that includes consideration of both an entity's financial statements and its value chain.

CONTROLS OVER INFORMATION TECHNOLOGY SYSTEMS

COSO Guidance

COSO describes framework for considering IT-related controls that groups these controls into two types: general computer controls and application-specific controls.

- *General controls* include controls over
  - Data center operations (e.g., job scheduling, backup and recovery procedures)
  - Systems software controls (e.g., the acquisition and implementation of operating systems)
  - Access security
  - Application system development and maintenance controls (e.g., the acquisition and implementation of individual computer software applications)

- *Application controls* are designed to control data processing and help ensure the completeness and accuracy of transaction processing, authorization, and validity. Application controls also encompass the way in which different applications interface with each other and exchange data.

The COSO report does not mandate this approach to assessing the effectiveness of internal controls but states that this is one set of groupings of IT-related control activities that can be used.

The COBIT Framework

Since the release of the COSO, the ISACA has developed its COBIT framework, which provides a generally applicable and accepted standard for IT security and control practices. Among IT audit professionals, COBIT is widely accepted.

The COBIT framework is similar to COSO in that it puts controls within the context of an entity's need to achieve certain business objectives and the risks it faces toward achievement. Within that context, the overall goal of an entity's IT-related control structure is to

Ensure the delivery of *information* to the business that addresses the required information criteria.

This goal is enabled by

Creating and maintaining a system of process and control excellence that considers all IT resources.

In defining the goals of IT governance and control, COBIT takes a rather broad brush and does not limit itself to the financial reporting process. COBIT describes the following high-level goals for IT governance.

- IT is aligned with the business, enables the business, and maximizes the benefits to the entity.
- IT resources are used responsibly.
- IT-related risks are managed appropriately.

For our purposes, which relate only to the reliability of financial reporting, only the third COBIT objective, the management of IT-related risks, will be considered.

Information Needs. COBIT emphasizes the "information" piece of "information technology." Given that management needs information in order to achieve the entity's stated objectives, COBIT asks, "What are the necessary qualities of that information to enable that process?" For example, the information management uses to make decisions must be accurate.

The following summarizes *all* of the information qualities identified in COBIT. These qualities are then divided into "primary" qualities, which have a direct effect on the reliability of financial information, and "secondary" qualities, which do not affect the financial statements directly but which relate to the purely operational aspects of the business.

1. Primary (direct effect on the reliability of financial reporting)
   - *Integrity* relates to the *accuracy* and *completeness* of information as well as to whether transactions are valid and authorized.
   - *Availability* relates to the information's *being available when required by the business* now and in the future. It also concerns the *safeguarding* of necessary resources and associated capabilities.
   - *Compliance* deals with *complying with externally imposed business requirements*, such as the preparation of financial statements, tax returns, regulatory requirements, and the like. Compliance relates to the provision of appropriate information for management to exercise its financial and compliance reporting responsibilities.
2. Secondary information qualities (no direct impact on financial reporting)
   - *Effectiveness* deals with information's being relevant and pertinent to the business processes as well as being delivered in a *timely, correct, consistent,* and *usable* manner.
   - *Efficiency* concerns the provision of information through the optimal use of resources
   - *Confidentiality* concerns the protection of sensitive information from unauthorized disclosure.

For the purposes of assessing the effectiveness of internal control over financial reporting, you typically will limit your consideration of IT-related controls only to those that have a direct effect on the reliability of financial reporting.

IT Processes. COBIT describes a framework in which IT processes manage IT resources to produce information that has the qualities necessary to manage the business. Within this overall framework, COBIT groups the IT processes into four categories, each of which is critical in delivering information that meets the stated criteria. Exhibit 2.6 summarizes the four main process categories and the key processes within each category.

Note that the delivery and support category of processes is analogous to the COSO category of application controls. The other categories identified by CO-BIT approximate the general controls described by COSO but are somewhat broader in scope.

You will consider IT-related controls at all stages of the engagement process, from planning to the identification, documentation, and testing of significant

Exhibit 2.6 COBIT IT Processes

Category	Description	Key Processes
Planning and Organization	These processes cover strategy and tactics and concern the identification of the way IT can best contribute to the achievement of stated business objectives, both now and in the future.	• Define a strategic plan • Define the information architecture • Define the IT organization and relationships • Communicate management aims and direction • Manage human resources • Ensure compliance with external requirements • Assess risks • Manage quality
Acquisition and Implementation	To realize the IT strategy, IT solutions need to be identified, developed or acquired, as well as implemented and integrated into business processes.	• Acquire and maintain application software • Acquire and maintain technology infrastructure • Develop and maintain procedures • Install and accredit systems • Manage changes
Delivery and Support	These processes include the actual processing of data by application systems.	• Define and manage service levels • Manage third-party service levels • Manage performance and capacity • Ensure continuous service • Ensure systems security • Educate and train users • Manage the configuration • Manage problems and incidents • Manage data • Manage facilities • Manage operations
Monitoring	All IT processes need to be regularly assessed over time for their quality and compliance with control requirements.	• Monitor the processes • Assess internal control adequacy • Obtain independent assurance

controls. At each stage, your work should address each of the four categories of IT processes summarized here.

Recent Developments. In November 2003, the Information Technology Governance Institute (ITGI) in conjunction with the Information Systems Audit and Control Association (ISACA) published *IT Control Objectives for Sarbanes-Oxley*. This publication is intended for IT professionals to help them understand management's required reporting on the effectiveness of internal control and to plan and perform procedures to help management comply with these requirements. The document also provides an important bridge between the control components described in the COBIT framework and those described by COSO.

The document also can be used by management or those who assist them in the evaluation process as a means for understanding the overall objectives and general procedures for an IT review of internal control over financial reporting. The document can be downloaded from either the ITGI Web site at *www.itgi.org* or the ISACA Web site at *www.isaca.org*.

DISCLOSURE CONTROLS AND PROCEDURES

As described in Chapter 1, management is required to assess and report on the effectiveness of the entity's disclosure controls and procedures on a quarterly basis. This section provides further guidance on how to comply with this requirement.

The Relationship of Disclosure Controls and Internal Controls over Financial Reporting

As described in Chapter 1, *disclosure controls* are broadly defined to include "the controls and procedures designed to ensure that information required to be disclosed by the issuer in the reports and filed or submitted under the Exchange Act is recorded, processed, summarized, and reported within the time period specified by the SEC's rules and forms." Thus, disclosure controls and procedures cover *all* information required to be reported. Internal controls over financial reporting is a *subset* of disclosure controls and procedures that covers only the preparation of the financial statements and disclosures required under GAAP. Exhibit 2.7 summarizes this relationship between disclosure controls and internal controls over financial reporting.

With respect to any information required to be disclosed, management should first determine whether the information is included in the consideration of internal controls. If it is, then the evaluation of the entity's internal controls will satisfy the requirement to assess disclosure controls. If the required disclosure information is *not* included within internal controls, then a separate disclosure control should be designed and implemented. It is this group of separate controls that we will refer to as *disclosure controls* going forward.

Exhibit 2.7 Relationship between Disclosure Controls and Internal Controls over Financial Reporting

Disclosure Control Considerations

The objective of disclosure controls is to provide reasonable assurance that all material required disclosure information is captured, evaluated, and, if necessary, reported.[4]

There is no equivalent of a COSO framework for establishing control criteria for system of disclosure controls. However, when evaluating the effectiveness of such a system, you should consider the following:

- *Role of the disclosure committee.* As described in Chapter 1, the SEC has recommended that registrants form a disclosure committee to oversee the process by which disclosures are created and reviewed. For example, you might expect the disclosure committee to

  - Develop a process for capturing disclosure information.
  - Assume the primary responsibility for evaluating this information to determine if and how it should be reported.

  The existence and effective functioning of this committee is a significant part of an entity's disclosure control system that has a pervasive effect on the entire system.

- *Quantitative information.* Quantitative information includes both *internally* generated and *externally* generated information. The entity's disclosure controls should include methods for gathering both types of information reliably and in a timely manner. More time may be required to gather external information than internal information.

- *Qualitative information.* The reliable identification and capture of qualitative information usually is more difficult than the identification and capture of quantitative information. By definition, disclosure controls should capture "information that is relevant to an assessment of the need to disclose *developments and risk* that pertain to the issuer's business." Additionally, Exchange Act Rule 12b-20 requires the entity to report "material information, if any, as may be necessary to make the required statements, in light of the circumstances under which they are made, not misleading."

These types of broad disclosure requirements rely primarily on management's unique insights into the business and not necessarily from a reading of the financial statements. As such, it is difficult, if not impossible, to identify this information in advance and design controls and procedures that ensure its capture and evaluation. Instead, an entity's disclosure "control" may consist of

- Identifying those individuals in the entity most likely to spot and assess trends and developments that may require disclosure
- Making inquiries of these individuals by those with the requisite knowledge of the SEC's disclosure obligations

- *Monitoring internal control effectiveness.* As described in Chapter 1, the SEC rules require management to disclose material weaknesses and changes in the entity's internal control. In order to comply with this requirement, the disclosure committee should assume some responsibility for monitoring the continued effectiveness of internal control, and identifying

  - Material weaknesses
  - Changes to internal control

An earlier section of this chapter describes the monitoring component of internal control, as defined by COSO, in more detail.

- *Documentation.* If the CEO and chief financial officer (CFO) are to certify that they have reviewed the entity's disclosure controls, those controls and procedures should be documented. In addition, significant determinations of the disclosure committee normally would be documented, either in the committee's minutes or in some other fashion.

APPENDIX 2A
Example Value Chains

ALOHA HAWAIIAN SPORTSWEAR

Description of the Company and Its Operations

The Company. Aloha Hawaiian Sportswear is a leader in the design, manufacture, and distribution of premium sportswear and accessories. The company offers a full line of men's, women's, and children's apparel and a wide variety of accessories that include footwear, eyewear, and leather goods.

AHS competes primarily on the basis of fashion, quality, and service. Its main strategies for achieving this competitive advantage include

- The production of innovative and attractive brands and marketing as a way to shape consumer taste
- Maintaining and creating brand equity

- Providing strong and effective marketing support to its business partners
- Effectively presenting products at the retail level
- Ensuring product availability

The company operates in the following areas:

- *Wholesale.* The company sells its products through department stores, specialty stores, and golf and tennis pro shops throughout the United States and Europe.
- *Retail.* The company owns and operates 30 full-price retail stores. In addition, the company has 57 outlet stores that are located in retail outlet malls.
- *Licensing.* AHS enters into licensing agreements that grant its licensing partners the right to manufacture and sell at wholesale certain specified products. In exchange, AHS earns a licensing royalty. The company retains control and oversight of all aspects of the design, production, packaging, distribution, and marketing process of licensed products.

Sourcing, Production Distribution and Service. The company does not own or operate any production facilities. All of its products are manufactured by independently owned manufacturers under long-term contracts. The company has two basic approaches to production.

1. *Purchase finished goods.* AHS buys finished products from the supplier, who is responsible for the purchasing and carrying of raw materials, in addition to the manufacture of the product.
2. *Cut, make, and trim.* AHS buys raw materials and piece goods and then moves these to finished product assemblers.

The company uses a third-party warehouse distributor to store and ship its products.

As a way to prevent costly "stock outs," the company maintains a high level of "basic" products, such as knit shirts and shorts. Customers can order these products at any time, and they will be shipped within 5 business days.

Information Technology Systems. The apparel industry is characterized by long lead times from the design of a product to its ultimate offering for sale at the retail level. Industry-wide, these long lead times result in significant lost sales revenue due to forced markdowns and high inventory carrying costs, which are necessary to avoid stock outs.

Like others in the industry, AHS has adopted a technology-based "quick response" system that captures necessary information on a real-time basis and transmits it electronically to decision makers both at the business partner level and within the company. For example, the company uses point-of-sale terminals at all its retail stores to track sales and inventory levels. This information is monitored constantly and new orders are placed—electronically—when inventory stock reaches certain predetermined levels. The entity's production information system also tracks the purchase and movement of its "cut, make, and trim" production activities.

Value-Chain Analysis

Primary Activities. Since the company has no warehouse facility, its inbound activities are moderate, limited only to the tracking of raw materials for the "cut, make, and trim" production. It has effectively outsourced its distribution, so it has no outbound activities. Likewise, it has no operations.

However, the company is highly involved in marketing and brand management. Maintaining and increasing brand equity is a significant part of its competitive strategy and a large part of how the company provides value to its customers and its licensing partners. The service element of the company's business is somewhat important, as it works to ensure that wholesalers do not "stock out" of basic, high-sales-volume items.

Secondary Activities. The company has a relatively complex network of suppliers, outsource business partners, and licensees, all of whom must be closely monitored to ensure quality. Additionally, AHS must negotiate, create, and monitor a variety of legal documents with these third parties.

Information technology is important as a means to efficiently capture and distribute information that is critical for decision-making purposes.

By far the most significant secondary activity is procurement. Since the company has no operating facilities, it must buy all of its finished goods. Sourcing raw materials also can be a significant activity.

The Value Chain. Exhibit 2.8 is an illustration of the AHS value chain with the size of the various activities reflecting their relative significance. Note how the primary activities do not include operations or outbound activities.

WD WEATHERS

WD Weathers Inc. is involved in the acquisition, ownership, management, and leasing of regional and community shopping centers. The company owns 38 regional malls and 27 community shopping centers ("strip malls") across the country. The company is organized and operates as a real estate investment trust (REIT). As a REIT, it generally is not subject to federal and state income taxes provided that it continues to meet certain dividend distribution tests, share ownership requirements, and other qualifying tests provided in the Internal Revenue Code of 1986. As a property owner, the company also may be liable for the costs of removal or remediation of certain hazardous substances, as required by federal and state law.

The company competes against approximately 10 to 15 other similar entities,

Exhibit 2.8 Aloha Hawaiian Sportswear Value Chain

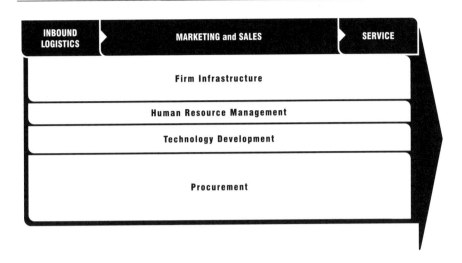

primarily in the acquisition of properties and in attracting and retaining tenants. The company believes that its business requires highly specialized skills in a wide variety of disciplines. In order to achieve its business objectives, it has recruited, trained, and attempted to retain high-quality personnel with expertise in property acquisition, finance, leasing, legal, and property management.

The company is committed to a decentralized structure in which all of its properties are managed by on-site property managers. These property managers are responsible for operating the property, maintaining it and providing security, marketing, and other services to tenants.

The company is actively involved in property acquisition and disposition. Over the course of a year it may buy or sell three to five properties, depending on market conditions.

One of the company's core competencies is in the redevelopment and subsequent repositioning of older, less successful malls. The company's in-house staff is highly experienced at shopping center revitalization, and they are responsible for developing, implementing, and overseeing all redevelopment plans. Weathers Contractors, the company's wholly owned subsidiary, is the general contractor responsible for all redevelopment construction work. In that capacity, it works closely with the redevelopment team to implement the plan. It coordinates the acquisition of construction materials and either performs the construction work itself or engages specialized subcontractors.

Value-Chain Analysis

WD Weathers has two different (though complementary) businesses: a property management business and a general contractor. It is helpful to consider these two businesses separately. In this example, we will analyze only the REIT.

Primary Activities. The property management company is a service business. It does not produce a product, so there are no inbound logistics, operations, or outbound logistics.

Its marketing and sales activities consist primarily of its leasing activities—attracting new tenants, signing them to long-term lease agreements, and then retaining them under new leases when the existing leases expire. The company also may sell properties it owns, and these activities also are considered part of its sales and marketing efforts.

As a service provider, all of the company's on-site property management operations are considered to be postsale service activities. The company provides utilities, common area maintenance, security, and other services to its tenants.

Secondary Activities. The acquisition and disposition of properties together with the constant leasing activity requires a significant amount of legal work. Compliance with the environmental remediation laws and the maintenance of the company's status as a REIT also require legal attention.

The company's business strategy emphasizes the hiring, development, and retention of highly qualified and competent people.

Finally, in addition to the typical procurement activities that are a part of every business, WD Weathers is involved in the regular acquisition of properties to add to its portfolio.

The Value Chain. Exhibit 2.9 is an illustration of the WD Weathers value chain with the size of the various activities reflecting their relative significance. Note how the primary activities do not include inbound, operations, or outbound activities, reflecting the service nature of the business.

Exhibit 2.9   W.D. Weathers Value Chain

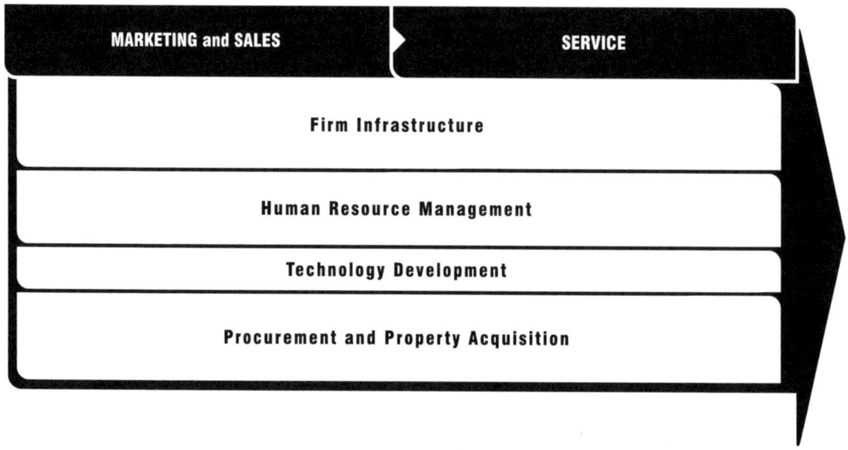

Notes

1. In 2003, COSO published a draft of a document entitled *Enterprise Risk Management Framework*, whose purpose was to provide guidance on the process used by management to identify and manage risk across the enterprise. This new framework does not supersede or otherwise amend its earlier internal control framework. Internal control is encompassed within and an integral part of enterprise risk management. Enterprise risk management is broader than internal control, expanding and elaborating on internal control to form a more robust conceptualization focusing more fully on risk. *Internal Control—Integrated Framework* remains in place for entities and others looking at internal control by itself.

2. The value-chain analysis was developed by Michael Porter and first presented in his book *Competitive Advantage*, published by the Free Press in 1985.

3. Prior to the formation of the PCAOB, auditing standards were issued by the Auditing Standards Board of the American Institute of Certified Public Accountants. The auditing literature referred to here is Statement of Auditing Standards No. 55, (as amended) Internal Control in a Financial Statement Audit. This standard will remain in effect unless and until it is superseded by a PCAOB standard. Additional guidance on the information and communication component of internal control can be found at AU§319.47-.53 of *Professional Standards*, Vol. 1, published by the AICPA.

4. The SEC rules have not explicitly qualified the definition of disclosure controls with the terms *materiality* and *reasonable assurance*. We have inferred these limits based on the CEO's and CFO's required certification of disclosure controls and on the SEC's definition of internal control.

Chapter 3

Project Planning

Chapter Summary

Assess information needs and identify sources of information required to effectively perform an assessment of internal control effectiveness.
- Determine overall scope of the project.
- Establish the terms of the working relationship, both within the project team and between the project team and the client.
- Coordinate the project with the independent auditors.

THE OBJECTIVE OF PLANNING

There are two main objectives for project planning:

1. *Prepare for key decisions.* During your engagement, you will be required to make important judgments regarding
   - The focus of your work
   - The types of procedures you will perform
   - The scope of your project

   During the planning phase of the project you will gather information to help you make broad, preliminary judgments on these matters. The knowledge you gain from gathering this information will then provide you with the background necessary to make informed decisions as the engagement proceeds.

2. *Organize the project team.* You will want to perform your work as effectively and efficiently as possible. To accomplish this, you will need to create a project team with the required skills, knowledge, and experience to achieve the engagement objectives. The work of each team member will need to be defined and coordinated with other members.

Planning is an iterative process. The two objectives listed here are *not* performed once at the beginning of the engagement and then remain static. Rather, they are revisited continuously throughout the project, as more information becomes available and the decisions you are required to make become more specific and narrowly focused.

INFORMATION GATHERING FOR DECISION MAKING

There are several key questions that will arise during the engagement that you will want to consider early on in order to gather the necessary information. Broadly, these key questions are

- Which control objectives are most significant to the entity's overall internal control structure?
- What areas should receive the most attention?
- What is a "significant deficiency" or "material weakness" in internal control?
- What is the overall scope of the project, and what work has already been performed to achieve the engagement objectives?

Significant Control Objectives

As described in Chapter 2, the COSO framework acknowledges that, within the context of internal control taken as a whole, some controls are more significant than others. For example, one entity may have a highly centralized decision-making and control structure in which management involvement, supervision, and review are more important than many of the individual control procedures performed by entity personnel. In contrast, another entity may have a more decentralized structure in which senior management relies on others in the entity to make decisions and control certain aspects of the entity's business. In that situation, the hiring and training of entity personnel and the effective communication of the entity's business and control objectives becomes much more significant than they would when senior management maintains central control.

As indicated in Chapter 1, one of the first objectives of your project will be to identify significant control objectives. To prepare for that decision, you should consider obtaining an understanding of the following:

- *Key business activities.* Chapter 2 provides a discussion of the value chain as a means to identify an entity's most significant business activities. Typically, significant controls are those related to the value-chain activities that are most critical to the entity's overall success.
- *Industry characteristics.* The entity's business activities often can be understood more completely when considered in the context of the overall industry in which it operates. For example, information about specialized industry performance metrics (both financial and nonfinancial) and the overall financial health of the industry can help you determine which business activities or reporting processes require significant control or oversight.
- *Significant risks.* As described in Chapter 2, internal control should be considered within the context of an entity's overall risk management strategy. Significant control objectives are those that help the entity manage its most significant financial reporting risks.

- *Financial reporting considerations.* A primary objective of the engagement is to assess internal control over financial reporting. Therefore, to assess significant controls you should have a good understanding of the entity's

  – Significant financial statement accounts, balances, and classes of transactions

  – Financial reporting process

  – Critical accounting policies

- *Mandated significant controls.* As described in Chapter 1, the Public Company Accounting Oversight Board's (PCAOB's) proposed internal control auditing standard requires the independent auditors to evaluate the effectiveness of management's process for evaluating internal control. As part of that evaluation, the proposed standard requires management's process to include the testing of certain specified controls. Any controls that the auditing standard describes as "generally should be included as part of management's evaluation process" also should be designated as "significant" for your engagement.

Areas of Focus

Like any other project, you will want to focus your efforts on those areas that are most critical for achieving the engagement objectives. As a starting point, you will plan on addressing those control objectives deemed to be significant. In addition, you also should consider

- Areas of known or suspected control weakness, for example, which may have been communicated to management from the internal auditors or the independent auditors as part of their audit of the entity's financial statements.

- Financial statement accounts with a high inherent risk for material misstatement. The term *inherent risk* is defined in the auditing literature as the risk of material misstatement in an account irrespective of any internal controls. Many factors can affect inherent risk. For example, account balances that require complex calculations or significant judgment or estimation usually have a higher inherent risk than other accounts.

Defining Internal Control Deficiencies

There is a presumption that the design and performance of the project will be sufficient to enable you to detect significant deficiencies and material weaknesses in internal control.[1] In order to plan the project, particularly its scope, you should therefore establish a preliminary understanding of the types and magnitude of internal control weaknesses that will rise to the level of "significant deficiency" or "material weakness." To the extent possible, you, client management, the independent auditors, and possibly the entity's legal advisors should reach a consensus on this preliminary understanding of internal control weaknesses.

Chapter 8 provides detailed guidance on the factors to consider when assessing internal control deficiencies. In general, those factors include

- The *likelihood* that the internal control deficiency could result in a misstatement of the financial statements. For example, suppose that an entity has both a preventive control and a detective control designed to achieve the same control objective. A deficiency in the preventive control may not result in a misstatement if the detective control is operating effectively. However, absent an effective detective control, a deficiency in the preventive control would be much more likely to result in a misstatement.
- Whether such a misstatement, if it were to occur, would be *material*. In developing a working definition of materiality, you should consider that
  - The auditing and accounting literature as well as the relevant legal standards describe materiality *from the user's point of view*. That is, materiality is described as the magnitude of an error or omission that would affect a *user's* decision about the entity.
  - Financial statement materiality includes both quantitative *and qualitative* factors[2]
  - Disclosure controls and procedures pertain to both financial and nonfinancial information. Determining materiality related the disclosure of nonfinancial information will involve a great deal of judgment and may require the input of the entity's legal counsel.

Your preliminary judgments about the nature and magnitude of errors that will be considered significant deficiencies or material weaknesses will be greatly influenced by your determination of which controls are considered significant. For example, a weakness in either the design or operating effectiveness of a significant control is more likely to be considered a "significant deficiency" than a comparable weakness in a control not considered significant.

As described in Chapter 1, the proposed new auditing standard provides definitions for the key terms "internal control deficiency," "significant deficiency," and "material weakness." The proposed standard also states that

- Certain control deficiencies are at a minimum "significant deficiencies."
- Other deficiencies are a strong indicator that a material weakness in internal control over financial reporting exists.

These matters are discussed in detail in Chapter 8 and are incorporated into the guidance provided in this and subsequent chapters.

Additionally, you should consider obtaining information relating to the following matters during the planning phase of the project:

- Any material weaknesses identified by the entity or its independent auditors during the most recent audit of the entity's financial statements

- Any significant deficiencies that have been communicated to management and the audit committee that remain uncorrected after a reasonable period of time
- Any restatement of previously issued financial statements to reflect the correction of a misstatement
- The nature of any material weaknesses reported by competitors or others in the entity's industry
- The common financial and nonfinancial metrics used by investors, analysts, and other users of the entity's financial statements to make decisions about the entity
- Financial statement materiality, both the quantitative and qualitative aspects
- The existence of any fraud on the part of senior management
- For entities that operate in highly regulated industries, the nature and overall effectiveness of the entity's regulatory compliance program
- For larger, more complex entities, the general nature and effectiveness of the entity's internal audit function

Project Scope and Existing Efforts to Assess Internal Control Effectiveness[3]

As you develop an overall strategy for conducting your engagement, you will need to consider the overall breadth and depth of the project. Those matters may be affected by one or more of the following:

- Operations in multiple locations
- Internal controls that reside at third parties, such as service organizations
- Recent internal audit projects
- Work performed by the disclosure committee and others

Multiple Locations. When the entity has multiple locations or business units, you will need to determine which of those locations or business units will be included in the scope of your engagement. To make this determination, you may wish to consider

- *Relative significance.* To assess the relative significance of the location or business unit, you should consider the following:
  - *Financial significance.* From a financial perspective, you should consider locations or business units that contribute significantly to material transactions, balances, or classes of transactions. For example, a business unit that contributes significantly to revenue are more likely to be included in the scope of your project than one that is inactive or makes little contribution to revenue.
  - *Operational significance.* A location or business unit may not be significant from a financial perspective but may be significant operationally. For example, an entity may have a separate business unit responsible for developing and maintaining the technology infrastructure that supports its

e-commerce activities. Financially, this business unit contributes no direct revenues to the entity, and its assets, liabilities, and expenses may be minimal. But if the entity's e-commerce activities are significant, then so too is the technology business unit that supports those activities. That business unit exposes the entity to certain risks, which you should consider when planning the engagement.

– *Risk exposure.* A location or business unit may seem relatively insignificant in terms of assets, profitability, or other financial statement measures. However, it may expose the company to specific significant risks. For example, a business unit may have the ability to create obligations, commitments, or liabilities that affect the entire entity. Business units that have the potential to expose the entity to additional risk should be considered within the scope of your engagement.

• *Aggregation of several locations or business units.* You should consider whether certain locations, though individually not considered significant, would be considered significant when combined.

• *The entity's approach to controlling its various locations or business units.* The way in which the entity establishes control over its multiple locations or business units will influence your engagement strategy and approach. For example, suppose that entity A maintains highly centralized processes and financial reporting applications, and the various locations share a common methodology for reporting and controlling activities. Entity B has relatively decentralized processes, and, because of recent acquisitions, its business units operate rather autonomously and no two financial reporting systems are alike. For entity A, you may decide to test the centralized processes and controls together with the common processes at just one or two locations. For entity B, which lacks common procedures for its business units, it may be more appropriate to expand the scope of the engagement to include the evaluation of controls at more locations and business units. Other factors you may wish to consider include

– Whether the location or business unit could create an obligation on the part of the entity

– The entity's risk assessment process

– The entity's policies and procedures for monitoring the activities of separate locations or business units

– The effectiveness of other entity-level controls

The proposed auditing standard described in Chapter 1 provides detailed guidance to the independent auditors that they will follow in deciding which locations or business units to test. Those proposed requirements are consistent with the guidance offered above and specifically require the following:

• *Individually important.* The auditor will first determine which locations or business units are individually significant. They will then audit the internal control relating to the entire location or business unit.

- *Specific risks.* Some locations or business units may present specific, significant risks to the entity. The auditor will audit the controls related to these specific risks.
- *Aggregation of locations or business units.* The auditor is required to consider which remaining locations (that is, those that are not individually important or do not pose certain specific significant risks) when aggregated, represent a group with a level of significance that could create a material misstatement. For that group, the auditor will evaluate the effectiveness of entity-level controls. Ineffective entity-level controls will result in the auditor testing controls at some of the locations or business units.
- *No work required.* No work is required on locations or business units that are not able to create, either individually or in the aggregate, a material misstatement.

Service Organizations. An entity may engage a third-party service organization to perform certain aspects of its information processing. These service organizations may provide a wide variety of services, ranging from performing a specific task under the direction of the entity to replacing entire business units or functions. The types of services such an organization may provide include

- *Information processing.* Information processing is probably the most common type of service organization. An information-processing service organization may provide standardized services, such as entering the company's manually recorded data and processing it with software that produces computer-generated journals, a general ledger, and financial statements. At the other end of the spectrum, the information-processing service organization may design and execute customized applications.
- *Trust departments.* Service organizations, such as the trust department of a bank or an insurance company, may provide a wide range of services to user organizations, such as employee benefit plans. This type of service organization could be given authority to make decisions about how a plan's assets are invested. It also may serve as custodian of the plan's assets, maintain records of each participant's account, allocate investment income to the participants based on a formula in the trust agreement, and make distributions to the participants.
- *Transfer agents, custodians, and record keepers for investment companies.* Transfer agents process purchases, sales, and other shareholder activity for investment companies. The custodian is responsible for the receipt, delivery, and safekeeping of the company's portfolio securities; the cash related to transactions in those securities; and the maintenance of records of the securities held for the investment company. Record keepers maintain the financial accounting records of the investment company based on information provided by the transfer agent and the custodian of the investment company's investments.
- Other service organizations include
  - Insurers that maintain the accounting for ceded reinsurance

  - Mortgage servicers or depository institutions that service loans for others
  - Value-added networks

When an entity uses a service organization to process transactions, the controls over that processing reside *outside the entity*, at the service organization. When developing an engagement strategy under these conditions, you will need to determine whether the scope of the engagement should be restricted to those controls that remain directly administered by the entity or extended to include the controls at the service organization. In making that determination, you should consider

- The significance of the processing activity
- The degree of interaction between the entity and the service organization

When assessing the significance of the processing activity, you may wish to treat the service organization as if it were a separate business unit or location and follow the guidance discussed previously. For example, you would consider the materiality of the transactions processed, relative to the financial statements taken as a whole. In addition, you would consider whether the nonfinancial or operational information processed by the service organization is significant to the entity and should be subject to disclosure controls and procedures.

The *degree of interaction* between the entity and the service organization is a term used in Statement on Auditing Standards (SAS) No. 70 (as amended), *Reports on the Processing of Transactions by Service Organizations*. The term refers to the extent to which the entity (the "user organization") is able and elects to implement effective controls over the processing performed by the service organization.

- If the services provided by the service organization are limited to recording user organization transactions and processing the related data, and the user organization retains responsibility for authorizing the transactions and maintaining the related accountability, there will be a high degree of interaction. When there is a high degree of interaction between the user and service organizations, then you are more likely to be able to obtain the information necessary to evaluate internal control by focusing solely on the controls maintained by the user.
- Alternatively, when the service organization is authorized to initiate and execute transactions without prior authorization of each transaction by the user, there will be a lower degree of interaction. Under these arrangements, the user must record activity from information provided by the service organization because the user has no means of independently generating a record of its transactions. In these situations, you will be more likely to *extend* the scope of your engagement to include an assessment of the service organization's controls.

It is not uncommon for the service organization to take action to help its customers gain a better understanding of the design and operating effectiveness of its controls. For example, the service organization might

- Engage its own auditor to review and report on the systems it uses to process the company's transactions
- Engage a service auditor to test the effectiveness of the controls applied to the company's transactions to enable the company to evaluate controls at the service location as part of management's assessment of its internal control

In either case, the service organization will produce a report describing the work of the service auditor and his or her findings, and that report should be useful to you when planning your project.

When considering the implications that an outside service organization has on your engagement, you may find the guidance contained in SAS No. 70 and the related Audit Guide (*Service Organizations: Applying SAS No. 70, as Amended*, published by the American Institute of Certified Public Accountants [AICPA]) to be helpful.

Internal Audit Activities. A fundamental objective of the internal audit function is to help the entity maintain effective controls by evaluating their adequacy and effectiveness. Standards established by the Institute of Internal Auditors state that this evaluation should include the

- Reliability and integrity of financial and operational information
- Effectiveness and efficiency of operations
- Safeguarding of assets
- Compliance with laws, regulations, and contracts

In planning the scope of your project, you may wish to incorporate some of the conclusions reached by the internal auditors into your findings about the effectiveness of the entity's internal control. Keep in mind that the objectives of the engagements performed by the internal auditors may not have been performed primarily for the purpose of reporting on internal control within the context of the Sarbanes-Oxley Act Section 404. Therefore, when determining how internal audit engagements and conclusions affect the scope of your engagement, you should consider

- The scope of the internal auditor's engagements and whether it is sufficient to meet the objectives of your project. For example, an internal audit engagement may have evaluated internal controls for only a limited number of business units, excluding one or more of those you consider significant. In that case, you would want to include an evaluation of the other significant business units in the scope of your project.
- The timing of the work and whether it is within a time frame that would permit you to draw a conclusion as to the effectiveness of the entity's internal control as of the end of the year. If a significant amount of time has elapsed since the internal auditors performed their engagement, additional testing may need to be performed to determine whether the conclusions reached are still appropriate

- The documentation of the internal auditors' procedures and whether this is sufficient for the independent auditors. If you plan to incorporate the work of the internal auditors, you should evaluate the documentation of their work to ensure that the independent auditors can rely on the conclusions reached. For considering an internal auditor's work in an audit of internal control, the independent auditors will refer to the auditing standard, which refers them to SAS No. 65, *Auditor's Consideration of Internal Audit Function.* That standard states that the auditor should consider such factors as whether the internal auditors'
  - Audit programs are adequate.
  - Working papers adequately document work performed, including evidence of supervision and review.
  - Conclusions are appropriate in the circumstances.
  - Reports are consistent with the results of the work performed.

Disclosure Committee. Chapters 1 and 2 describe the responsibilities of the entity's disclosure committee for overseeing the process by which Securities and Exchange Commission (SEC)-mandated disclosures are created and reviewed. When planning your engagement, you should consider the policies and processes of the committee and the extent to which their work product can be used to support the entity's evaluation of its internal control. Policies and processes of the disclosure committee that may affect the planning of your project include

- Areas of the entity's business that should be monitored for disclosure issues
- Individuals within each monitored area who are best able to identify potential disclosure issues
- Methods for communicating identified disclosure issues to the disclosure committee
- Disclosure documents (in addition to Exchange Act filings) that are the responsibility of the disclosure committee. These documents may include
  - Reports and letters to shareholders
  - Earnings releases
  - Presentations to analysts
- Any comparisons of the entity's disclosures to those of its competitors, which the committee may have done to benchmark the company's disclosures
- If applicable, the impact on the entity's disclosure controls and procedures of any significant changes to the entity, for example—
  - New information systems
  - Significant acquisitions or dispositions
  - Changes in lines of business
  - Geographic expansion
  - Changes in personnel with significant control responsibilities

INFORMATION SOURCES

A great deal of information exists about publicly traded companies and the industries in which they operate. When planning your project, you are more likely to encounter problems related to having too much, rather than too little, information. For that reason, your information-gathering strategy should focus on selectivity. Chances are that most of the information you need to plan an engagement can be provided by just a few sources. Rather than try to read an entire 10K, for example, you should instead target a few key sections of the 10K and then perform a thorough, in-depth reading. Following is a discussion of the information sources that are most likely to provide the information you need to achieve the planning objectives described earlier in this chapter.

SEC Form 10K

Annually, publicly traded companies are required to file their Form 10K within 90 days of their year-end (soon to be 60 days under a proposed SEC rule). This form provides a great deal of narrative information about the entity, its industry, competitors, and business risks in addition to the most recent financial statements. A targeted, in-depth reading of the 10K can provide you with a sound background for understanding key elements of the entity and its industry that affect risk and the design of internal control. You should consider your client's 10K as a primary source of information needed for planning.

When reading the entity's 10K, keep in mind that your main objective is to

* Learn about the characteristics of the entity and the industry.
* Highlight possible areas of focus.

It would be unlikely that one single area or item of disclosure will be able to provide you with all the information you need. Instead, as you read the targeted areas of the document, look for patterns and recurring themes about the company and how it does business.

In general, the 10K is divided into four parts. The first of these parts provides information on the entity's operations, and the second part covers the financial statements and Management's Discussion and Analysis. These are the two parts of the 10K that probably will be most useful for your purposes. The following is a brief summary of the information contained in a 10K that typically is most valuable to understanding and planning an evaluation of an entity's internal control.

Description of the Business. The 10K starts off with a general description of the entity's business. Usually, these descriptions are succinct and help you quickly understand how the company makes money. For example, the entity is required to disclose its principal products or services, how those products are distributed, and the sources and availability of raw materials, if applicable. Some companies also include a brief overview of other matters that will be helpful, such as their organizational structure or key business strategies. Mergers, acquisitions, major restructurings of the entity's operations also will be disclosed in this section of the 10K. These types of significant changes to an entity frequently pose challenges to internal control that can diminish its effectiveness. See the discussion of the risk assessment of internal control provided in Chapter 2 for additional details.

The SEC rules emphasize the need for a discussion of the entity's operating segments, and this information can be quite helpful. Not only will it give you a better understanding of how the company does business, this discussion also will allow you to identify the presence of multiple business units or locations, which will have an effect on the scope of your procedures, as discussed earlier.

Item 1 of an entity's 10K typically includes a discussion of the entity's competitive condition, which includes a description of the particular markets in which it competes. This discussion usually is quite informative about the characteristics of the industry and the dynamics of how it operates. You also may learn about the key financial and nonfinancial measures that investors and others use to judge the company's performance, and this knowledge can help you make preliminary determinations about materiality. In turn, materiality judgments are critical for determining which accounts, balances, and classes of transactions are significant and which internal control deficiencies may be considered material weaknesses.

Other information in this section of the 10K that may provide additional insight about either the industry, the entity, or its internal controls include

- The extent to which the company's business is seasonal
- The practices of the entity or the industry relating to inventory management, the extension of credit to customers, and other methods for managing working capital
- Information about key customers, if the entity is highly dependent on one or a few customers
- Backlog for the company's products
- Research and development activities
- The number of employees and a general description of the workforce
- Legal proceedings

Risk Factors Affecting the Business. The SEC has long recognized that investors value "forward-looking" information that describes the company's plans and its projections about future performance. However, companies were hesitant to provide this type of information for fear of litigation in the event that the entity did not realize its plans. In an attempt to encourage the disclosure of forward-looking information while protecting companies who made such disclosures in good faith from unreasonable litigation, the Private Securities Litigation Reform Act of 1995 created a "safe harbor" provision for forward-looking statements.

The safe harbor provides public companies with a defense in securities disclosure litigation challenging such forward-looking statements. This defense is available, however, only if the statements are clearly identified as forward-looking and are coupled with cautionary language as mandated by the Act. You will find that cautionary language in the company's 10K, usually identified as "risk factors" that affect the company's business.

Note that boilerplate language will not invoke the protections of the safe harbor. Instead, the cautionary statement should articulate each risk, why it is relevant to the forward-looking statements, and how it could actually influence whether those statements turn out to be true. The disclosure begins with a brief, one-sentence summary of the risk (highlighted in some fashion), followed by a more detailed discussion. In reading this section of the 10K, be alert for the following:

- *Risks that have a direct impact on one or more components of the entity's internal control.* For example, consider the following risk factor, described in the 2002 10K of Sangamo BioSciences, Inc., a biotechnology research and development company:

    Failure to attract, retain and motivate skilled personnel and cultivate key academic collaborations will delay our product development
    Our success depends on our continued ability to attract, retain and motivate highly qualified management and scientific personnel . . . Competition for personnel . . . is intense . . . If we lose the services of personnel with these types of skills, it could impede significantly the achievement of our research and development objectives.

    The way in which the entity responds to this risk will have a direct effect on the control environment component of its internal controls. As described in Chapter 2, one of the key components of an entity's control environment is its human resource policies and the methods used to attract, train, motivate, and retain personnel. In this example, the entity's success depends on its ability to compete effectively for qualified personnel. In planning an engagement to assess internal control effectiveness, one should consider the strategies the company has developed for meeting this challenge (e.g., a stock-based compensation program) and how these strategies contribute to or detract from an effective control environment.

- *Risks that will affect the entity's disclosure controls and procedures.* As described in Chapter 1, an entity's disclosure controls and procedures should "capture information that is relevant to an assessment of the need to disclose developments and risks that pertain to the entity's business." Thus, the business risks described in the entity's 10K will provide you with valuable insight as to the types of information that should be encompassed by the entity's disclosure controls and procedures. For example, consider these two risks, which were disclosed in the 2002 10K for Polo Ralph Lauren Corporation:

    1. Our business could suffer as a result of a manufacturer's inability to produce our goods on time and to our specifications
    We do not own or operate any manufacturing facilities and therefore depend upon independent third parties for the manufacture of all of our products . . .

2. Our business could suffer if we need to replace manufacturers

  We compete with other companies for the production capacity of our manufacturers and import quota capacity . . . If we experience a significant increase in demand, or if an existing manufacturer or ours must be replaced, we may have to expand our third-party manufacturing capacity. We cannot assure you that this additional capacity will be available when required on terms that are acceptable to us.

  Given this information, one would expect that the company's disclosure controls and procedures would be able to identify and report to senior management significant changes in the company's relationships with its third-party manufacturers. If the entity's system were *not* capable of capturing and communicating this information, one would have to question whether a system that could not monitor one of the company's main business risks was truly effective.

- *Descriptions of risk that provide further insight into the business and industry operating characteristics.* Note that the two risk disclosures described above clarify Polo Ralph Lauren Corporation's operations: It is *not* a manufacturing entity but instead relies on others to manufacture its products.

  Finally, as described in Chapter 2, the entity's risk assessment process is a component of its internal control. The first steps in that process are to identify and then assess the various risks faced by the company. The entity's 10K disclosures of those risks will provide you with insight into this process at the entity level, which for many companies will be considered a significant control.

Management's Discussion and Analysis. Item 7 of the 10K is the MD&A—management's discussion and analysis of financial condition and results of operations. This is an important section of the 10K, which can provide you with an in-depth understanding of the entity and some of its main internal control challenges. The SEC has stated that the MD&A is "intended to provide, in one section of a filing, material historical and prospective textual disclosure enabling investors and other users to assess the financial condition and results of operations of the registrant, with particular emphasis on the registrant's prospects for the future." When a technically correct application of generally accepted accounting principles (GAAP) provides an incomplete picture of a company's financial condition, MD&A is intended to complete that disclosure.[4]

  Guidance from the National Investor Relations Institute suggests that an entity's MD&A include the following items, all of which will be helpful to you in planning your engagement to assess internal control:

- A brief description of the company's business that clarifies how it makes money.
- The primary factors or trends, both short and long term, causing revenues to increase, decrease or remain flat. The company should also explain clearly and simply any changes to its policies on revenue recognition or expense deferment from those disclosed in the Annual Report/Form 10K.

- A brief discussion of what drives other key data, such as gross profit; sales, general and administrative (SG&A) expenses; other income (expense); interest expense; income taxes; and the effect of currency translation or transaction on net income.
- An explanation of any charges, including both pre- and after-tax numbers and whether there will or could be additional charges of a similar nature in future quarters.
- A brief discussion of liquidity and capital resources, including debt levels and key ratios, the adequacy of cash resources, cash provided from operations, capital expenditures, any anticipated changes in financing, and any share repurchases.
- Key measures specific to its industry that a company uses to evaluate performance, such as same-store sales growth for retailers or net interest margin for financial institutions.
- Any material changes in accounting practices adopted during the quarter, either due to changes in Financial Accounting Standards Board (FASB) requirements or by company choice.
- The company's current expectations for sales and earnings (if the company provides such guidance at all).

Critical Accounting Policies. The SEC's MD&A rules require disclosure about trends, events, or uncertainties known to management that would have a material impact on reported financial information. However, the Commission believes that companies should provide investors with a greater awareness of the sensitivity of financial statements to the methods, assumptions, and estimates underlying their preparation. To achieve this awareness, the Commission encourages companies to disclose their "critical accounting policies," which are defined as "the judgments and uncertainties affecting the application of those policies, and the likelihood that materially different amounts would be reported under different conditions or using different assumptions."[5]

The review of a company's critical accounting policies, combined with an analysis of the financial statements, can help you make preliminary judgments about significant controls. For example, in its 2003 10K, Krispy Kreme Doughnuts, Inc. identified the accounting for intangible assets as one of its critical accounting policies. Significantly, the company highlighted the accounting for impairment losses on intangible assets, which requires significant judgment. A review of the balance sheet indicates that total intangible assets were approximately $48 million, or approximately 12 percent of total assets. Given this information, an evaluation of internal controls should consider the procedures the entity has in place to identify the events or changes in circumstances that could indicate that one or more of these assets has been impaired.

Other Information Sources

The 10K should be your primary source of information about the company and its industry. However, a review of other sources can help you confirm the knowledge gained through reading the 10K, and possibly update or identify other conditions that were not included in the 10K. Other helpful sources of information include

- The entity's annual report
- Any recent 8Ks filed by the entity
- The entity's "Investor Relations" section on its Web site and on the Web sites of its competitors
- Analyst reports on the entity, its competitors or industry

Inquiries

Making inquiries of key personnel at the initial planning stage of your project is an excellent way to

- Probe deeper into issues identified based on your review of the 10K and other written documentation.
- Confirm your understanding of information already gathered.
- Establish a relationship with individuals you will need to work closely with during the engagement.

In addition to senior management, you should consider making inquiries of entity personnel involved in operations, internal audit, and investor relations. You also may wish to gather information from the entity's independent auditors and SEC counsel.

Additional Guidance

Appendix 3B provides detailed guidance on the questions you should consider when performing research and gathering the information needed to plan your engagement.

STRUCTURING THE PROJECT TEAM

During the planning phase of the project you should describe the overall responsibilities of the project team and how the team will be configured to achieve its objectives.

Establishing Responsibilities and Lines of Reporting

The project team should have the responsibility for overseeing and coordinating all of the activities relating to the evaluation of and reporting on the effectiveness of the entity's internal control. As a condition for assuming this responsibility, the team should have the authority to conduct the evaluation in a way that is appropriate given the nature, size, and complexity of the organization.

Exhibit 3.1 shows an example of how a project team for evaluating internal

Exhibit 3.1   Example Project Team Organization

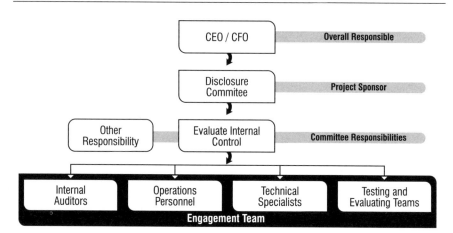

control fits into an entity's overall financial reporting structure. As described in Chapter 2, internal control over financial reporting are a subset of an entity's disclosure controls and procedures. Thus, Exhibit 3.1 describes the internal control evaluation engagement team as reporting to the disclosure committee. Alternatively, the engagement team could report directly to the chief executive officer (CEO) and chief financial officer (CFO), who are responsible for certifying the effectiveness of the entity's internal control.

However the lines of reporting are configured, you should be sure that the project team reports to one of the senior committees or executives at the entity in order to emphasize that

- The successful completion of the evaluation is important for the entity.
- Communications and requests from the engagement team should be given a high priority.

Project Team Members

The project team should be comprised of individuals with the knowledge, skills, and authority within the entity to oversee a successful engagement. Collectively, the group should have a high-level knowledge of the entity's operations and strategies and have the authority to make important decisions and obtain and allocate the necessary resources. Exhibit 3.1 describes an example project team consisting of key operating personnel, technical specialists, and one or more testing and evaluation teams.

Internal Auditors. Internal auditors can be a valuable resource in helping an entity assess the effectiveness of internal control. In general, internal audit can provide assistance in two different ways.

- *Use of work product.* The work that internal auditors perform as part of their normal, routine responsibilities may provide you with
  - Documentation about the design of internal control
  - Evidence to support the effectiveness of the design, operations, or both of specific controls

    The section entitled "Internal Audit Activities" included earlier in this chapter identified some of the issues you may encounter when using the work of internal auditors in this capacity. Additionally, as described in Chapter 1, the PCAOB's proposed auditing standard relating to internal control reporting places limits on the degree to which independent auditors may rely on the internal auditor's work product.
- *Project team member.* The internal auditor can be a member of the project team, working under the direct supervision of the engagement team leader to perform procedures designed specifically to comply with the Sarbanes-Oxley internal control reporting requirements.

Exhibit 3.1 depicts internal auditor participation as part of the project team. As project team members, internal auditors may provide assistance in any number of areas, including

- Enhancing the understanding of entity operations, significant risks, and controls
- Providing insight or a preliminary analysis on the relative strengths and weaknesses of each component of internal control
- Providing technical expertise in areas such as information technology (IT) auditing
- Assisting in the design or testing of controls

Operations Personnel. Operating personnel from the entity's major business segments or activities should be involved with the project team. These individuals will contribute an in-depth understanding of the entity's operations, the business risks of various activities, and existing controls. Having these individuals on the project team will also help establish important communication channels between the team and entity employees who will be responsible for providing information to the team or implementing its recommendations.

Technical Specialists. The project team may need technical expertise in order to successfully meet its objectives. In some industries it is typical for entities to establish certain quality control groups; for example, financial institutions will have a credit review committee whose responsibilities include setting underwriting criteria and ensuring that the entity's lending practices conform to those criteria. Individuals with this type of expertise can be invaluable to project teams seeking to understand an entity's operations and internal control structure.

Information technology specialists may be required whenever the entity uses

IT to enable key business activities or process significant transactions. The presence of one or more of the following conditions may indicate that IT expertise is needed on your engagement:

- Technology development is a significant value-chain activity (as described in Chapter 2).
- The entity has recently implemented a new IT system or made significant modifications to its existing system.
- The entity has significant e-commerce activity.
- Data is shared extensively between computer applications.
- The entity uses emerging or unproven technologies.

It is anticipated that information technology expertise will be required on most projects. An IT specialist is essential for helping the project team

- Identify risks related to these IT system
- Document and test IT controls
- Design and implement missing IT controls, if any
- Monitor the continued effectiveness of IT controls

As described in Chapter 2, the Information Technology Governance Institute (ITGI) and the Information Systems Audit and Control Association (ISACA) have published *IT Control Objectives for Sarbanes-Oxley*, which provides guidance to IT auditors who assist management in the testing and evaluation of internal control. In addressing the planning for these projects, the authors of the document note the following:

> To meet the demands of Sarbanes-Oxley, most organizations will require a change in culture. More likely than not, enhancements to IT systems and processes will be required, most notably in the design, documentation and evaluation of IT controls. Because the cost of noncompliance can be devastating to an organization, it is crucial to adopt a proactive approach and take on the challenge early.[6]

As a first step toward planning the IT component of the project, the document recommends the following:

- Management and the project leader should obtain an understanding of the risks inherent in IT systems and the effect these risks have on the project.
- IT management should obtain an understanding of the financial reporting process and its supporting systems.
- The Chief Information Officer should have an advanced knowledge of the types of IT controls necessary to support reliable financial information processing.

Testing and Evaluation Teams. Depending on the size and complexity of the entity, the project team may conduct the testing and evaluation of internal controls itself. Alternatively, it may act in more of a supervisory capacity and delegate the performance of the procedures to one or more testing and evaluation teams. If the engagement requires the use of multiple project teams, steps should be taken to ensure the consistency and quality of the procedures performed. For example, training (either formal or informal) on the evaluation process and control documentation tools may be required.

COORDINATING WITH THE INDEPENDENT AUDITORS

It is vital that you coordinate your project with the entity's independent auditors. This coordination process begins at the planning phase of the project and continues at each subsequent phase. Proper coordination between your team and the independent auditors will facilitate an effective and efficient audit. A lack of coordination with the auditors could result in a variety of negative, unforeseen consequences, including

- Duplication of effort
- Reperformance of certain tests
- Performance of additional tests or expansion of the scope of the engagement
- Misunderstandings relating to the definition or reporting of material weaknesses

As a starting point for understanding the auditors' expectations related to your engagement, you should have a working knowledge of the standards the independent auditors are required to follow when auditing an entity's internal control. As described in Chapter 1, at the time this manuscript was prepared, those standards were in the process of being developed by the PCAOB.

Reach Consensus on Planning Matters

You should reach a consensus with the entity's independent auditors on key planning decisions, including

- The overall engagement process and approach
- The scope of your project, including locations or business units to be included
- Preliminary identification of significant controls
- The nature of any internal control deficiencies noted by the auditors during their most recent audit of the entity's financial statements
- Tentative conclusions about what will constitute a significant deficiency or material weakness

- The nature and extent of the documentation of controls

- The nature and extent of the documentation of tests of controls

- The degree to which the auditors will rely on the results of your testwork to reach their conclusion

Additionally, some firms have developed guidance on the factors to consider when determining whether internal control, as a whole, is effective. You should determine if your client's auditors have developed such guidance and, if so, obtain that guidance, as it will help you design and, subsequently, evaluate the effectiveness of significant controls. For example, Chapter 6 describes the Internal Control Reliability Model as a tool that can help evaluate overall effectiveness of internal control. Some audit firms may have similar models.

During the early phases of the project, it may not be possible to obtain a definitive understanding with the auditors on all significant planning matters. In those situations, you should still work with the auditors to reach a consensus regarding

- A clear understanding of the issue(s) that need resolution

- The additional information required to reach a resolution

- The process to be followed to resolve the matter

- An estimated time frame for the process to be completed and the issue(s) to be resolved

DOCUMENTING YOUR PLANNING DECISIONS

You may wish to document your planning decisions. Having a written record of these decisions can help

- Clarify and confirm the understanding of your engagement with management, the entity's independent auditors and others. Circulating this planning document and receiving feedback on it can greatly improve the communications process among all those affected by the engagement.

- Establish a concise record of significant facts and circumstances that influenced the design of your engagement, which can be used by others who review the entity's internal control going forward.

- Provide a permanent record of the entity's compliance with the requirement to review the effectiveness of its internal control.

Your documentation need not be extensive, and may be simply a summary of key planning considerations and conclusions. Items that you may consider documenting include

Background Information

- Sources of written information you considered in planning the engagement
- Excerpts of key passages from those documents, for example, the description of the entity's business or its risks, in the entity's 10K
- Discussions you had with management, the entity's auditors, or others. Include a general description of what was discussed and when the discussions were held.

Tentative Conclusions

- Significant controls
- Definitions of materiality, significant internal control deficiencies, and material weaknesses
- Considerations for determining effectiveness of internal control
- Project scope, including the effects of
  - Responsibilities and activities of the disclosure committee
  - Internal auditors' efforts to document or evaluate internal control
  - The use of an outside service organization to process certain transactions
  - Multiple locations and business units

Project Team Organization and Project Administration

- Lines of reporting (i.e., to whom the project team will report)
- Timetable for completion of key phases of the project
- Plans for coordinating with the client, external auditors, legal counsel, and others, as appropriate
- The involvement of specialists

Discussions with Independent Auditors

- Project matters discussed with the independent auditors
- Conclusions reached on key planning matters
- Open items and any issues that remain to be resolved

Before finalizing any documentation, it would be advisable to consult with the entity's legal counsel regarding the nature and extent of the documentation.

APPENDIX 3A
Action Plan:
Project Planning

The following action plan is intended to help you implement the suggestions contained in this chapter for planning your project.

1. Information Sources

Identify and obtain sources of information about the entity that will be useful for planning purposes. For example:

- Consider published sources of information, including

  - Form 10K and other SEC filings

  - Annual report

  - Information available in the entity's investor relations section of its Web site

  - Analyst reports

- Identify key individuals to be the subject of inquiries that will help you supplement the knowledge gained through reading written materials.

2. Preliminary Understanding of Significant Control Objectives and Areas of Focus

Based on your research, develop a preliminary understanding of the entity's significant control objectives and areas of emphasis for your engagement. For example:

- Identify possible significant control objectives by considering—

  - The entity's key business activities

  - Industry characteristics

  - Significant risks facing the entity and the industry

  - Financial reporting matters

  - Significant controls defined by the relevant auditing standard

- Identify other areas of focus, including those that

  - Have a known or suspected control weakness

  - Possess a high risk for material misstatement irrespective of any controls

3. Preliminary Definition of Material Weakness

Project scope and procedures must be designed to detect material misstatements. Therefore, in planning the engagement, you should develop a preliminary definition of what will constitute a material weakness. For example:

- Consider the definition of material weakness provided in the auditing literature.
- Describe how this definition will be applied to the specific circumstances of the entity. Consider
  - Factors that will affect the *likelihood* that an internal control deficiency will result in a misstatement of the financial statements
  - How the entity will determine materiality, including the qualitative factors that affect materiality
  - The nature of any material weakness reported by other companies in the same industry

4. Project Scope

Determine the overall scope of the project. Consider

- The locations, business units, or reporting segments that will be subject to documentation and testing
- The effect, if any, of information processing performed by third-party service organizations
- How the work already performed by internal auditors may be used to achieve your project objectives
- How the policies, processes, and work product of the disclosure committee may be used in your project

5. Project Team

You will need to form a project team to carry out your plan. To form this team may require you to

- Establish the overall responsibilities of the engagement team and obtain the concurrence of the CEO and CFO, who have the ultimate responsibility for forming an opinion and reporting on the effectiveness of the entity's internal control.
- Establish the lines of reporting for the team to ensure that it has the proper stature and authority in the organization to achieve its objectives.
- Identify the knowledge and skills required by the team as a whole. Choose individual team members based on these requirements.

6. Coordinate with Independent Auditors

Reach a consensus with the independent auditors regarding key planning decisions. For example:

- Communicate and reach agreement with the auditors on matters such as
  - The overall engagement process and approach
  - The scope of your project, including locations or business units to be included
  - Preliminary identification of significant controls
  - The nature of any control deficiencies noted by the auditors during their most recent audit of the entity's financial statements
  - Tentative conclusions about what will constitute a significant deficiency or material weakness
  - The nature and extent of the documentation of controls
  - The nature and extent of the documentation of tests of controls
  - The degree to which the auditors will rely on the results of your testwork to reach their conclusion

7. Documentation

Consider documenting planning decisions. For example:

- Consult with legal counsel regarding the nature and extent of possible documentation of planning decisions.
- Prepare documentation of key matters, including
  - Information used to make decisions
  - Tentative conclusions on significant planning matters
  - Project team organization, composition, and the like
  - Discussions with independent auditors

APPENDIX 3B
Summary of Planning Questions

Exhibit 3.2 summarizes some of the questions you should consider when planning your project to assess the effectiveness of a company's internal control. The second column provides guidance on how the answers to the questions are relevant for planning purposes. The third column offers suggestions on the most likely sources for obtaining the information.

Exhibit 3.2 Summary of Planning Questions

Planning Questions to Consider	Relevance for Engagement Performance	Information Sources
Company Operations and Industry Characteristics		
What are the primary characteristics of the entity's industry? Consider the effect of • Financial reporting practices • Economic conditions • Laws and regulations • Technological changes	• Determine significant controls • Establish materiality thresholds • Understand business and financial reporting risks	• SEC Form 10K and other filings • Inquiries of management or auditors • Analyst reports • Annual report to shareholders • Company and competitor Web sites • Industry publications
What are the fundamental operating characteristics of the entity?	Develop a preliminary understanding of the entity's value chain	Same as above
Which financial statement accounts, balances, or disclosures possess one or more of the following attributes? • Subjective in nature • Complex accounting • Accounting rules subject to interpretation • Dependent on external information	Make judgments about inherent risk, which will help identify those areas where strong controls are important	• Financial statements • Inquiries of management or auditors
Engagement Scope		
Which business activities or locations • Are financially most significant? • Are operationally most significant? • Have the potential to expose the entity to significant risk or obligation? • Lack adequate available information?	Determine scope of engagement	• SEC Form 10K and other filings • Annual report to shareholders • Inquiries of management
Does the entity use a service organization to process significant information?	Determine scope of engagement	Inquiries of management

(Continued)

Exhibit 3.2 (*Continued*)

Planning Questions to Consider	Relevance for Engagement Performance	Information Sources
What is the nature and extent of the entity's • Internal audit function? • Disclosure committee?	Determine scope of engagement	Inquiries of management
Internal Control Considerations		
What processes does the entity currently have in place to perform a self-assessment of its internal control?	• Determine scope of engagement • Plan the nature of the procedures to be performed	• Inquiries of management • Annual report and other filings
What have been the most significant recent changes to the company and its internal controls?	• Identify potential problem areas and set the focus for the engagement • Determine significant controls	• Inquiries of management and auditors • SEC Form 10K and Form 8K
What is the nature and extent of the entity's existing documentation of its internal control?	• Determine scope of the engagement • Assess needs	• Inquiries of management • Annual report to shareholders
What are management's current views regarding • The most important policies, procedures and practices it uses to control the business • Areas of potential weakness in internal control	• Determine significant controls • Determine scope of the engagement	Inquiries of management
Has management received communications from its independent auditors regarding control deficiencies observed during its audit of the entity's financial statements? What was the nature of these deficiencies?	• Determine significant controls • Determine scope of the engagement	

Has the company or its external auditors established guidance for • Defining "effective," for the purposes of assessing internal controls? • Defining "significant deficiency" and "material weakness?"	• Design procedures • Establish scope of procedures • Evaluate effectiveness of internal controls	Inquiries of management and auditor
If no guidance has been provided on defining a significant deficiency or material weakness, then— • What are the most significant financial and non-financial metrics used by third parties to evaluate the company? • What qualitative (i.e., disclosure information) would be most relevant to third parties?	Make preliminary judgments about materiality	• Inquiries of management, auditors, and attorneys • SEC Form 10K and other filings • Analyst reports

Existence of Significant Deficiency and Possible Material Weakness

In the past year, has there been a restatement of a previously issued financial statement to reflect the correction of a misstatement?	Identify significant deficiency and possible material weakness	Inquiry of management
In the past year, have the independent auditors identified a material misstatement in the financial statements that was not initially identified by the company's internal control?	Identify significant deficiency and possible material weakness	Inquiry of management
Are there any significant deficiencies that have been communicated to management that remain uncorrected after a reasonable time?	Identify significant deficiency and possible material weakness	Inquiry of management
Is the board aware of a fraud of any magnitude on the part of senior management?	Identify significant deficiency and possible material weakness	Inquiry of the board of directors

Notes

1. This presumption is not explicitly stated in any of the rules, regulations, or professional standards relating to internal control reporting. However, one would have to question the value of an engagement in which the detection of such deficiencies and weaknesses was not reasonably assured.

2. The auditing literature provides guidance to auditors on the qualitative factors that should be considered when assessing materiality. This guidance is provided by an auditing interpretation, which has been codified in the AICPA *Professional Standards*, AU Sec. 9312.15.

3. As described in Chapter 1, the PCAOB has proposed a new auditing standard relating to the independent auditor's audit of an entity's internal control. That planned standard will include guidance on several of the matters discussed in this section, including:
   - Consideration of multiple locations and business units
   - Planning and performance of tests related to service organizations
   - The auditor's use of and reliance on tests performed by internal auditors and others

   In planning your project you should become familiar with the PCAOB's guidance on these matters once the final auditing standard becomes available.

4. This second sentence represents the views of Karl Groskaufmanis, an SEC attorney with Fried, Frank, Harris, Shriver & Jacobson. The comments were taken from his article on MD&A disclosure that appeared on the Web site of the National Investor Relations Institute, *www.niri.org.*

5. See SEC release No. 8040 (*www.sec.gov/rules/other/33-8040.htm*). The SEC currently is considering rules that would provide further guidance on what should be considered a critical accounting policy.

6. Christopher Fox and Paul A. Zonneveld, *IT Control Objectives for Sarbanes-Oxley* (Information Technology Governance Institute and the Information Systems Audit and Control Association, 2003), p. 9.

Chapter 4

Identifying Significant Control Objectives

Chapter Summary

Describe entity-level control objectives that typically are significant:
- Corporate culture
- Personnel policies
- General computer controls
- Alignment between entity objectives and control structures
- Risk identification
- Top-level financial reporting processes
- System-wide monitoring

Provide guidance on identifying significant activity-level control objectives.

INTRODUCTION

The COSO framework recognizes that, within the context of an internal control structure (taken as a whole), some controls are more significant than others. When assessing the effectiveness of internal control, your engagement should be sure to encompass these significant controls, and often the engagement will be limited to testing these controls only.

Controls vary between entities. Moreover, the way in which individual controls combine to create an overall internal control structure also will vary. Different entities may achieve the same control objective by different controls or combinations of controls. For example, suppose that both Company A and Company B have several subsidiaries, each of which reports financial results that must be consolidated. Both companies have the same control objective: to make sure that the results reported by the subsidiaries are accurate, complete, and prepared in a way that facilitates the consolidation. They may take different approaches to achieving this same objective; for example, suppose that

- Company A's subsidiaries are all in similar lines of business, and the company relies on standardized financial reporting packages and procedures to collect information. Preparers at each subsidiary have different levels of accounting expertise, but all are highly trained on how to properly complete the standard reporting packages. The company's internal auditors periodically review each subsidiary to ensure that their processes for preparing the packages are reliable. At the corporate level, the subsidiaries' financial reports are analytically reviewed and any unusual relationships are identified and investigated. In this system, the more significant controls involve

- The design of the standard reporting packages
- The effectiveness of the training on how to prepare these packages
- The monitoring of the process done by the internal auditors

The reviews performed at the corporate level, though important, are somewhat secondary.

- Each of company B's subsidiaries are in substantially different lines of business, several of which require the application of highly specialized accounting standards. To ensure the proper application of these standards, the company requires all the subsidiary controllers to have extensive experience in the industry's accounting practices. The company does not have standardized reporting packages but, instead, requires the subsidiaries to provide trial balances and other disclosures to facilitate the preparation of the consolidated financial statements. This information is the subject of agreed-upon procedures engagements that are performed by external certified public accountants (CPAs). At the corporate level, individual accountants closely review the information submitted by the subsidiaries together with the agreed-upon procedures reports. For company B, the more significant controls are

- The hiring policies for subsidiary controllers
- The review and monitoring performed by the corporate accounting staff
- The agreed-upon procedures engagements

To recognize that different controls and combinations of controls can achieve the same objective, this chapter focuses on identifying significant control *objectives*. The guidance provided in this chapter assumes that

- Certain entity-wide control objectives should be presumed to be significant for most entities.
- Some activity-level control objectives will be more significant than others, and so guidance is needed to identify these significant activity-level objectives.

The guidance contained in this chapter is built on the COSO framework introduced in Chapter 2. However, it does not follow the COSO framework exactly. Some of the control components and ideas described in COSO have been reorganized in this chapter in order to facilitate their explanation and the subsequent documentation and testing provided in Chapters 5, 6, and 7.

ENTITY-LEVEL CONTROL OBJECTIVES PRESUMED TO BE SIGNIFICANT

Entity-level control objectives have a pervasive effect on the design and operating effectiveness of activity-level controls. Certain of these control objectives are presumed to be significant for most entities.[1]

Corporate Culture

Scholars define culture in many different ways (see Exhibit 4.1). Most of these definitions describe a culture as a system of beliefs and values that are shared among members of a group. More often than not, this process of sharing is informal and communicated indirectly through symbols and symbolic activities. For example, in a work environment, the physical space in which one works is a symbol of that person's status within the organization. A corner office means something; a cubicle in an interior "bullpen" means something else.

Members of a group must become socialized to the culture of the group. This socialization process seeks to make the individual a functioning member of the group. The process teaches individuals what is acceptable and not acceptable within that particular culture. For example, an individual starting work at a new job will quickly learn the acceptable style of dress. In some organizations, a business suit may be seen as making the individual overly formal, aloof, and unapproachable. In another organization, blue jeans and a collarless shirt may be viewed as too informal and reflective of careless, undisciplined work habits.

The socialization process teaches individuals within the group

- *Values.* These are the guidelines for behavior accepted by members of the organization. For example, the organization may value informal relationships and communications styles.

Exhibit 4.1   Some Definitions of Culture

Culture is . . .

- Behavior, cultivated through social learning
- The behaviors, beliefs, values, and symbols accepted by a group, generally without thinking about them, and communicated and imitated among its members
- Symbolic communication whose meanings are learned and deliberately perpetuated
- Patterns of and for behavior that are communicated by symbols. On one hand, culture may be considered as a product of actions taken by individuals; on the other hand, as conditioning influences upon further action.
- The sum total of the learned behavior of a group of people

Source: Adapted from a list prepared by Gee Ekachai, associate professor, Department of Speech Communications at Southern Illinois University at Carbondale, for his course "Communications Across Cultures."

- *Norms.* These are the specific ways that organizational values are expressed in behavior. For example, members of the organization may dress in a casual style.
- *Shared beliefs.* These are the ways that the organization expects individuals to behave in particular situations. For example, if someone has a question to ask the person in the office next to him or her, the accepted method of communication might be to ask the person directly or possibly through instant messaging, but not through writing a formal memo or e-mail.

In these discussions and definitions of culture, there is a direct link between culture and behavior. An organization's culture—its values, norms, and beliefs—drive the behavior of its members. It is this link between culture and behavior that led to the conclusion in the COSO report that

- The effectiveness of an entity's internal control can not rise above its ethical values, and therefore,
- Ethical values are essential elements of internal control because they affect the design, administration, and monitoring of other control components.

Based on the COSO framework, minimum control objectives related to an organization's culture should include

- Definition and communication of ethical and behavioral norms. Note that formal, documented statements about values often paint only a partial (or even inaccurate) picture of the company's values. "Accidental values" can arise spontaneously without being formally defined, and these values can take hold in the entity over time.[2]
- Removal or reduction of incentives and temptations that could motivate people act outside of the organization's defined ethical norms
- Reinforcement of stated ethical values and norms through observable behavior of the entity's leaders
- Appropriateness of remedial action taken in response to departures from approved policies and procedures or violations of the entity's code of conduct
- Attitudes and actions related to intervention or the override of established control procedures

Personnel Policies

Internal control is a people-dependent process. That is, the effectiveness of an entity's internal control ultimately depends on how effectively its personnel perform their control-related responsibilities.

Each person in an organization brings a unique background and ability to his or her assignments. People have different needs and priorities. They do not always understand, communicate, or perform consistently. Thus, at the entity level, the organization must institute a set of policies and procedures aimed at improving the effectiveness with which its people perform their control-related tasks.

Personnel-related controls generally can be grouped into three levels.

1. *Understanding and awareness of the individual's control-related responsibilities.* Before individuals can effectively contribute to the entity's internal control, they must know what is expected of them. See Exhibit 4.2 for an example.

2. *Appropriate organizational structure.* The way in which an organization is structured can greatly improve the effectiveness of individual performance. By way of analogy, consider a basketball team. The coach of the team must make certain strategic decisions about offense, defense, substitution patterns, and the like, in order to help the team win. Players with certain skills will perform better in some systems than others. For example, a player who is quick and athletic, but relatively small, will be more effective playing in a system that takes advantage of those skills than she would be in another system that features big, strong, but somewhat slow players.

   Similarly, in a work environment, an organization should create a structure that allows its personnel to be most effective. Consideration should be given to

   – Formal and informal job descriptions or other means of defining tasks that comprise particular jobs

Exhibit 4.2   What People Must Know to Be Effective

The effectiveness of any internal control system rests primarily on how effectively entity personnel perform their control-related responsibilities. *All* personnel play a role in internal control. As a starting point for improving performance, they need to be aware of the elements of their jobs that contribute to the company's internal control structure. For example, employees should be able to answer the following questions:

- What is the level of authority and the authority of those around you?
- What behaviors are expected or acceptable, and what is unacceptable?
- What policies and procedures should you follow in your job?
- How do you avoid conflicts of interest?
- How do you appropriately protect the company's data?
- If you see something you think is wrong, dishonest, or detrimental to the company, what should you do about it?
- What is proprietary, confidential, and secret in your company?
- What is your role in protecting company assets?

Source: This list was prepared by Mike Lambert and Marsha Carter and was printed in "The Missing Link in Implementing Effective Internal Controls," *Compliance Week* (April 24, 2003) at *www.complianceweek.com.*

    – Hiring policies, which serve as a critical starting point for creating an environment in which people can succeed. The entity should have a process for identifying the skills and knowledge needed in the entity, identifying qualified candidates, and hiring new employees who possess the necessary qualities.

    – The delegation of responsibility, authority, and accountability. Clear delegation involves establishing well-defined boundaries.

    – The establishment of clear reporting relationships

    – Monitoring activities that are commensurate with the significance of the duties delegated and the competence of the personnel

3. *Provide the necessary resources.* In order to be effective, people must have the necessary resources made available to them. These include

    – Ongoing training

    – Performance appraisal and feedback

    – Compensation policies that are aligned with entity-wide objectives

Understanding and Awareness of Control Responsibilities. Every individual in an organization has some role in effecting internal control, and these roles and responsibilities will vary. The COSO report provides guidance on the responsibilities of those in the organization who contribute most significantly to the effectiveness of internal control, and Exhibit 4.3 summarizes this guidance.

Importance of the Audit Committee. The proposed auditing standard described in Chapter 1 emphasizes the importance of the audit committee in the company's overall system of internal control. Under the proposed standard, auditors will be required to evaluate the effectiveness of the audit committee, and an ineffective committee will be regarded as at least a significant deficiency in internal control and is a strong indicator of a material weakness.

    Under the proposed auditing standard, when auditors evaluate the effectiveness of a company's audit committee, they should consider the following:

- Independence of the audit committee members from management
- Clarity with which the audit committee's responsibilities are articulated and how well the audit committee and management understand those responsibilities
- Level of involvement and interaction with the independent auditor
- Level of involvement and interaction with internal audit
- Committee's compliance with applicable listing standards
- Whether the committee includes one or more financial experts
- Amount of time that the audit committee devotes to control issues, as well as the amount of time that audit committee members are able to devote to committee activity.

Exhibit 4.3   Control Responsibilities of Entity Personnel Summary of
COSO Guidance

Individual	Control-Related Responsibility
Chief executive officer	• Ultimate responsibility for internal control system. Ensures that all components of internal control are in place • Sets the overall "tone at the top" • Establishes a management philosophy and operating style • Influences selection of the board of directors • Provides leadership and direction to senior management that shapes the corporate culture • Meets with senior managers to review control-related responsibilities and gains knowledge of controls and their effectiveness
Management	• Establishes more specific internal control procedures • Monitors and reports on effectiveness of controls • May perform some control procedures themselves
Finance officers	• Primary responsibility for the design, implementation, and monitoring of the entity's financial reporting system • Provide input to the establishment of entity-wide objectives and risk assessment
Board of directors	• Provides guidance and oversight to management • Through selection of management, helps define expectations for integrity and ethical values • High-level objectives setting and strategic planning • Investigates any issues they deem important
Audit committee	• Investigates how top management is carrying out its financial reporting responsibilities • Requires corrective action for internal control and financial reporting deficiencies • Identifies and takes action when top management overrides internal controls or otherwise seeks to misrepresent reported financial results
Internal auditors	• Directly examine internal controls and recommend improvements
Other entity personnel	• Perform with due care control-related activities • Communicate to a higher organizational level problems in operations, noncompliance with the code of conduct, or other violations of policy or illegal actions

General Computer Controls

General computer controls are entity-wide controls that apply to many if not all application systems and help ensure their continued, proper operation. For example, the effectiveness of an entity's controls relating to the access of its database will determine whether it will be successful in maintaining the integrity of that data, which may be used in a number of different applications. General computer controls have a pervasive effect on the entity's information technology (IT) system, and, therefore, the related control objectives usually are considered significant to the entity's overall internal control structure. If there are inadequate general controls, it may not be possible to depend on computer controls at the application level, which rely on the system itself functioning properly.

The Control Objectives for Information and related Technology (COBIT) framework (summarized in Chapter 2) describes general computer control objectives in four separate domains:

1. *Planning and organization.* This domain covers strategy and tactics and concerns the identification of the way IT can best contribute to the achievement of the business objectives. Furthermore, the realization of the strategic vision needs to be planned, communicated, and managed. Finally, a proper organization as well as technological infrastructure must be put in place.

2. *Acquisition and implementation.* To realize the IT strategy, IT solutions need to be identified, developed, or acquired, as well as implemented and integrated into the business process. In addition, this domain includes changes in and maintenance of existing systems.

3. *Delivery and support.* This domain is concerned with the actual delivery of required services, which range from traditional operations over security and continuity aspects to training. In order to deliver services, the necessary support processes must be set up. Included in this domain are controls related to data center operations and access security, which COSO describes as examples of general computer controls.

4. *Monitoring.* All IT processes need to be regularly assessed over time for their quality and compliance with control requirements.

With the exception of planning and organization, all of the COBIT domains are encompassed by the COSO framework, though in a slightly different organization.

Significant general computer control objectives typically include the following:

- IT systems manage the quality and integrity of information
- The entity maintains access controls over IT systems and related applications
- Computer applications include an authorization process
- Information is provided on a timely basis and is available when needed

- The confidentiality of sensitive information is maintained
- Continued reporting is supported by recoverability controls

Chapter 6 provides more detailed guidance to help you understand and evaluate IT general controls.

Alignment between Entity Objectives and Control Structures

As described in Chapter 2, internal controls have no intrinsic value. Organizations do not adopt control policies and procedures because they are "good" and to not have them would be "bad." Rather, internal controls are driven by an entity's desire to achieve certain business objectives. Clearly defined business objectives are a prerequisite for effectively designed controls.

Exhibit 4.4 shows this relationship. At the top of the diagram are the entity's business objectives. These should be defined in a way that is broad enough to provide guidance on what the entity desires to achieve in a number of areas, yet at the same time, they should be specific enough to relate directly to the entity. The broad business objectives drive strategy, which in turn dictates certain activities that are

Exhibit 4.4   Alignment of Objectives and Controls

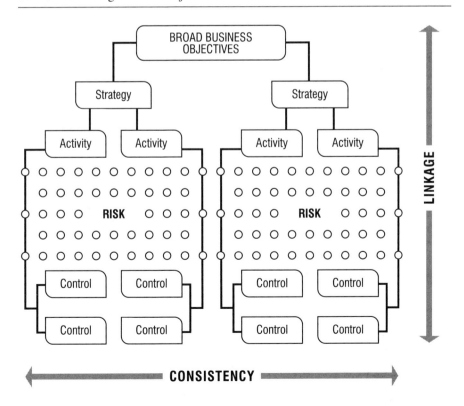

necessary to implement the strategy. In defining these activity-level objectives, it is important that all levels of management be involved in the objective-setting process and that they identify those objectives that are most important to the achievement of entity-wide objectives.

Reading further down the diagram, risks exist that could prevent the company from successfully achieving its objectives, and controls are designed to manage these risks.

To be effective, these controls should be aligned with the company's stated business objectives and its operating structure. As indicated in Exhibit 4.4, alignment is achieved when the following occur:

- *Linkage.* Control activities are *linked* directly to the company's strategies and objectives, as indicated along the vertical axis.
- *Consistency.* Looking horizontally across the diagram, control activities for each of the various activities should be consistent with each other.

Exhibit 4.5 describes a situation in which the entity lacks linkage. The entity has described certain activities for which there are no controls (the right side of the

Exhibit 4.5   Lack of Linkage between Controls and Activities

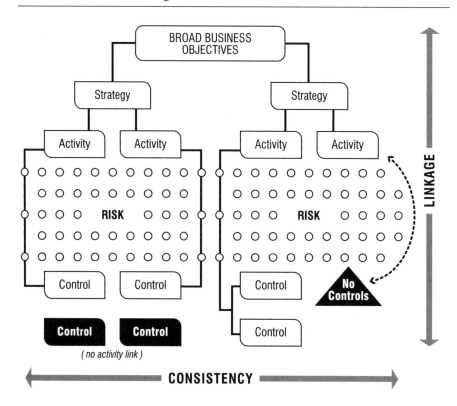

diagram), and they perform some activities that are unrelated to the achievement of any specific objective (the left side of the diagram). When an entity's control objectives are not directly linked to its business objectives, the effectiveness of the internal control system may be diminished. In Exhibit 4.5, the entity has an entire class of activities that are uncontrolled.

Exhibit 4.6 shows a situation in which control activities are not consistent with each other. Most of the activities have control procedures that are similar (indicated in white), but one activity has adopted controls that are at another end of the spectrum (black). The lack of consistency among control objectives raises questions about the effectiveness of the overall system. Assuming that there is consistency at the strategy level, why would the entity choose one approach to controls for one activity and a different approach for another activity? Are the two activities so dissimilar that they require different control objectives? It may be that the answer to that question is "yes," but if the two activities are similar, then one would have to consider how greater effectiveness is achieved by having dissimilar sets of control objectives.

Case Study: Johnson & Johnson. To illustrate how the alignment of objectives can be analyzed, consider the example of Johnson & Johnson, which is en-

Exhibit 4.6   Lack of Consistency among Controls

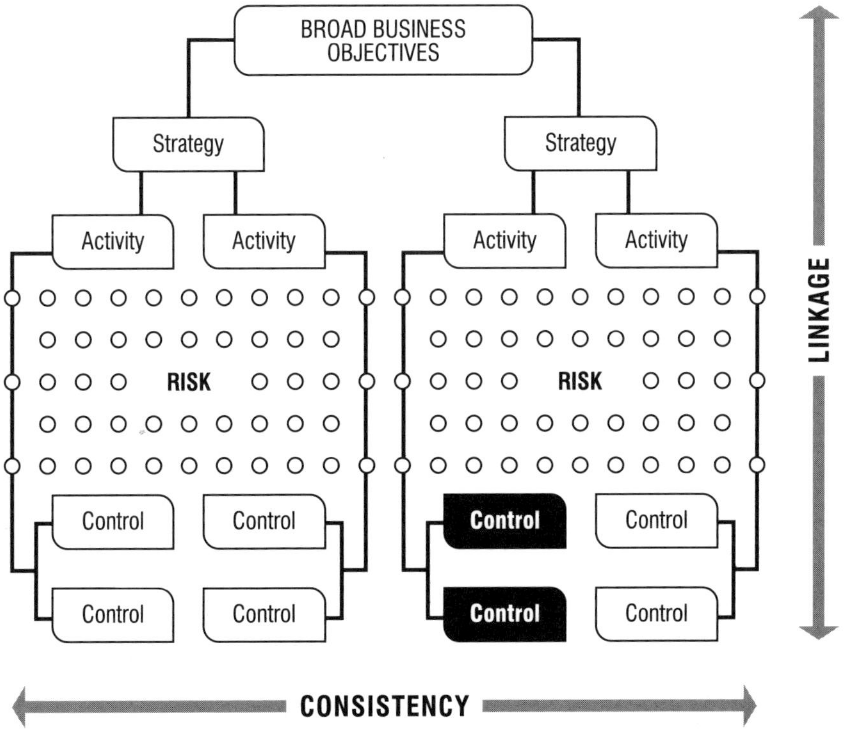

gaged in the manufacture and sale of a broad range of products in the health care field.

Here are the first two paragraphs of the company's 2003 management discussion and analysis (MD&A), in which it describes its business objectives and strategies.

> The Company's objective is to achieve superior levels of capital efficient profitable growth. To accomplish this, the Company's management operates the business consistent with certain strategic principles that have proven successful over time. To this end, the Company participates in growth areas in human health care and is committed to attaining leadership positions in these growth segments through the development of innovative products and services. In 2002, approximately $4.0 billion or 10.9% of sales was invested in research and development, recognizing the importance of on-going development of new and differentiated products and services.
>
> The Company's system of management operates on a decentralized basis. With over 200 operating companies located in 54 countries, the Company views this management philosophy as an asset and fundamental to the success of a broadly based business. It also fosters an entrepreneurial spirit, combining the extensive resources of a large organization with the ability to react quickly to local market changes and challenges. Businesses are managed for the long term in order to sustain leadership positions and achieve growth that provides an enduring source of value to shareholders.

In these brief paragraphs, you can see how the company has *linked* its overall business objective (achieve superior levels of capital efficient, profitable growth) to certain strategies:

- Through research and development (R&D) and other initiatives, participate in growth areas in human health care.
- Decentralize operations.
- Manage for the long-term.

The company has three primary business units: consumer products, pharmaceutical products, and medical devices and diagnostics. One would expect that the broad business strategies described for the overall company would be incorporated at the business level. For example, research activities are a significant activity for each business unit.

The company's internal control structure should be aligned with its business strategies. For example, decentralized operations and a culture that fosters the entrepreneurial spirit create certain risks that need to be managed. What boundaries does the company place on entrepreneurial-minded managers? How does the entity monitor the activities of its various business units to make sure that the company's overall objectives are being met? The company addresses these issues in its 10K, stating the following:

> The Executive Committee of Johnson & Johnson is the principal management group responsible for the allocation of the resources of the Company. This Committee over-

sees and coordinates the activities of U.S. and international companies related to each of the Consumer, Pharmaceutical, and Medical Devices & Diagnostics businesses.

Again, one would expect that each of the business units, to the extent that they have adopted a decentralized approach and entrepreneurial spirit, would also establish control activities mirrored by the entity's overall structure that emphasizes a centralized oversight function.

Risk Identification

As described in Chapter 2, COSO includes the entity's risk assessment process as one of its five components of internal control. The first step in that process is the identification of the risks the entity faces to achieving its objectives. These risks can come from both internal and external sources, and the report provides a list of several factors to consider that may contribute to increased risks. Other than this list of factors, COSO does not provide any additional guidance on how management can most effectively identify risk. The following guidance has been adapted from guidance provided in the article "Predictable Surprises: The Disasters You Should Have Seen Coming," by Michael D. Watkins and Max H. Bazerman.[3]

Entities face risks from many different sources. Some of these risks cannot be foreseen, but the entity should be able to anticipate and identify many of them. Management fails to identify these risks when they remain oblivious to emerging threats or problems. In general, the reasons for failing to identify risks that should have been anticipated can be broken down into three categories.

1. *Management psychology.* As human beings, we all have cognitive biases, and some of these can lead us to ignore or underestimate identifiable risks. These biases include
   - A tendency to believe that conditions are better than they really are
   - An overemphasis on information that supports our (optimistic) vision of the future and an underemphasis on information that contradicts that vision
   - Overlooking threats posed from external sources
   - A tendency to procrastinate, to choose *not* to take action now that would mitigate future risks
   - Inability to treat as "real" risks that we have not experienced personally
2. *Organizational vulnerabilities.* It is common for companies to be organized into "silos." As a result, the information provided to management often is fragmented, and management may not always be successful in synthesizing this information to identify risks. Additionally, risks may be ignored because people assume, incorrectly, that someone else in another business unit will address the issue.
3. *Senior management may overvalue the interests of one group while undervaluing other, equally important groups.* This imbalance can create management blind spots.

Because of the severity of the consequences of *not* identifying risks, the control objectives related to this activity on the entity level usually are significant to the overall effectiveness of internal control.

Anti-Fraud Programs and Controls

The SEC's final rules relating to management's reports on internal control include an extensive commentary on the background of the rules and insight on how the rules should be interpreted and implemented. That commentary includes the following guidance:

> The assessment of a company's internal control over financial reporting must be based on procedures sufficient both to evaluate its design and to test its operating effectiveness. Controls subject to such assessment include, but are not limited to: . . . *controls related to the prevention and detection of fraud* [emphasis added].

In addition to the SEC guidance, the PCAOB, in its proposed auditing standard, has highlighted anti-fraud programs and controls as an important element of internal control.

The COSO framework does not include a discussion related to the prevention and detection of fraud. An established set of criteria for evaluating the effectiveness of fraud-related controls does not exist. Within the auditing literature the most definitive guidance on fraud-related controls is provided in the document *Management Anti-Fraud Programs and Controls*, which was published as an Exhibit to Statement on Auditing Standards (SAS) No. 99, *Consideration of Fraud in a Financial Statement Audit.*[4]

The guidance in the document is based on the presumption that entity management has both the responsibility and the means to take action to reduce the occurrence of fraud at the entity. To fulfill this responsibility, management should

- Create and maintain a culture of honesty and high ethics.
- Evaluate the risks of fraud and implement the processes, procedures, and controls needed to mitigate the risks and reduce the opportunities for fraud.
- Develop an appropriate oversight process.

In many ways, the guidance offered in *Management Anti-Fraud Programs and Controls* echoes the concepts and detailed guidance contained in the COSO report. The primary difference is that the anti-fraud document reminds management that it must be aware of and design the entity's internal control to specifically address material misstatements caused by fraud and *not* limit their efforts to the detection and prevention of unintentional errors.

A Culture of Honesty and Ethics. A culture of honesty and ethics includes the following elements:

- A value system founded on integrity
- A positive workplace environment in which employees have positive feelings about the entity
- Human resource policies that minimize the chance of hiring or promoting individuals with low levels of honesty, especially for positions of trust
- Training—both at the time of hire and on an ongoing basis—about the entity's values and its code of conduct
- Confirmation from employees that they understand and have complied with the entity's code of conduct and that they are not aware of any violations of the code
- Appropriate investigation and response to incidents of alleged or suspected fraud

Evaluating Anti-Fraud Programs and Controls. The entity's risk assessment process (as described in Chapter 2) should include the consideration of fraud risk. With an aim toward reducing fraud opportunities, the entity should take steps to

- Identify and measure fraud risk.
- Mitigate fraud risk by making changes to the entity's activities and procedures.
- Implement and monitor an appropriate system of internal control.

Develop an Appropriate Oversight Process. The entity's audit committee or board of directors should take an active role in evaluating management's

- Creation of an appropriate culture
- Identification of fraud risks
- Implementation of anti-fraud measures

To fulfill its oversight responsibilities, audit committee members should be financially literate and each committee should have at least one financial expert. Additionally, the committee should consider establishing an open line of communication with members of management one or two levels below senior management to assist in identifying fraud at the highest levels of the organization or investigating any fraudulent activity that might occur.

Top-Level Financial Reporting Processes

Top-Level versus Routine, Systematic Processes. An entity's financial reporting processes can be separated into two general types:

1. *Routine, systematic transaction processing.* These processes usually are distributed across the organization and include all levels of entity personnel. The processing of sales transactions or the payment of payables are two examples of this type of routine processing.

2. *Top-level financial reporting procedures.* These procedures address financial reporting events, rather than routine transactions with external parties. The recognition of an asset impairment loss, the posting of general ledger adjustments, and the preparation of accounting estimates are some examples of top-level financial reporting procedures. Unlike routine, systematic transactions, these top level processes usually are centralized and performed by senior financial executives within the organizations.

The nature of the controls and their relative significance is different for the two types of activities. For example, routine transaction processing is built around a processing "stream" that captures and then manipulates data, changing it from raw data into accounting information (e.g., debits and credits). Typical steps in this processing stream include

- The initiation of the transaction, including the capture of relevant information
- The processing of information, usually through multiple steps, with controls designed to ensure the integrity of the data processed.
- The creation of debits and credits, which are then posted to the general ledger and other accounting records

The Nature of Top-Level Processes. Top-level financial reporting activities are characterized by an information gathering, analysis, and decision-making process, rather than data manipulation. Key control objectives in this process include the following:

- *Awareness and understanding.* Management is aware of and understands the need for the top-level activity. For example, they are aware of the need to periodically assess the recoverability of long-lived assets to determine whether an impairment loss should be recognized.
- *Gather relevant and reliable information.* A process exists to identify and communicate information that is relevant for decision-making purposes. For example, management monitors internal and external information sources to identify events or changes in circumstances that indicate an asset may be impaired.
- *Analysis and decision making.* Using the information gathered, management analyzes the situation and develops an appropriate response. For example, if an impairment loss should be recognized, management should estimate the amount of the loss.
- *Review and approval.* Top-level adjustments and entries to the accounting records should be communicated to, reviewed, and approved by an appropriate level of authority within the organization. In some instances, that level of authority may be the board of directors or audit committee.

The Need to Consider Top-Level Processes. Many reports of financial reporting failures cite weaknesses in top-level financial reporting processes as the main cause of the failure. Fraudulent financial reporting schemes frequently are perpetrated through an abuse of these processes. For those reasons you should identify the entity's top-level financial reporting practices and consider whether the control objectives related to these practices are significant to the entity's internal control.

Processes you should consider include those relating to

- The recording of nonroutine, nonsystematic entries or other post-closing adjustments such as consolidating adjustments or reclassifications
- The preparation of significant accounting estimates
- The consideration of asset valuation issues
- The recognition of obligations that meet the criteria for liability recognition, including contingent liabilities and off-balance-sheet financing
- The recording of journal entries to the general ledger
- The recording of recurring and non-recurring adjustments to the financial statements, for example, consolidating adjustments, report combinations, and reclassifications

The Selection and Application of Accounting Principles. The selection and application of accounting principles may have a significant effect on an entity's reported financial results and on the design of its internal control. For example, suppose that ABC Company manufactures and sells products and related services that usually are bundled together in a variety of configurations and offered to its customers as a complete solution package. In the selection and application of its revenue recognition accounting principles, company management must make several important decisions, including

- How revenue should be recognized when some elements of the bundle are delivered before other elements
- How the fee should be allocated among the elements when revenue is recognized at different delivery dates

These decisions may have a significant effect on how much revenue ABC will recognize in any given year. Additionally, once the decisions are made, the company will need to implement control policies and procedures to ensure that the accounting policy is applied appropriately. For example, if management determines that revenue from the product elements of the bundle should be recognized when the product is shipped, then the company should have procedures to capture the information necessary to determine what products were shipped when.

For these reasons, your consideration of an entity's financial reporting processes should include an assessment of the controls over management's selection and application of accounting principles.

The entity's financial statements should be *"presented fairly* ... in accordance with GAAP."* The overriding requirement is "presents fairly." The phrase "in accordance with GAAP," is *subordinate* to the requirement for a fair presentation. Ultimately, an entity's accounting principles must be appropriate under the circumstances, and they must report transactions and events in accordance with their substance.

The auditing literature provides guidance on the meaning of "present fairly." In part, that guidance states that a "fair presentation" means

- The accounting principles selected and applied have general acceptance.
- The accounting principles are appropriate in the circumstances.
- The financial statements, including the related notes, are informative of matters that may affect their use, understanding, and interpretation.
- The information presented in the financial statements is classified and summarized in a reasonable manner, that is, neither too detailed nor too condensed.
- The financial statements reflect the underlying transactions and events in a manner that presents the financial position, results of operations, and cash flows stated within an acceptable range, that is, limits that are reasonable and practicable to attain in financial statements.

In those instances in which there are no established principles for reporting a specific transaction or event, it might be possible to report the event or transaction on the basis of its substance by selecting an accounting principle that appears appropriate when applied in a manner similar to the application of an established principle to an analogous transaction or event.[5]

No definitive guidelines exist on the controls that should be in place to ensure the appropriate selection and application of accounting policies. However, when considering your entity's process, you should consider whether the following objectives have been met:

- Management identifies events and transactions for which accounting policy choices should be made or existing policies reconsidered.
- The accounting policies chosen by management have general acceptance and result in a fair presentation of the financial statement information.
- Information processing and internal control policies and procedures are designed to appropriately apply the accounting principles selected.

SYSTEM-WIDE MONITORING

Chapter 2 describes the characteristics of the monitoring component of internal control. Under the SEC rules relating to the evaluation of and reporting on internal control, the monitoring component of the COSO framework takes on increased importance. There are two reasons why monitoring is now so important and may be considered a significant control objective.

1. As described in Chapter 1, management is required to report on both a quarterly and annual basis all material weaknesses in internal control and any material

changes to internal control. In order to comply with this requirement, it is vital that the entity's monitoring of its internal control be functioning effectively.

2. As a practical matter, most entities will perform a substantial portion of their tests on the operating effectiveness of internal control at various points in time that may be well in advance of the report date. In order to draw a valid conclusion about the continued effectiveness of those controls at the report date, the entity must be able to rely on the monitoring component of its internal control. Without an effective mechanism for monitoring the continued effectiveness of internal control, entities would have to perform all of their testwork close to their reporting date.

IDENTIFYING SIGNIFICANT ACTIVITY-LEVEL CONTROL OBJECTIVES

The scope of your project should include those control objectives that relate to the relevant assertions[6] related to all significant financial statement accounts and disclosures. To determine which activity-level control objectives are significant, you normally will begin with a reading and analysis of the entity's financial statements. In performing this analysis, you normally would consider

- The magnitude of the account balance and how this compares to financial statement materiality. The proposed auditing standard described in Chapter 1 instructs auditors that "an account is significant if there is more than a remote likelihood that the account could contain misstatements that individually or when aggregated with others, could have a material effect on the financial statements."
- Qualitative considerations of materiality and the accounts and classes of transactions that have the greatest impact on these qualitative assessments.
- The inherent risk associated with the account balance, which is defined as the risk of material misstatement irrespective of internal controls. Inherent risk is affected by factors such as the complexity of the related accounting standards or the degree of judgment required in the recognition or measurement of the item.
- The critical accounting policies disclosed in the Form 10K, as described in Chapter 3.

The proposed auditing standards described in Chapter 1 provide guidance to auditors that:

- In some cases, separate components of an account may also need to be considered a significant account because of the company's organizational structure
- An account also may be considered significant because of the exposure to unrecognized obligations represented by the account.

The advantages to basing your definition of significant activity-level control objectives on a financial statement analysis include

- The relatively objective nature of the process
- The familiarity you probably already have in performing such an analysis

However, as discussed in Chapter 2, the COSO model defines *activities* not in terms of financial statement accounts, but rather, as the entity's business process activities. The COSO example practice aids are modeled after these value-chain process activities. The drawback to a purely financial statement–based approach is that you can become too narrow in your definition of the activity. Consider the example of Aloha Hawaiian Sportswear, which was described in Appendix 2A. The company designs and sells sportswear and accessories, and a value-chain analysis identified procurement as one of its most significant business activities. Suppose that the company's policy was to pay its accounts payable as quickly as possible, particularly at the balance sheet date. Because of the relatively small balance in accounts payable, a simple financial statement analysis may not identify payables as a significant financial statement account. But the volume of activity through the payables account and the significance of the procurement activity would make it important for the company to have strong controls relating to accounts payable. Financial statement analysis alone could miss this point.

Thus, in determining which activity-level control objectives are significant, you should consider a blended approach that combines both a financial statement and a value-chain analysis. To help you adopt this approach, Exhibit 4.7 maps the value-chain activities to example-related financial statement line items.

Subsequent Reconsideration of Significant Activity-Level Controls

As described in Chapter 6, your evaluation of internal control typically begins with the evaluation of entity-level controls. The results of that evaluation may cause you to reconsider your definition of significant activity-level control objectives. If weaknesses exist in entity-level controls, the entity may effectively compensate for this weakness through strong activity-level controls. For example, suppose that the entity's compensation program for sales personnel includes a bonus plan based on the achievement of certain sales goals. Depending on how aggressive these goals are, the presence of such a plan could motivate salespeople to recognize revenue prematurely. You may consider this a control weakness. However, if the entity has strong activity-level controls over revenue recognition, it may successfully mitigate this weakness and allow you to conclude that, overall, internal control operates effectively.

Example Activity-Level Control Objectives

Appendix 4B provides a list of example control objectives, including activity-level control objectives. Chapter 7 provides additional examples of control objectives and related control procedures.

Exhibit 4.7   Value Chain Activities and Financial Statement Accounts

Value-Chain Activity	Example Related Financial Statement Account(s)
Support Activities	
Firm infrastructure	• Investments
	• Long-term debt
	• Equity
	• Income taxes
	• Goodwill and other intangible assets
	• General and administrative expenses
Human resource management	• Payroll and other compensation
	• Employee benefits, pension liabilities, 401(k) plans, etc.
Technology development	• Fixed assets
	• E-commerce sales
Procurement	• Accounts payable
	• Cash disbursements
	• Fixed asset additions
Primary Activities	
Inbound activities	• Raw materials inventory
Operations	• Work-in-process inventory
Outbound activities	• Finished goods inventory
	• Cost of sales
Sales and marketing	• Revenue
	• Accounts receivable
	• Selling costs
	• Cash receipts
Service	• Warranty obligations

COORDINATING WITH THE INDEPENDENT AUDITORS

Once you have identified the significant control objectives that will be the focus of your testing and evaluation, you should communicate with the external auditors to reach consensus on the following matters:

- The process used to identify significant control objectives, including the criteria used to distinguish significant from less significant objectives
- The list of control objectives determined to be significant

---

APPENDIX 4A

Action Plan:
Identifying Significant Control Objectives

The following action plan is intended to help you implement the suggestions contained in this chapter for identifying significant control objectives.

1. Entity-Level Control Objectives

Based on your understanding of the entity, the control criteria used to evaluate effectiveness, and the expectations of the independent auditors determine significant entity-level control objectives. For example:

- Consider the entity-level control objectives described in this chapter as significant.
    - Corporate culture
    - Personnel policies
    - General computer controls
    - Alignment between entity objectives and control structures
    - Risk identification
    - Anti-fraud programs and controls
    - Top-level financial reporting processes
    - System-wide monitoring
- Consider the relevant auditing standards for internal control reporting that will be followed by the independent auditors in their engagement.[7] Determine that all controls that independent auditors are required to deem significant have been considered significant for the purposes of your engagement.
- Consider the following to determine whether your list of significant entity-level control objectives is complete:
    - The business activities of the entity and the industry in which it operates
    - The most significant financial reporting risks facing the entity
    - The overall design of the entity's internal control

2. Activity-Level Control Objectives

Based on your understanding of the entity's financial statements and business activities, determine significant activity-level control objectives. For example:

- Review the entity's financial statements and identify the relevant assertions for the most significant

- – Account balances
- – Classes of transactions
- – Disclosures
- To make this determination, consider
  - – Magnitude of the accounts
  - – Qualitative factors that affect materiality
  - – Inherent risk
  - – The entity's critical accounting policies disclosure
- Consider the entity's most significant value-chain activities to assess whether your list of significant activity-level control objectives is complete.

3. Coordinate with Independent Auditors

Reach a consensus with the independent auditors regarding key decisions about significant control objectives. For example:

- Communicate and reach agreement with the auditors on matters such as:
  - – The process used to identify significant control objectives
  - – The list of control objectives determined to be significant

---

APPENDIX 4B

Example Significant Control Objectives

Exhibit 4.8   Example Significant Control Objectives

Business Objective	Example Control Objectives
Corporate Culture	
Establish a culture and a "tone at the top" that fosters integrity, shared values, and teamwork in pursuit of the entity's objectives.	• Articulate and communicate codes of conduct and other policies regarding acceptable business practice, conflicts of interest, or expected standards of ethical and moral behavior. • Reduce incentives and temptations that can motivate employees to act in a manner that is unethical, opposed to the entity's objectives, or both. • Reinforce written policies about ethical behavior through action and leadership by example.

(Continued)

Exhibit 4.8   *(Continued)*

Business Objective	Example Control Objectives
Personnel Policies	
The entity's personnel have been provided with the information, resources, and support necessary to effectively carry out their responsibilities.	• Identify, articulate, and communicate to entity personnel the information and skills needed to perform their jobs effectively. • Provide entity personnel with the resources needed to perform their jobs effectively. • Supervise and monitor individuals with internal control responsibilities. • Delegate authority and responsibility to appropriate individuals within the organization.
General Computer Controls	
The entity's IT governance structure and policies create an environment in which computer application programs and controls can operate effectively.	• Develop, communicate and plan an overall IT strategy that enables the achievement of entity-wide controls. • Provide resources and organizational infrastructure necessary to implement the IT strategy. • Identify, acquire, and integrate IT applications and solutions that are necessary for implementing the IT strategy. • Monitor IT processes to ensure their continued effectiveness.
Alignment between Objectives and Organizational and Control Structures	
The entity's business objectives, organizational structure, and internal control structure are linked to and consistent with each other.	• Articulate and communicate entity-wide objectives and related business strategies. • Design and periodically review activity-level objectives and resources to ensure they are linked to and consistent with each other and the entity-wide objectives.
Risk Identification	

Implement a process that effectively identifies and responds to conditions that can significantly affect the entity's ability to achieve its objectives.	• Develop mechanisms to anticipate, identify and react to
	  – Routine events or activities that affect the entity or activity-level objectives
	  – Unusual, significant events that can have a more dramatic and pervasive effect on the entity

Exhibit 4.8   *(Continued)*

Business Objective	Example Control Objectives
Anti-Fraud Programs and Controls	
Reduce the incidence of fraud.	• Create a culture of honesty and high ethics. • Evaluate anti-fraud processes and controls. • Develop an effective anti-fraud oversight process.
Top-Level Financial Reporting Processes	

Nonroutine, nonsystematic financial reporting adjustments are appropriately identified and approved.	• Management is aware of and understands the need for certain financial reporting adjustments.
	• Information required for decision-making purposes is
	  – Identified, gathered, and communicated.
	  – Relevant and reliable
	• Management analyzes the information and responds appropriately.
	• Management's response is reviewed and approved.

Selection and application of accounting principles result in financial statements that are "fairly presented."	• Management identifies events and transactions for which accounting policy choices should be made or existing policies reconsidered. • The accounting policies chosen by management have general acceptance and result in a fair presentation of financial statement information. • Information processing and internal control policies and procedures are designed to appropriately apply the accounting principles selected.
System-Wide Monitoring	
Identify material weaknesses and changes in internal control that require disclosure.	• Reach a common understanding of internal control deficiencies and changes that are considered "material" and require disclosure. • Identify material weaknesses in internal control on a timely basis. • Identify material changes to internal control on a timely basis.

(Continued)

Exhibit 4.8 *(Continued)*

Business Objective	Example Control Objectives
Activity-Level Control Objectives	
Adequately control the initiation, processing and disclosure of transactions	• Identify, analyze, and manage risks that may cause material misstatements of the financial statements.
	• Design and implement an information system to accurately record, process, summarize, and report transactions.
	• Design and implement control activities, including policies and procedures applied in the processing of transactions that flow through the accounting system in order to prevent or promptly detect material misstatements.
	• Monitor the design and operating effectiveness of activity-level internal controls to determine if they are operating as intended and, if not, to take corrective action.

APPENDIX 4C
Map to the COSO Framework

Chapter 2 described the COSO internal control integrated framework as consisting of five separate components. This chapter describes a process for identifying significant control objectives within the overall COSO framework. The information presented in this chapter does not follow the exact organization of the COSO report but, rather, has been interpreted and organized in a way that will facilitate the identification of significant controls and their documentation and testing. Exhibit 4.9 maps the five components of internal control described in the COSO framework to the main topics presented in this chapter.

APPENDIX 4D
Map to the Auditing Literature

As described in Chapter 1, the proposed auditing standard for the independent auditor's audit of internal control requires the auditor to evaluate management's process for assessing internal control. The proposed standard also describes certain controls that should be tested by management as part of its evaluation of internal control. Exhibit 4.10 maps these controls that the independent auditors expect management to test to the main topics presented in this chapter.

Exhibit 4.9   Internal Control in the COSO Framework

COSO Control Components	Chapter 4 Reference								
	Culture	People	Computer Controls	Alignment	Risk Identification	Anti-Fraud	Top-Level Processes	System-Wide Monitoring	Activity Level Controls
Control Environment									
Integrity and ethical values	X								
Commitment to competence		X							
Board of directors or audit committee		X							
Management philosophy	X								
Organizational structure				X					
Assign authority and responsibility		X							
HR policies and practices		X							
Risk Assessment									
Objectives and linkage				X					
Entity-level risk assessment					X				
Activity-level risk assessment									X
Managing change					X				
Control Activities									
Computer general controls			X						
Computer application controls									X
Information and Communications									
Information									X
Communication									X
Monitoring									
Ongoing monitoring activities			X		X			X	X

Exhibit 4.10 Auditing Standard Requirements

	Culture	People	Computer Controls	Alignment	Risk Identification	Anti-Fraud	Top-Level Processes	System-Wide Monitoring	Activity Level Controls
Initiation, recording, processing and reporting of significant accounts and disclosures									X
Selection of accounting principles							X		
Anti-fraud programs									
Controls on which other controls are dependent	X	X	X	X	X		X	X	
Nonroutine and nonsystematic transactions							X		
Period-end financial reporting process							X		

Notes

1. The *presumption* that certain control objectives are significant is based on the proposed auditing standard for internal control. As described in Chapter 1, the planned standard will designate certain controls as significant for the purposes of the independent auditor's audit of the entity's internal control. The control objectives you determine to be significant should include all the required significant controls designated as such in the final attestation standard. Appendix 4D links the significant control objectives described in this chapter to the proposed auditing standard.

2. The term *accidental values* is described by Patrick Lencioni in his article "Make Your Values Mean Something," which appeared in the July 2002 edition of the *Harvard Business Review*.

3. This article originally appeared in the March 2003 issue of the *Harvard Business Review*.

4. This document may be downloaded free of charge from the AICPA Web site at *www.aicpa.org/antifraud/homepage.htm*. From the "Select a topic" menu, choose "Prevent Fraud" and you will be linked to a new page; select "Instituting Antifraud Programs and Controls" to link to the documents.

5. See Statement on Auditing Standards No. 69, *The Meaning of "Present Fairly in Conformity with GAAP*," paragraphs .04 and .09 (AICPA *Professional Standards* vol. 1, sec. 411.04 and 411.09).

6. Chapter 7 and Exhibit 7.1 provide detailed guidance on financial statement assertions.

7. As described in Chapter 1, these standards, which will be issued by the PCAOB, are expected to be made available in final form by early 2004.

Chapter 5

Documentation of Significant Controls

Chapter Summary

Describe the importance of adequate documentation of internal control.

Summarize contents of anticipated key documents for significant entity-level control objectives.

Describe documentation requirements for activity-level controls.

Provide an example flowcharting method for documenting activity-level controls.

Describe the necessary design features and key implementation issues related to automated documentation tools.

DOCUMENTATION: WHAT IT IS . . . AND IS *NOT*

The Importance of Documentation

The adequate documentation of internal control is important for the following reasons:

- *Improved reliability of internal control.* As described in Chapter 6, documentation of internal control policies and procedures improves the effectiveness and reliability of internal control. Without adequate documentation, the performance of the system depends exclusively on the skills and competence of the individual responsible for performing the control procedure. As such, performance can vary greatly between individuals or over time. Adequate documentation reduces this variability by facilitating the consistent dissemination of critical information, namely, the policy or procedure to be performed, by whom, when, and for what purpose. Additionally, by clearly stating the parameters within which a control procedure should be performed, it becomes easier to identify deviations from the policy or procedure—that is, material weaknesses can be identified.

- *Enable effective monitoring.* As described in Chapter 1, management is required to report material changes in internal control on a quarterly basis. Thus, one of the most important features of the monitoring component of the entity's internal control system is its ability to identify change. Documentation facilitates this monitoring element. Documentation is *not* internal control any more than a reflection of yourself in the mirror is actually you. However, like the image in a mirror, internal control documentation should be a highly accurate representation of the actual system. Changes in the documentation should represent changes to internal control itself. By monitoring these changes to the documentation, you effectively monitor changes to internal control.

In addition to enhancing the overall effectiveness of internal control, documentation also will facilitate management's assessment of effectiveness by providing a basis for

- Evaluating design effectiveness
- Planning tests of operating effectiveness

Finally, as described in Chapter 1, the PCAOB's proposed auditing standard would consider inadequate documentation to be a deficiency in internal control that may rise to the level of material weakness.

What Documentation Is Not

As the analogy of the reflection in the mirror suggests, the documentation of internal control should never be confused with internal control itself. In a similar vein, the mere documentation of a control policy or procedure provides *no evidence* to support the operating effectiveness of the control. For example, the documentation of an entity's values and its commitment to integrity and ethical values gives you a starting point for determining whether its corporate culture is conducive to effective controls. Based on reading this statement of values, you may determine that the intent of the policies is consistent with a strong control environment, however, this documentation, by itself, will not allow you to draw a conclusion about whether the policy is operating as designed. To support a conclusion about operations, you will need to gather evidence by performing testwork. An entity that automates certain control-related business process is not relieved of this obligation to test control performance.

The Objective of This Phase of the Project

In almost every entity there is a difference between the way in which a system is *supposed to work* and the reality of how it *actually works*. Sometimes these differences are minor, and sometimes they are not. At this phase of your project your goal is to gather and analyze documentation about how the system *is supposed to work*. In the next phase of the project you will gather evidence to determine how the system really works in practice.

A lack of documentation does not mean that a control does not exist. In many instances it may only mean that the existing control (which may have been developed informally) has not been documented. In some instances, you may need to expand the scope of your project to include the documentation of controls when adequate documentation does not exist.

To avoid misunderstanding between you and the project business owner, it usually is best to perform the documentation phase of the engagement in two steps:

1. Asses the adequacy of documentation
2. Create additional documentation as required

Automated Documentation Tools

Most entities will use a computer-based tool to aid in the accumulation, creation, and storage of internal control documentation. The guidance provided in this chapter is applicable to *all* forms of documentation, whether facilitated by a computerized system or not. Appendix 5C provides guidance on evaluating the design and implementation of automated documentation tools.

ASSESSING THE ADEQUACY OF EXISTING DOCUMENTATION

As described in Chapter 1, at each phase of your engagement, you will begin by assessing the efforts already taken by management to determine whether these effects have been sufficient to meet the engagement objective. For this phase of the engagement, you will want to identify the client's existing documentation of controls and assess whether it provides adequate support for management's assertion to the independent auditors about whether controls have been suitably designed. In assessing the adequacy of documentation, you should determine whether

- *All significant controls objectives have been considered.* Control policies and procedures should be documented for *all* significant control objectives. If control policies have *not* been documented for certain identified significant control objectives, then you must determine whether
  - Controls do not exist to achieve the stated control objective, in which case, the entity must design, implement, and document new control procedures
  - Controls exist to achieve the control objective; however they are informal, communicated verbally, or otherwise not documented. In this case, suitable documentation must be developed to facilitate an evaluation of the effectiveness of the design of the control.
- *Documentation is sufficient.* To be sufficient, the documentation should allow management and the independent auditor to
  - Determine whether the policy or procedure is adequately designed to
    - Create an environment that enables the effective functioning of activity-level controls
    - Prevent or detect material financial statement misstatements in a timely manner by people performing their assigned functions
  - Design and perform procedures to test the operating effectiveness of the controls.

Exhibit 5.1 describes this process for evaluating the adequacy of existing documentation. The steps in the process in black represent step 1 in the process, which is an assessment of the adequacy of documentation. Steps in white represent step 2 in the process, which is the creation of existing documentation.

What Should Be Documented

Documentation of controls should contain the following elements:

- A link between the control objective and the control policy or procedure
- A description of the control policy or procedure that achieves the control objective. Appendix 5C includes example control policies and procedures, organized by significant control objective.

Exhibit 5.1   Assessing the Adequacy of Existing Client Documentation

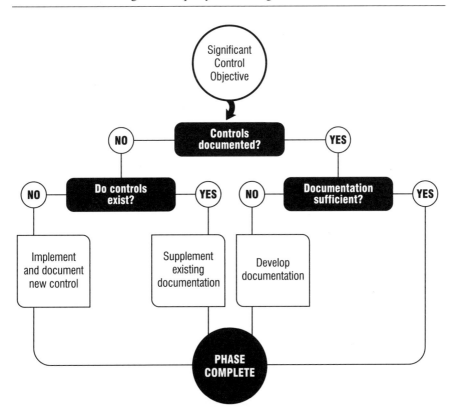

- Information about:
  - How transactions are initiated, recorded, processed, and reported
  - The flow of transactions to identify where material misstatements due to error or fraud could occur
- A description of
  - How the control procedure is to be applied
  - Who is responsible for performing the procedure
  - How frequently the procedure is performed

DOCUMENTATION OF ENTITY-LEVEL CONTROL POLICIES AND PROCEDURES

Corporate Governance Documents

Several of the entity-level control objectives described in Chapter 4 fall under the general topic of corporate governance. One of the more popular definitions of corporate governance is the following:

> Corporate governance is the system by which business corporations are directed and controlled. The corporate governance structure specifies the distribution of rights and responsibilities among different participants in the corporation, such as the board, managers, shareholders and other stakeholders, and spells out the rules and procedures for making decisions on corporate affairs. By doing this, it also provides the structure through which the company objectives are set, and the means of attaining those objectives and monitoring performance.[1]

The rules of the Securities and Exchange Commission (SEC), the stock exchanges and other laws and regulations (e.g., the Federal Sentencing Guidelines) generally result in public companies' having relatively formal, well-documented policies that describe entity-level controls related to the following broad control areas:

- Corporate culture
- Alignment between objectives and controls
- Risk identification
- Disclosure controls and procedures
- Top-level financial reporting processes

To evaluate the adequacy of the documentation related to the entity's corporate governance policies, you may wish to supplement your reading of the entity's documentation with a review of the documentation of the entity's competitors or others in the industry. That documentation frequently is available on those entities' Web sites in the investor relations section. You also should consider consulting with the entity's SEC counsel to determine the normal and customary corporate governance documentation available for similar companies.

The following is a brief description of relevant corporate governance documentation that may address these entity-wide control objectives.

Board of Directors Charter. The entity should have a document that describes the functioning of its board of directors. These documents, typically described as "charters," will vary between entities. Most charters generally contain the following, which can provide you with the documentation necessary for a number of significant entity-level controls:

- Mission or purpose
- Membership in the board, including number of members, their qualifications, independence requirements, continuing education, and selection
- Roles and responsibilities of the board. For the purposes of documenting significant controls, this section of the board of directors' charter should be considered carefully. Exhibit 5.2 provides a list of example board responsibilities.

Typically, an entity's board will carry out its responsibilities largely through committees, and each of these should have a charter similar to the board charter. Committees that are relevant for internal control purposes include those with responsibilities for

- Independent audit engagements (i.e., the audit committee)
- Compensation and employee benefits
- Risk management
- Technology planning
- Ethics

In order to carry out its responsibilities, it is critical that the board and its committees receive reliable and accurate information on a timely basis. When considering the entity's documentation related to responsibilities of the board, you should address the ways in which information about the company is gathered and communicated to the board.

Code of Conduct.[2] A written code of conduct can help the entity achieve certain significant control objectives in a variety of ways, including

- Increased awareness of and sensitivity to ethical issues among its personnel
- Clear guidance on permissible and impermissible behavior

Exhibit 5.2   Example Board of Directors Responsibilities

The following are example board of director responsibilities that directly address significant control objectives. These examples were adapted from actual board of directors' charters of several entities. Related control objectives are in parentheses.

- Monitor and manage potential conflicts of interest of management and the board. (Corporate culture)

- Review and approve key policy statements developed by management relating to corporate governance, including ethics and codes of conduct. (Corporate culture)

- Monitor and assess its own performance. (Corporate culture)

- Monitor the overall effectiveness of the entity's corporate governance practices. (Corporate culture)

- Ensure that members of senior management possess the qualifications, experience and integrity to perform their assigned roles. (Entity personnel)

- Evaluate the performance of the entity's chief executive officer. (Entity personnel)

- Review and approve the entity's overall strategic plan, including major deviations from the approved plan. (Alignment of objectives and controls)

- Review and approve operating plans and budgets. (Alignment of objectives and controls)

- Identify the principal risks of the entity, and implement and monitor a system of risk management. (Risk identification)

- Evaluate the adequacy and form of compensation and other incentives provided to key management personnel. (Risk identification)

- Review and approve significant transactions. (Top-level financial reporting)

- Approve annual and quarterly financial statements, including Management's Discussion and Analysis. (Top-level financial reporting)

As described in Chapter 4, a corporate culture is a socialization process that involves the establishment of values, norms, and shared beliefs. A written code of conduct will aid greatly in this process.

The form and content of a code of content can vary greatly. Typically, a code of conduct addresses

- A statement of the entity's values
- The people or group of people who are affected by the entity, for example, shareholders, customers, suppliers, and employees
- A discussion of the types of ethical problems that entity personnel are likely to encounter and guidance on how these situations should be resolved
- The identification of key behaviors that are accepted and not accepted in the workplace

- How to identify and resolve conflicts of interest
- How to report violations of the code and to whom
- Consequences of violating the code
- In general, how reported violations will be investigated

Disclosure Committee Charter. The disclosure committee charter is structured in a way that is similar to other board or committee structures. For example, it normally should contain a description of its purpose, the composition and qualification of members, and its responsibilities. Key elements of the charter include

- Composition and qualifications of disclosure committee members
  - The SEC has indicated that the committee should include the principal accounting officer or controller, the in-house or external SEC counsel, the entity's principal risk management officer, and the chief investor relations officer.
  - Members should have adequate experience or training in SEC reporting and disclosure matters.
  - Members should have access to information and the stature within the company to allow them to identify and evaluate disclosure items.
- Roles and responsibilities
  - Define the documents that the disclosure committee is responsible for reviewing. Establish a disclosure drafting and review process.
  - Establish and monitor the process for the identification, processing, summarizing, and disclosure of matters required to be disclosed.
  - Establish procedures to communicate disclosure matters to senior management.
  - Provide guidelines and a process for evaluating disclosure issues.
  - Establish communication channels with the chief executive officer (CEO) and chief financial officer (CFO), the independent auditors, and SEC counsel.
  - Determine an appropriate means for documenting the work of the committee, for example, the preparation of minutes or other periodic reports.
  - Evaluate the effectiveness of the entity's disclosure controls and procedures on a regular basis.

Other Documentation

Human Resource Policies and Personnel Handbook. Most companies document their human resource policies and communicate these to their employees through a personnel manual or handbook. Human resource policies may cover dozens of issues, which run the gamut from attendance and cell phone use to vacation plans and workplace diversity. For the purpose of evaluating internal controls, you should focus on the documentation of those policies that are most directly related to

- Demonstrating the entity's commitment to competence
- Communicating messages to employees regarding expected levels of integrity, ethical behavior, and competence

Both of these elements of the entity's control environment were discussed in Chapter 2.

Personnel policies that typically have significant internal control implications include those related to

- Recruiting potential employees and board members, including screening and background checks
- Hiring new employees
- New employee orientation, including senior management hired from outside the company
- Ongoing training, including board member training
- Compensation and benefits
- Promotion
- Performance appraisal and feedback
- Disciplinary measures
- Employee termination procedures

Issues such as conflicts of interest and acceptable use of company property may be included in the entity's personnel handbook. For our purposes, we have included these policies in our discussion of the entity's code of conduct.

Accounting Manuals. The entity's accounting manual should provide you with information relating to the procedures used to capture and process accounting information, the documents required in the processing, and the related control procedures. Typically, this information is most useful for documenting activity-level controls. However, the accounting manual may provide some documentation that is relevant for entity-wide controls, particularly those related to top-level financial reporting control objectives.

For this purpose, when reviewing the entity's accounting manual, look for documentation related to

- Procedures and related controls for closing the books at the end of the accounting period
- The process used to identify nonroutine, nonsystematic journal entries and the approvals that are required before these are recorded.
- Reclassifications and other adjustments that are required to combine the financial information of various business units or otherwise prepare the financial statements
- The process used to prepare significant accounting estimates

DOCUMENTING ACTIVITY-LEVEL CONTROLS

The processing of accounting transactions is a relatively linear process, as indicated in Exhibit 5.3.

Reading from left to right, the entity enters into a transaction, for example, the purchase of raw materials. That transaction generates data, some of which is significant for accounting purposes, some of which is not. For example, the description of the items purchased, the amount paid, and when the goods were received all have significance in the recognition, measurement, presentations, or disclosure of the transaction in the financial statements. The vendor's invoice number also is included as part of the transaction data, but this information has no relevance for accounting purposes.[3]

Raw transaction data must be transformed into information that can be processed by the accounting system, that is, information that will eventually result as a debit and credit to the general ledger. Once the accounting information has been prepared, the transaction enters the accounting system to be recognized and measured for financial reporting purposes. As indicated in Exhibit 5.3, several discreet processing steps may be required before the information ultimately is posted in the general ledger and other accounting records.

This entire process, which begins with the capture of raw transactional data and ends with posting to the general ledger, is the activity-level processing stream. Through this journey, raw data is changed—combined with other data, added, multiplied, subtracted and divided, or otherwise manipulated to create new information. Controls are needed to ensure that, throughout this multistep transformation process, the information retains its original integrity. It must remain complete and accurate. The processing stream itself also must retain its integrity, accepting all valid transactions and preventing unauthorized ones from entering the stream.

When evaluating the effectiveness of significant activity-level controls, you will assess the internal controls of the processing stream taken as a whole. Thus, when documenting activity-level controls, you should seek to understand the control structure for the entire stream, starting with the transaction data, all the way through to the posting of debits and credits.

Exhibit 5.3 Processing Accounting Transactions

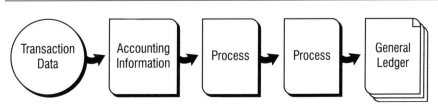

Documentation Requirements

Earlier in this chapter we described what should be included in the documentation of controls. Essentially, you should indicate how the control procedure is related to the control objective, and you should provide a description of the control that is sufficient to gauge the effectiveness of design.

There are many different forms your documentation may take, including narratives, "walk-through" descriptions of key documents, and flowcharts. Computerized documentation tools may be used to facilitate this process. (See Appendix 5B for additional information). In deciding how to best document activity-level controls, the principle that "form follows function,"[4] is a good one to follow. Remember that the purpose of your documentation is to describe your understanding of how the activity-level processing system works and to use that understanding to evaluate the effectiveness of the design of its overall control structure. Regardless of the form you use to document activity-level controls, certain key principles, if followed, will allow you to reach that understanding and convey meaning in a more direct, effective way. The following is a discussion of these key documentation principles.

Follow the Flow of Information. Accounting manuals and other traditional means of documenting accounting processes frequently focus on the flow of documents through the system. For example, if a four-part receiving form is completed to document the receipt of raw materials, one approach to documentation would be to track the processing and eventual disposition of each of the four copies of the form. For the purpose of understanding activity-level controls, it usually is more effective to track the flow of *information* rather than the flow of documents. By tracking the flow of information you are better able to identify the processes that change that information. Whenever information is changed, the risk of error enters the system, and that risk must be controlled.

To focus on the flow of information, you should consider working *backwards*, beginning with the posting to the general ledger. Obtain answers to a series of questions that seek to determine what *information* is created throughout the process and *how it is processed.* For example:

- *What is posted as a debit to inventory and a credit to accounts payable?*
  Monthly purchases.
- *How is this information created?*
  It is an accumulation of individual transactions throughout the month.
- *How is the information related to individual transactions created?*
  Invoices are matched with receiving reports and purchase orders and entered into the system on a real-time basis.

In this short example, you have quickly determined how information is created and processed, from initiation through posting. The fact that one copy of the purchase order is sent to the vendor or that production managers receive updates on raw material receipts is not considered.

Exhibit 5.4 describes this process. To highlight this method of working "backwards" we have reoriented the flowchart vertically, rather than the horizontal process depicted in Exhibit 5.3. In this depiction, the general ledger accounts are at the top of the flowchart. We have then worked *downward* to eventually identify the documents that captured the original transaction data.

Define the Boundaries of the System. Accounting systems have limits, and it is important that you clearly define them. The entity's control procedures start at the perimeter of its accounting system.

For example, an entity's purchase of raw materials may begin when the entity orders raw materials. The process continues through the vendor's selection, packing, and shipment of the product. Ultimately, the entity receives the materials it ordered.

In this scenario, the entity's controls begin when it receives the goods. It would be unreasonable to extend the control system any further upstream, for example, to the vendor's procedures for selecting and packing the materials.

For our purposes, the boundary of the activity-level accounting system is defined as the point at which the transaction information is approved and authorized and is in a format that is usable for accounting purposes (i.e., allows for the posting of debits and credits).

This definition of the accounting system boundary has several important implications. As a "gatekeeper" to the system, the system boundary must include control policies and procedures to ensure that

- Only valid, authorized transactions are allowed to enter the processing stream.
- *All* valid, authorized transactions are captured for processing.
- The accounting information that is captured accurately reflects the terms of the transaction.

Your documentation of the activity-level controls should include a description of the control policies and procedures that meet these boundary control objectives.

Exhibit 5.5 describes how the control boundary functions. Note that invalid, unauthorized transactions may attempt to enter the system at any point in the processing. Thus, the control boundary is depicted as a perimeter that encompasses the entire processing stream. For example, controls should exist to ensure that unauthorized journal entries are prevented from being posted directly to the general ledger account and thereby bypassing the processing stream and the controls built into that stream. Note that the boundary is established after the determination that a valid transaction exists, at the point where the information is presented in a form that contains accounting information. In this example, this occurs after entity personnel match the receiving reports and purchase order with the vendor invoice.

Exhibit 5.4 Capturing Information Flow

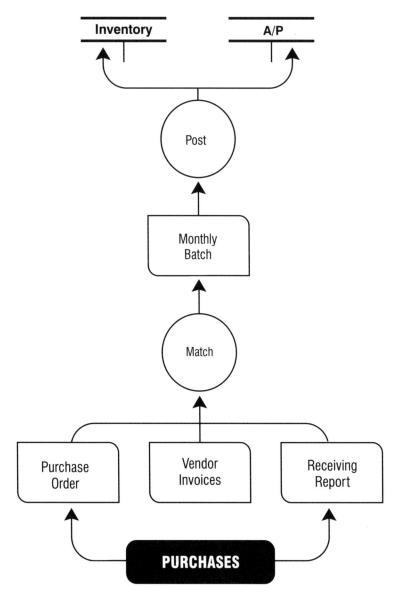

Transactions versus Events. Accounting information can be generated from either transactions or events. So far we have discussed the control implications related to business transactions, for example, the purchase of raw materials. But what about the recording of depreciation expense? The process of calculating and posting depreciation expense is initiated not from a transaction with an external party, but rather with an event—namely, the passage of time.

Exhibit 5.5   Control Boundary

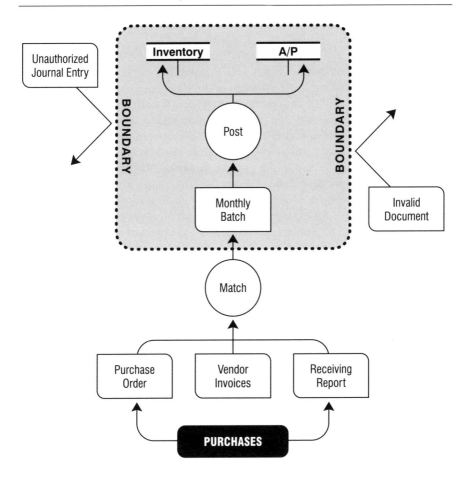

Like transactions, events occur at the perimeter of the accounting system. The "gatekeeper" control objectives relating to events are the same as those relating to transactions. However, the way in which those objectives are achieved usually varies.

At the boundary, *transactions* usually are controlled in real time, on a transaction-by-transaction basis. Proper authorization of each transaction is critical. *Events* can be triggered merely by the passage of time. For example, the recording of depreciation expense is initiated by the arrival of the end of the month. Authorization of each individual event is not as critical. The processing of the event may be initiated by the system itself. The control procedures usually are performed after the fact, not at the time the event is processed. For example, the controller may scan the general ledger to ensure that depreciation expense was recorded once and only once.

Preventive versus Detective Controls. Controls can be designed to either

- Identify errors as they occur and prevent them from further processing
- Detect and correct errors that already have entered the system

There are trade-offs for each approach. *Preventive* controls are more timely and help ensure that errors are never recorded in the accounting records to begin with. However, to design and perform preventive controls at each step in the processing stream may be costly. *Detective* controls may be cheaper to design and perform. For example, performing a reconciliation once a month between the general ledger and a subsidiary ledger may be more efficient than performing preventive controls on each transaction at each step in the process. However, the drawback to detective controls is that they are performed after the fact, sometimes well after the fact. The lack of timely performance of a detective control could mean that errors remain in the accounting records for extended periods of time. Most systems rely on a combination of preventive and detective controls, and it is common to build some redundancy into the system, in which more than one control meets the same objective.

Preventive and detective controls share one important thing in common. Both types of controls contain both an error detection and a correction component. The fact that a control procedure can identify an error does not make the control effective. It is the process of communicating identified errors to individuals who can then make corrections that makes the control complete.

Information Storage and Retrieval. It is common for systems to capture data, store it, and then retrieve it for later use. For example, an entity may maintain a database of approved vendors. This database is updated regularly as vendors are added or removed. When the time comes to authorize a payment, the control procedure requires someone to access the database and determine whether the vendor has been approved. If the vendor is in the database, then payment is authorized; if not, then the matter is brought to someone of appropriate authority to take follow-up action.

Databases and other types of information storage repositories should be considered part of the activity-level processing stream and therefore "protected" by the control boundary. All of the boundary control objectives should be addressed for gaining access to the information storage repository. In this example, controls should exist to ensure that

- All approved vendors are in the database.
- No unapproved vendors are in the database.
- Only authorized users have the ability to access and modify the information maintained in the database.

Computer Application Controls. Many control procedures are programmed into the entity's computer system. For example, the process of matching a vendor to a database of preapproved vendors may be completely computerized. A user may submit an invoice for payment, the computer performs the match, and, if the vendor is on the list, processing is allowed to continue. The user is informed only when the computer detects an error, namely, that the vendor has not been preapproved. It is then the user's responsibility to take the appropriate follow-up action. Again, the follow-up of the identified errors is a critical component of the control.

Ultimately, the effectiveness of computer application controls will depend on the effectiveness of computer general controls, including

- *Systems development.* The application was properly developed and tested to make sure that the control functions as designed.
- *Access.* Access to the program is monitored to ensure that unauthorized changes to the program cannot be made.

The control objectives for computer application controls are the same as the objectives for manual controls—information must remain complete and accurate at all phases, from initiation (data input) through processing.

Case Study

Appendix 5D provides a example documentation of an activity-level processing stream. The example is based on the W.D. Weathers Inc. case study introduced in Chapter 2.

COORDINATING WITH THE INDEPENDENT AUDITORS

Early in this phase of the project, you will want to coordinate your efforts with the client's independent auditors. Before proceeding too far, you should reach consensus on significant matters such as

- The criteria you will use to determine whether documentation is sufficient
- In general, what the documentation will contain
- The process you will follow for gathering and assessing documentation
- Plans for addressing documentation deficiencies

The form and content of an entity's documentation of internal control can vary greatly. For that reason, you also should work with the independent auditors to develop a process that allows them to review documentation periodically, as you determine it is adequate. For example, you may wish to "pilot test" the documentation of significant activity-level processes and controls and provide this to the auditors as soon as it becomes available. Providing them with examples of actual documentation will help you reach a consensus quicker on what should be documented.

APPENDIX 5A
Action Plan:
Documentation

The following action plan is intended to help you implement the suggestions contained in this chapter for evaluating an entity's documentation of its internal control.

1. Assess Existing Documentation

Determine whether existing documentation is sufficient to evaluate the design and plan tests of operating effectiveness. For example:

- Determine that documentation exists for all significant control objectives:
  - If documentation does not exist, then determine whether: (a) controls do not exist, or (b) ad hoc, informal controls exist but have not been documented.
  - If controls do not exist, design, document, and implement new control procedures.
  - If controls exist but are not documented, document existing controls.
- Determine that documentation contains the following elements:
  - A link between the control objective and the control policy or procedure
  - A description of the control policy or procedure that achieves the control objective. Appendix 5C includes example control policies and procedures, organized by significant control objective.
- Information about:
  - How transactions are initiated, recorded, processed, and reported, and
  - The flow of transactions to identify where material misstatements due to error or fraud could occur
  - A description of
    - How the control procedure is to be applied
    - Who is responsible for performing the procedure
    - How frequently the procedure is performed

2. Evaluate Automated Documentation Tool

Assess the adequacy of the documentation warehouse of the entity's automated compliance tool. For example:

- Determine that users have an adequate understanding of the entity's operations, internal control concepts, and financial reporting processes.

- Information integrity is maintained through the use of
  - Logical access controls
  - Controls over the systematic updating of documentation
- Changes to documentation are captured and monitored for possible disclosure

3. Entity-Level Controls

Assess the adequacy of the documentation of significant entity-level controls. Take corrective action as necessary. For example:

- Consider key documents such as—
  - Corporate governance documents
  - Human resource policies and the personnel handbook
  - Accounting policies manual

4. Activity-Level Controls

Assess the adequacy of the documentation of significant activity-level controls. Take corrective action as necessary. For example:

- Determine whether the documentation includes
  - The flow of information from initiation through posting to the general ledger
  - Clear delineation of processing stream boundaries
  - Consideration of both transactions and events
  - Maintenance of the integrity of information stored by the system for later use (e.g., the approved vendor master file)

5. Coordinate with Independent Auditors

Reach a consensus with the independent auditors regarding key decisions about the documentation of internal control. For example:

- Communicate and reach agreement with the auditors on matters such as
  - The criteria you will use to determine whether documentation is sufficient
  - In general, what the documentation will contain
  - The process you will follow for gathering and assessing documentation
  - Plans for addressing documentation deficiencies

APPENDIX 5B

Evaluating the Design and Implementation
of Sarbanes-Oxley Automated Compliance Tools

FUNCTIONS OF AN AUTOMATED SARBANES-OXLEY TOOL

Since the passage of the Sarbanes-Oxley Act, many companies with a wide variety of expertise have developed computer software products that aid in complying with the internal control provisions of the Act. These software tools typically center on helping companies automate the documentation of internal control policies and procedures, although some products automate other processes as well. In general, Sarbanes-Oxley automated compliance tools are designed to facilitate one or more of the following:

- *Warehouse of internal control documentation.* The program provides a repository for all of the entity's documentation relating to the design of internal control. In those instances in which the documentation of the control or the control itself either does not exist or otherwise is deficient, the software allows the company to efficiently either document existing policies or design and document new ones.
- *Automate business processes.* Many software programs are designed to automate business processes. Within the context of Sarbanes-Oxley, this automation can occur on two different levels:
  1. *Testing and evaluation of internal controls.* In order to support its assessment of internal control, management must test both its design and operating effectiveness. Software tools can help manage this process, for example, by tracking the progress of testwork or accumulating the conclusions reached about the achievement of significant control objectives.
  2. *Implementation of internal control policies and procedures.* Software tools can automate or make systematic the performance of a wide variety of business tasks, including the performance of control procedures. For example, the software tool automatically may send an e-mail to an employee to remind him or her to prepare the monthly bank reconciliation. The software may then facilitate the actual performance of this control procedure, including its subsequent review by a supervisor. Within this context, the software can help monitor the performance of control procedures, for example, by providing summaries for supervisors on which control tasks have been completed.

Note that these two functions are not mutually exclusive but, rather, closely aligned. It is the design of the internal control procedures, as maintained in the internal control documentation warehouse, that drives any automation of business processes. That is, without a well-defined control system, there would be no business process to automate. The design of internal control policies and procedures must precede the automation of either their implementation or tests of effectiveness.

Implementation Is Critical

The installation of an automated Sarbanes-Oxley software tool is analogous to the installation of an accounting software package. The installation of a new general ledger system does *not* ensure reliable financial statements prepared in accordance with generally accepted accounting principles (GAAP); the installation of a Sarbanes-Oxley compliance tool does *not* guarantee compliance with the Act. Ultimately, the effectiveness of any automated tool will depend on how well the entity identifies and addresses critical implementation issues. Even the most well-designed tool can be rendered ineffective it if is deployed improperly. The following discussion highlights several of the most important design and implementation issues that should be considered.

ASSESSING THE CONTROL WAREHOUSE FUNCTION

The warehouse function of an automated Sarbanes-Oxley tool serves as a central repository for the description of the entity's internal control policies and procedures. In assessing this function, you should consider the following.

What to Document

As indicated in Chapter 5, the documentation of controls should be adequate in that

- *All controls objectives have been considered.* Control policies and procedures have been documented for *all* significant control objectives.
- *Documentation is sufficient.* To be sufficient, the documentation should allow management and the independent auditor to
  - Evaluate the effectiveness of design.
  - Design and perform procedures to test the operating effectiveness of the controls.

The documentation of individual control policies and procedures should contain

- A link between the control objective and the control policy or procedure
- A description of the control policy or procedure that achieves the control objective
- Information about:
  - How transactions are initiated, recorded, processed, and reported, and
  - The flow of transactions to identify where material misstatements due to error or fraud could occur

- A description of
  - How the control procedure is to be applied
  - Who is responsible for performing the procedure
  - How frequently the procedure is performed

Documentation Process

Automated documentation tools typically use a combination of the following methods for creating and accumulating internal control documentation:

- *Reference existing documentation.* In many instances, the documentation of a policy or procedure already exists, for example, the company's code of conduct. When that is the case, the automated tool should simply allow this existing documentation to be reviewed by the user. To allow for this sharing of existing information, the automated tool may have to
  - Interface with existing systems
  - Import existing data

  The ease and accuracy with which the tool accomplishes this task will greatly affect its utility.
- *Menu-driven responses.* To create documentation for a new or existing control procedure, the automated tool may provide users with choices from a pull-down menu. For example, in order to describe a control objective, the user may be presented with a choice of: "ensure proper authorization of transactions," "verify accuracy," "ensure the capture of all valid transactions," and so on.
- *Free responses.* Instead of choosing from a predetermined list of possibilities, users may enter their own response into a text box.

Regardless of the method used to document new or existing controls, the goal remains the same—to accurately describe the entity's control policies and procedures as they currently exist. Whether that goal is achieved depends primarily on the qualifications, knowledge, and training of the user. To effectively document the entity's control policies and procedures, the user should have an in-depth understanding of all of the following:

- The entity's operations and existing control policies and procedures
- Internal control concepts, as described in the COSO framework (or other framework, if the entity does not use COSO)
- The financial reporting process
- The assertions that are represented in the financial statements (See Chapter 7 for a discussion of financial statement assertions.)

Note that a new control policy or procedure does not end with the creation of the documentation. If a control is found to be missing and a new one must be created, then the new policy or procedure must be communicated to all affected parties and placed in operation.

Review Features

One of the objectives of documentation is to facilitate the review of internal control design and to allow for the planning of tests of control effectiveness. To enable these objectives, the automated tool must allow for the effective review of the documentation stored in the warehouse.

Different reviewers will have different objectives, and the tool should accommodate multiple perspectives.[5] At a minimum, controls should be able to be reviewed from the following perspectives:

- *By control objective.* This perspective will allow the user to review the control policies and procedures for each significant control objective.
- *By business process.* This perspective is one way for the user to evaluate significant activity-level control objectives.
- *By general ledger account.* This perspective is the other way for a reviewer to assess activity-level controls, and it provides a direct link between the financial statements and internal control.

Maintaining Information Integrity

If the documentation exercise is successful, then ultimately, the documentation maintained in the warehouse will be a true and accurate reflection of what *actually should be occurring* in the day-to-day operations of the entity. Once that verisimilitude is achieved, it must be maintained. Reviewers must be able to rely on the accuracy of the documentation.

In order to maintain the integrity of the information kept in the warehouse, the automated tool should have the following features.

- *Logical access controls.* The ability to modify documentation should be tightly controlled in the same way that access to all of an entity's sensitive information and computer applications is controlled. Individual users should be granted access privileges only to those areas of documentation that pertain to their assigned responsibilities. Once they have documented the controls in their area and the documentation has been reviewed, the access privileges should be revoked until the documentation needs to be updated. Someone on your project team should assume the responsibility for administering logical access controls over the documentation warehouse.
- *Standardized updating procedures.* The company's internal control will change over time. Additionally, testing of control effectiveness may reveal that the documentation is not an accurate reflection of what actually occurs in the entity, and the documentation will need to be changed. Changes to documentation should be controlled. When required changes are identified, the affected control objectives,

business process, and general ledger accounts also should be identified immediately so that users know that the documentation in these areas is subject to change and should not be relied on. Modifications to the documentation should be done in an orderly fashion that ensures that *all* required changes are made. Once the changes have been made, they should be reviewed.

Monitoring Documentation Changes

Once the documentation warehouse becomes established as an accurate reflection of internal control, and standardized updating procedures are in place, then any changes to the documentation should represent actual changes to internal control. Management is required to report material changes in internal control. Identifying and capturing changes to the internal control documentation will enable this requirement to be met.

The automated documentation tool should have a means for identifying changes since the last reporting date. In order to help reviewers evaluate their significance, these changes should be able to be grouped in a variety of ways, including business process, control objective, and financial statement account grouping.

AUTOMATED TESTING OF CONTROLS

Management must support its assessment of the effectiveness of internal control by testing significant control objectives. Once these objectives and the related control policies and procedures have been documented and stored in the warehouse, it would be natural for the automated compliance tool to link to the documentation and help manage the testing process. In this capacity, the automated tool *neither*

- Performs testwork *nor*
- Draws conclusions about effectiveness

Rather, the function of the system is to assist in the coordination of the testing and evaluation of controls by enabling the effective flow of information. To achieve this objective, the automated tool should include the following features:

- *Project administration.* All of the information necessary to manage the engagement and coordinate and direct team members should be accumulated, stored, and made available to the team. For example, this information might include the overall work plan, identification and contact information for project team members, due dates, project status summary, and so on.
- *Work programs.* The system should allow work programs to be created, stored or both. These programs should link automatically to the controls as documented in the warehouse. Changes to the documentation should be flagged so that work programs can be reviewed and updated as necessary.

- *Monitor testing status and results.* As work program steps are completed and conclusions reached about whether control objectives have been met, the progress of the engagement team should be captured and made available for review.

- *Communication and collaboration.* Individual participants in the project do not work in a vacuum. They are part of a team. Timely, effective communication and collaboration among all participants is required for the team to function at its highest level. As described in Chapter 1, the participants in your project include both internal and external parties, which include the entity's independent auditors, SEC legal counsel, and any consultants assisting in the project. E-mail lists are a common method for facilitating this communication. However, a chat room type of feature may be more effective at creating a more collaborative environment in which different perspectives can be exchanged and considered by all participants and a consensus more quickly reached.

- *Resource library.* During the performance of the engagement, questions will arise constantly. A self-help resource library can provide project team members with the information necessary to research issues related to the testing, evaluation, and reporting of internal control. With this research, individuals can either resolve the issue themselves or form an opinion that can be vetted among the group members to reach a consensus. The resource library should be dynamic, allowing for the easy posting of relevant, helpful guidance as it becomes available.

AUTOMATED CONTROL PROCEDURES

Once a control procedure has been defined, that process can be automated. For example, the entity may define a process for the review, approval, and payment of vendor invoices or the identification, preparation, and review of a significant accounting estimate.

The compliance tool can be used to automate many elements of the control procedures, for example, by

- Providing required information on a timely basis to the person responsible for performing the procedure
- Routing the work product (e.g., a check request or an accounting estimate) to the person responsible for initiating the next phase in the process
- Tracking the progress and results of the procedure to allow for monitoring of control performance at a supervisory level
- Initiating follow-up action in those instances in which control procedures have not been performed in a timely manner

The overall objective of automating control procedures is to enhance their effectiveness and efficiency. To achieve this objective, the system should include the following features:

- *Interface with existing systems.* The compliance tool should "sit on top of" and interface with the entity's existing systems. It should do so in a way that is minimally invasive and has a relatively benign effect on the existing system. This ability to interface with other systems is necessary if the tool is to successfully extract the information needed to perform the control procedure.

- *Ease of use.* The software should be easy to use and intuitive. Little training should be required for users to use the system effectively.

- *Flexibility.* The software must be easily configurable to accommodate a virtually limitless number of control processes.

- *Handling of exceptions and special circumstances.* It is inevitable that unusual transactions or events will arise. To enable the effective functioning of internal control, the system should

  - Identify the existence of those unusual transactions or events.

  - Provide guidance or a structured escalation procedure to the individual who processes and controls the activity.

- *Resource library.* Individuals may have questions about company policies, techniques for performing certain procedures, or other matters that affect the performance of their tasks. Guidance on these matters should be provided in a reference library to allow for the effective and efficient resolution of issues as they arise.

- *Monitoring.* The progress and results of the performance of the control procedure should be captured to allow for the monitoring required at a supervisory level.

THE VALUE OF AN AUTOMATED COMPLIANCE TOOL

Almost all entities will adopt an automated tool to assist in the documentation, testing, and evaluation of internal control. At first, the necessity of adopting such a tool probably will be driven by a need for engagement efficiency. The sheer magnitude of the task will require the entity to automate certain aspects.

As entities begin to deploy the tool, they will quickly realize significant additional benefit. Formal documentation of policies and control procedures will enhance the reliability of internal control. Entities that use a software tool to automate business processes will need to make decisions about how the tool should be configured and deployed. To make these decisions will require management to consider carefully the processes they put in place, the information resources people need to perform their assigned task, and how controls are monitored and exceptions handled. All of these considerations will add further definition to the entity's internal control and improve its effectiveness.

APPENDIX 5C
Linkage of Significant Control Objectives to
Example Control Policies and Procedures

The following table summarizes the significant control objectives described in Appendix 4B and links these objectives to example control activities. Note that Appendix 6D provides example control activities related to significant general computer control objectives.

Exhibit 5.6   Linkage of Significant Control Objectives to Example Control Policies and Procedures

Control Objective	Example Control Policy or Procedure
Corporate Culture	
Articulate and communicate codes of conduct and other policies regarding acceptable business practice, conflicts of interest, or expected standards of ethical and moral behavior.	• Comprehensive codes of conduct are developed and maintained and are periodically acknowledged by all employees. • Procedures are established that allow employees to take appropriate action to report unacceptable behavior they observe. • The board of directors evaluates corporate culture and "tone at the top." • The entity's code of conduct and ethical standards are communicated to outside parties such as vendors and customers. • Feedback mechanisms with outside parties exist that allow them to report concerns about corporate culture and ethical behavior.
Reduce incentives and temptations that can motivate employees to act in a manner that is unethical, opposed to the entity's objectives, or both.	• Management identifies compensation policies and other incentives that can motivate unethical behavior • Management and the board of directors monitor identified incentives and motivations (including compensation) to identify unintended consequences (e.g., possible violation of codes of conduct).
Reinforce written policies about ethical behavior through action and leadership by example.	• Management and the board of directors take appropriate remedial or disciplinary actions in response to violations of acceptable behavior. • Actions in response to unacceptable behavior are communicated to employees as a means of providing an effective deterrent.

(Continued)

Exhibit 5.6 *(Continued)*

Control Objective	Example Control Policy or Procedure
Corporate Culture (cont'd)	• Management takes appropriate action on all complaints, suggestions, and feedback about ethical behavior and possible control weaknesses, including that received from outside parties.
Personnel Policies Identify, articulate, and communicate to entity personnel the information and skills needed to perform their jobs effectively.	• Responsibilities and expectations are communicated clearly to individuals, especially those in supervisory positions and new personnel. • Job descriptions are developed and maintained. • Job descriptions contain specific references to control-related responsibilities. • Management determines the information needs of personnel and the board of directors. • Information is provided to the right people in sufficient detail and on time to enable them to carry out their responsibilities efficiently and effectively.
Provide entity personnel with the resources needed to perform their jobs effectively.	• Organizational structure is designed to facilitate the flow of information upstream, downstream, and across all business activities. • Senior management is comprised of individuals from several functional areas, not just a few. • Recruiting and hiring policies ensure that only competent individuals are hired. • Training needs are evaluated and appropriate training provided to all entity personnel (possibly including the board of directors). • Management evaluates the adequacy of the workforce—both in numbers and experience—necessary to carry out company objectives.
Supervise and monitor individuals with internal control responsibilities.	• Senior management has frequent interaction with operating management, particularly those operating from geographically remote locations. • Supervisory personnel provide performance evaluation feedback and suggestions for improvement to subordinates.

Exhibit 5.6   *(Continued)*

Control Objective	Example Control Policy or Procedure
	• Promotion, retention, and compensation criteria consider the individual's adherence to behavioral standards and standards of performance.
Delegate authority and responsibility to appropriate individuals within the organization.	• Authority, responsibility, and accountability are linked and delegated together. • Boundaries of authority are established and communicated. • The delegation of responsibilities considers the need to segregate incompatible activities. • Management periodically evaluates the entity's organizational structure to assess its continued effectiveness.

General Computer Controls

Control Objective	Example Control Policy or Procedure
Develop, communicate, and plan an overall IT strategy that enables the achievement of entity-wide controls.	• Management identifies and analyzes external reporting requirements for their IT impact and takes appropriate action to comply. • Management actively identifies, assesses, and responds to IT-related risks. • Planning, implementation, and maintenance of IT system appropriately considers user needs.
Provide resources and organizational infrastructure necessary to implement the IT strategy.	• Management budgets for the continued funding of IT systems development. • A structured approach exists to address training, service, and user documentation.

Identify, acquire, and integrate IT applications and solutions that are necessary for implementating the IT strategy	• Specific functional and operational requirements are developed.
	• The entity has policies such as the following to ensure that appropriate hardware and software are acquired and implented.
	  – Entity-wide standardized hardware and software standards
	  – Regular assessment of hardware and software performance
	• The entity has a formal migration, conversion, and acceptance plan for new systems and systems modifications.
	• Input and processing controls ensure that data remains complete, accurate, and valid during its input, processing, and storage.

(Continued)

Exhibit 5.6   *(Continued)*

Control Objective	Example Control Policy or Procedure

Personnel Policies (con't)	• Logical access controls restrict access to systems, data, and programs.
	• The entity's IT operating policies and procedures include the
	  – Development and testing of a business continuity plan
	  – Installation of suitable environmental and physical controls

Monitor IT processes to ensure their continued effectiveness	• Management has defined relevant performance indicators, which are reported and reviewed on a timely basis.
Alignment between Objectives and Organizational and Control Structures	
Articulate and communicate entity-wide objectives and related business strategies.	• Management develops and periodically updates the entity's strategic plan. • The entity's strategic plan is communicated to all employees and reviewed and approved by the board of directors. • Management obtains feedback from key managers, other employees, and the board on the entity's strategic plan.
Design and periodically review activity-level objectives and resources to ensure they are linked to and consistent with each other and the entity-wide objectives.	• Activity-level objectives are established for all value-chain activities. • Managers participate in establishing activity objectives for which they are responsible • The process for establishing activity-level objectives includes the consideration of past practices and performances or industry examples. • Activity-level objectives include the resources required for achievement, a definition of critical success factors, and measurement criteria for monitoring.
Risk Identification	
Develop mechanisms to anticipate, identify, and react to routine events or activities that affect the entity or activity-level objectives.	• Management identifies risks arising from both external and internal sources. • Risks are identified and addressed at sufficiently high levels in the organization so their full implications are identified and appropriate action plans considered.

Exhibit 5.6   *(Continued)*

Control Objective	Example Control Policy or Procedure
	• Risk identification is included in the entity's strategic planning process. • The board of directors oversees and monitors the risk identification and assessment process.
Develop mechanisms to anticipate, identify, and react to unusual, significant events that can have a more dramatic and pervasive effect on the entity.	• Risks related to significant change are identified, including those relating to – Changed operating environment – New personnel – New or redesigned information systems – Rapid growth – New technology – New lines, products, activities, and acquisitions – Corporate restructuring – Foreign operations – Changes in accounting principles
Anti-Fraud Programs and Controls Create a culture of honesty and high ethics	• Management is made aware that they are expected to set a high ethical standard within the entity. • Create policies that contribute to a positive workplace environment. • Personnel policies minimize the chance of hiring or promoting individuals with low levels of honesty. • Employees are trained about the entity's values and code of conduct. • Alleged incidents of fraud are appropriately investigated and disciplinary action is taken.
Evaluate anti-fraud processes and controls.	• Management actively identifies and assesses fraud risk. • Management makes changes to the entity's activities and business processes to mitigate identified fraud risks. • Internal control policies and procedures are designed to specifically address identified fraud risks.
Develop an effective anti-fraud oversight process.	• The audit committee provides an appropriate level of oversight with regard to – Management's identification of fraud risks – The implementation of anti-fraud measures – The creation of an appropriate culture and "tone at the top"

(Continued)

Exhibit 5.6   *(Continued)*

Control Objective	Example Control Policy or Procedure

Top-Level Financial Reporting Processes

Control Objective	Example Control Policy or Procedure
Management is aware of and understands the need for certain financial reporting adjustments.	• Senior management, the board of directors, and the audit committee include individuals with appropriate levels of financial expertise. • Senior management, the board of directors, and the audit committee stay current on financial accounting and reporting matters. • When the entity is structuring nonsystematic, nonroutine transactions, accounting personnel are consulted early in the process.

Relevant and reliable information required for decision-making purposes is identified, gathered, and communicated.	• Management considers information from both external and internal sources that may affect
	  – The assumptions underlying significant accounting estimates
	  – The valuation of assets
	  – The recognition of liabilities
	• Information used to make estimates and consider the recognition and measurement of assets and liabilities is consistent with industry conditions, entity plans, budgets, and its past performance.
	• Information gathering and communication processes are reviewed and updated to reflect changed accounting and reporting needs.
	• Support is provided for nonroutine, nonsystematic journal entries.

Management analyzes the information and responds appropriately.	• Management develops and maintains a process for closing the books and preparing financial statements at the end of an accounting reporting period. • Nonroutine, nonsystematic journal entries are identified • Management seeks advice from independent auditors on significant accounting issues.
Management's response is reviewed and approved	• Management reviews significant accounting estimates and support for significant unusual transactions and non-routine, non-systematic journal entries. • Board of directors assesses the quality of the entity's accounting principles.
Management identifies events and transactions for which accounting	• Management regularly reviews its significant accounting policies and considers

Exhibit 5.6   *(Continued)*

Control Objective	Example Control Policy or Procedure
policy choices should be made or existing policies reconsidered.	– Accounting principles applied by the entity for which acceptable alternative principles are available – Judgments and estimates that affect the financial statements – Evolving business and accounting issues and choices that affect financial reporting – The accounting for unusual arrangements
The accounting policies chosen by management have general acceptance and result in a fair presentation of financial statement information.	• Management assesses the clarity and transparency of the entity's financial statements and disclosures. • Management considers input from auditors,[a] regulators, and others when choosing or reconsidering its existing choice of accounting principles. Based on this input, it takes appropriate action. • When considering new or reevaluating existing accounting policies, management obtains input from financial accounting experts. • Other matters, such as the accounting policies of other entities that report the same or similar events or transactions, is considered. • The choice of accounting principles is reviewed and approved by the board of directors.
Information processing and internal control policies and procedures are designed to appropriately apply the accounting principles selected.	• Company accounting policies are documented and communicated to all those that may affect their proper implementation. • Changes to accounting policies are communicated on a timely basis. • Training on the proper application of company accounting policies is provided as necessary.
System-Wide Monitoring Reach a common understanding of internal control deficiencies and changes that are considered "material" and require disclosure.	• Management describes internal control weaknesses and changes that are required for disclosure after considering input from the entity's – Independent auditors – SEC legal counsel

(Continued)

Exhibit 5.6 *(Continued)*

Control Objective	Example Control Policy or Procedure
System-Wide Monitoring (cont'd)	• Policies related to the disclosure of internal control deficiencies and changes are documented and communicated to the disclosure committee and others.
Identify material weaknesses in internal control on a timely basis.	• Management identifies significant controls that should be closely monitored and evaluated for deficiencies. • Management identifies individuals related to each significant control who are best able to identify potential material weaknesses that should be disclosed. • Management establishes policies for the timely communication of material weaknesses to the disclosure committee and the CEO and CFO. • The disclosure committee, audit committee, and board of directors review all material weaknesses identified by the independent auditors, and they take appropriate action.
Identify material changes to internal control on a timely basis.	• Changes to internal control documentation are captured and communicated to management. • Changes to internal control that may *not* have been reflected in the documentation are captured and communicated to management. • Management reviews all changes to internal control and discloses these changes when appropriate.

[a]The auditing standards require auditors to discuss with the entity's audit committee the auditor's judgment about the quality, not just the acceptability, of the entity's accounting principles.

APPENDIX 5D

Documentation Example

As described in Chapter 2, W.D. Weathers Inc. is a real estate investment trust (REIT) that is involved in the acquisition, ownership, management, and leasing of shopping malls. The company's revenue stream has two different components: base rent (i.e., the minimum, fixed monthly rental paid by tenants) and percentage rent (i.e., additional rent calculated as a percentage of the tenant's gross sales).

BACKGROUND INFORMATION

Base Rent

Leases are negotiated at the local, property manager level, under broad guidelines provided by corporate. Leases must be approved at the corporate level before they become final. A lease abstract is used to capture leasing information, and this information is entered into a database that is maintained at the property level. Monthly, the system runs reports showing all changes to the lease information database, and these reports are reviewed by the property managers to ensure that all information was captured properly.

Monthly billing for base rent is handled locally and is totally automated. The billing application program accesses the database and prepares the monthly rent statements for the tenants. The program updates the rent receivable subledger. It also prepares a report that provides information on each space in the mall, including

- Tenant name
- Lease information summary, including base rent, scheduled rent adjustments, rent concessions, and the like
- Current month and prior month base rent

The property manager uses this report to check to see that all tenants got billed and at the right amount.

Cash receipts are physically received in the property manager's office. The process for capturing and reporting the information is largely manual.

- A receipt is prepared for each tenant.
- The receipts are batched and periodically input into the accounting system.
- The system processes the information by updating the accounts receivable ledger and posting a debit to cash.

At month end, the bank account is reconciled. The property manager reviews a printout of the accounts receivable subledger to identify large, unexpected receivables balances that may indicate that a rent payment was not processed properly. The accounts receivable subledger is reconciled to the general ledger account on a monthly basis.

Percentage Rent

Most tenants are required to pay additional rent based on an agreed-upon percentage of gross sales. This percentage rent is paid quarterly.

Quarterly, each tenant submits a report that shows gross sales, the percentage rent, and the total amount due. A check for the amount due usually is provided at the same time. The percentage rent reports are entered into the system. The program performs two checks on the data:

1. It compares reported quarterly gross sales to the comparable period for each of the last two years and calculates percentage changes in the reported amounts. It then prepares a report of this analysis for review by the property manager.
2. It compares the percentage used to calculate the amount due to the percentages maintained in the property management database. Any differences are identified and reported on an exception report.

Month-End Reporting

Each mall prepares a standardized month-end reporting package, which it then submits to the corporate accounting office. The process for combining these reports at the corporate level is not yet fully automated. Some manual processing still is required to enter information into the system for updating the corporate accounting records. Clerical level staff performs the input. In addition to updating the accounting records, the system also provides a number of operating reports that provide both financial and nonfinancial data. These reports group the malls by geographic region. The asset manager for each region reviews these reports for anomalies and possible errors by comparing rental income and cash flow to budget and looking for large, unusual accounts receivable balances.

Internal Audit Activities

Internal auditors perform two important control activities at the property management level:

1. Compare lease information maintained in the property management database to signed lease agreements.
2. "Audit" percentage rent reports by comparing gross sales information reported to the landlord to the sales records maintained by the client.

DOCUMENTATION EXAMPLE

The documentation of this system consists of two elements: a flowchart (see Exhibit 5.7; see also, Exhibit 5.8 for the flowchart legend) and an accompanying description of the related controls (see Exhibit 5.9).

Understanding the Flowchart

The flowchart follows the principles described in this chapter. In reading the flowchart, consider the following:

Exhibit 5.7 Flowchart (Read in conjunction with Exhibits 5.8 and 5.9.)

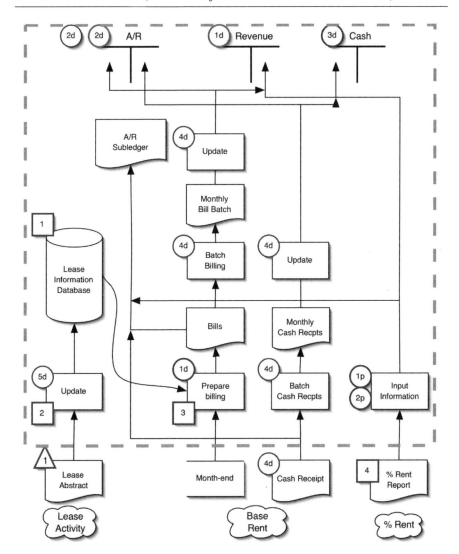

- *Organization.* At the top of the flowchart are T-accounts, which represent the general ledger accounts affected by revenue transactions. At the bottom of the chart is the initiation of the transactions. In between the general ledger and the initiation are the various information-processing steps.
- *Controls and processes.* Processes manipulate data. When data is changed, errors can occur. For example, one of the processes described on the flowchart is the batching of individual base-rent bills. In this process, it is possible that some individual bills could inadvertently be left out of the batch. Thus, each process

Exhibit 5.8   Flowchart Legend

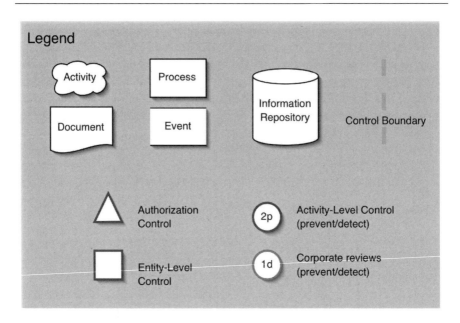

should have related controls to ensure that the integrity of the information (i.e., its completeness and accuracy) is maintained during processing.

- *Referencing control descriptions.* This flowchart has identified four different types of controls.
  1. Authorization controls, which are designed to ensure that only valid, authorized transactions are entered into the processing stream
  2. Entity-level controls
  3. Activity-level controls, which may be either preventive or detective
  4. Corporate controls, which are controls performed at the corporate, not property management, level. By their nature, these are detective controls.

- *Information repository.* This system includes an information repository, which is the database of lease information. This database is used to prepare billings and possibly other information used to monitor activities. As described in this chapter, the information repository should reside within the boundary of the system and protected from unauthorized access and changes.

Analyzing the Control Structure

This system relies primarily on detective and entity-level controls. This is a fairly high-level approach. Individual processes are not closely monitored, and there are very few preventive controls. For example, the entity does not perform any detailed

Exhibit 5.9   Description of Controls

W.D Weathers Inc.
Leasing Revenue
Description of Controls

Ref. No.	Description
Entity-Level Controls	
1	The entity maintains access control software to monitor and limit unauthorized access to the database of lease information.
2	Internal auditors periodically compare the lease information in the database to signed lease agreements.
3	Month-end base rent calculations are performed automatically by the computer system. Systems development and program change controls ensure that program functions properly. Access to program is controlled to protect against unauthorized changes.
4	Periodically, internal auditors audit percentage rent reports by comparing gross sales information to tenant records.
Authorization Controls	
1	New leases and lease modifications and changes are reviewed, authorized and approved by asset managers at the corporate level.
Activity-Level Controls	
1d	The property manager reviews a month-end report to ensure that all tenants got billed at their proper amount.
2d	The property manager reviews month-end receivables to identify unexpected balances.
3d	The bank account is reconciled monthly.
4d	The accounts receivable general ledger account is reconciled to the subsidiary ledger on a monthly basis.
5d	Monthly, the property manager reviews the changes made to the lease information database.
1p	Computerized controls compare quarterly sales to historical activity. Monthly, property manager reviews reports to identify possible errors in the reporting of percentage rent.
2p	Rent percentage used by the tenant to calculate percentage rent is compared to the lease information database. Control is computerized—all exceptions are printed to a report for follow-up by property management accountant on a monthly basis.

reviews of lease abstract information that is input into the lease information database. The leases themselves are authorized and lease abstracts are prepared, but there is no mention of anyone's reviewing these abstracts and comparing them to the signed lease agreements before they are entered into the system. Instead, the company relies on the internal audit department to perform this function at some later point. Similarly, the controls over the calculation of base rent are primarily reconciliations and analytical procedures performed by the property managers.

There is very little redundancy in this system. All processes are controlled, but usually only by one control procedure. Usually, the opposite is true—one control procedure addresses several control objectives. The advantage to such a structure is its efficiency.

The system is vulnerable because the failure of just one control could result in a financial statement misstatement. For example, the batching of base rent billings may be performed improperly—a tenant billing may not be included in the month-end total. The only control related to this process is the reconciliation of the sub-ledger to the related general ledger account. If this procedure is not performed properly, the error will go undetected.

Similarly, the primary reliance on detective controls means that errors may remain on the books and records for a long period of time. If there is a difference between the information maintained in the lease database and the signed lease agreement, that difference could go unnoticed until the internal auditors perform their review.

Notes

1. From the Organization for Economic Co-operation and Development (OECD), April 1999. This definition was reported by the *Encyclopedia about Corporate Governance, www.encycogov.com.*
2. The Center for the Study of Ethics in the Professions (*www.iit.edu/departments/csep*) has compiled a library of codes of conduct and ethics from a wide variety of entities. This is an excellent resource if you would like to compare your company's or client's code of conduct to other similar entities.
3. For the purpose of tracking or controlling the transaction, the entity may wish to capture the invoice number anyway, but this is purely optional. However, capturing the amount of the purchase is *not* an option.
4. Attributed to the American architect Louis Sullivan.
5. Reviewers may include
   - Engagement team personnel who review the documentation to ensure its accuracy
   - Management and independent auditors who evaluate the design and plan the tests of operating effectiveness of the controls

Chapter 6

Testing and Evaluating Entity-Level Controls

Chapter Summary

Define an internal control reliability model for evaluating effectiveness.

Using the reliability model, describe testing strategies and techniques for evaluating the effectiveness of significant entity-level controls.

Provide practice aids for testing and evaluation of entity-level controls.

INTRODUCTION

Two Dimensions of Effectiveness

The overall objective of your internal control project is to provide management with a basis for making an assertion about the effectiveness of the entity's internal control. Consider the following statement about effectiveness:

Sue is the most effective point guard in basketball.

This statement seems straightforward, but upon further consideration, you are likely to ask two important questions:

1. *Effective compared to whom?* In this example, the person making this statement would probably be comparing Sue to her peers—others who play her same position, at the same level of competition.
2. *Effective measured how?* Basketball, like most other sports, has a variety of statistical and nonstatistical measures of a player's effectiveness. The person making a claim about Sue could point to measures such as the average number of assists or turnovers per game or a variety of measures related to scoring points as a way to measure effectiveness.

Similarly, assertions about the effectiveness of internal control must be supported along two dimensions:

1. *Effective compared to what?* Typically, the entity's internal control will be compared to COSO as one means of assessing effectiveness. Chapter 2 pro-

vides a detailed discussion of the COSO integrated model for internal control.

2. *Effective measured how?* COSO provides an overall framework of the five integrated components of internal control. But it provides little guidance on how to measure relative effectiveness. There are no commonly accepted measurement techniques for internal control (as there are for basketball players). For example, COSO identifies integrity and ethical values as being an important piece of the entity's control environment, and the report makes a compelling argument for why this is so. But the report does not describe how to measure or otherwise evaluate whether an ethical climate is "effective." This chapter introduces an "internal control reliability model" that can be used as a tool to making such an evaluation.

Exhibit 6.1 describes this two-dimensional process for evaluating internal control effectiveness.

Across the horizontal axis are the entity's significant control objectives, which mirror the COSO framework. (Appendix 4C maps how these control objectives relate to the COSO framework.) The vertical axis depicts the internal control reliability model. As indicated, this model has five different levels of effectiveness, which will be described later in this chapter.

Exhibit 6.2 provides an example of a matrix that has been completed at the conclusion of one's test of effectiveness. The controls for each significant control objective have been evaluated and "scored" for effectiveness based on the reliability model. The result is a visual interpretation of the effectiveness of the entity-level controls *taken as a whole*.

Exhibit 6.1   Two-Dimensional Process for Evaluating Internal Control Effectiveness

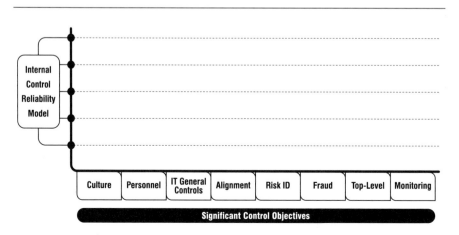

Exhibit 6.2 Visual Interpretation of the Effectiveness of the Entity-Level Controls

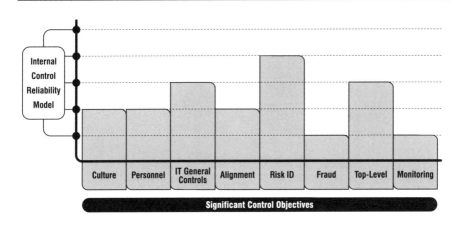

The Relationship between Testing and Evaluation

The way in which you plan to evaluate effectiveness ultimately drives the design of your engagement tests. Using the model summarized in Exhibit 6.1, you should plan your tests to include each of the significant control objectives identified across the horizontal axis. Additionally, the nature and scope of your tests should be sufficient to allow you to evaluate the control reliability level as indicated by the vertical axis.

This chapter provides guidance on the testing and evaluation of internal control. In practice you will test first and then evaluate. However, because the design of tests is so dependent on how you will evaluate effectiveness, this chapter will present guidance on evaluating test results *before* providing guidance on the design and performance of the tests themselves.

Chapter 2 provides a discussion of the COSO framework—that is, the horizontal axis. Following is a discussion of the second dimension of assessing effectiveness: the internal control reliability model.

INTERNAL CONTROL RELIABILITY MODEL[1]

Five Levels of Reliability

Over time, as businesses expand and change, their internal control evolves. What starts out as a relatively informal process can mature and become more well-defined and reliable. Exhibit 6.3 summarizes this development process. It identifies five distinct levels of internal control reliability, and describes what entities must do in order to for their systems to evolve from one level to the next.

Exhibit 6.3   Internal Control Reliability Model

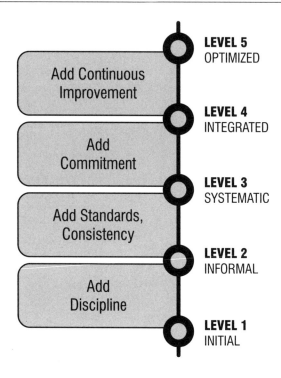

Reliability Level 1: Initial. Control objectives are not well defined or consistently understood throughout the organization. Policies and procedures are ad hoc and generally undocumented. As a result, control policies and procedures generally are not linked to objectives or are inconsistent with each other. The effectiveness of an initial system depends almost exclusively on the skills, competence, and ethical values of the individual. Because of this dependence on the individual rather than the organization, the reliability of this system can vary greatly over short periods of time or among business units.

Reliability Level 2: Informal. Common, intuitive control practices begin to emerge, but documentation is sporadic and inconsistent. Informal communication of information about internal control matters exists, but the lack of formal communication methods together with a lack of training prevents much of this information from reaching below the manager and supervisory levels. Management is aware of the need for controls but still views internal control as separate from, not integral to, the operation of the business. However, the emergence of repeatable processes and improved communication and dissemination of information improves the reliability of the system and reduces risk.

Reliability Level 3: Systematic. Management understands that internal control is an integral part of the company's business and that maintaining an effective system is one of their primary responsibilities. They begin to devote substantial resources in a coordinated effort to develop and maintain more reliable internal controls. Individual control components combine into a cohesive whole. Documentation of control policies and procedures is comprehensive and consistent; some training exists on control-related matters. With more formal, standardized controls in place, the system is more reliable as its overall effectiveness depends more on the organization and less on the capabilities of the individual.

Reliability Level 4: Integrated. Management understands the full requirements for maintaining an effective system of internal control. Control implications and issues are routinely considered as business decisions are evaluated and made. Controls are fully integrated into the strategic and operational aspects of the business. Comprehensive training exists. The company begins a formal process for the regular monitoring of the effectiveness of internal control.

Reliability Level 5: Optimized. Management commits to a process of continuous improvement of controls. The entity uses automation and sophisticated tools and techniques to monitor controls on a real-time basis and make changes as needed.

Exhibit 6.4 summarizes the Internal Control Reliability Model along five different characteristics used to gauge system reliability.

Exhibit 6.4   Summary of Internal Control Reliability Model

Reliability Level	Documentation	Awareness and Understanding	Attitude	Control Procedures	Monitoring
Initial	Very limited	Basic awareness	Unformed	Ad hoc, unlinked	
Informal	Sporadic, inconsistent	Understanding not communicated beyond management	Controls are separate from business operations	Intuitive, repeatable	
Systematic	Comprehensive and consistent	Formal communication and some training	Controls integral to operations	Formal, standardized	
Integrated	Comprehensive and consistent	Comprehensive training on control-related matters	Control processes considered as part of strategy	Formal, standardized	Periodic monitoring begins
Optimized	Comprehensive and consistent	Comprehensive training on control-related matters	Commitment to continuous improvement	Formal, standardized	Real-time monitoring

What the Model Can and Cannot Do

The internal controls reliability model provides you with a framework for

- Designing tests of control effectiveness
- Evaluating the effectiveness of controls
- Presenting and discussing your findings with your clients

Recognize that the boundaries between the various levels are hazy and that the levels of reliability themselves may not be discrete. In reality, components of an entity's internal control may exhibit qualities of more than one of the identified level. The purpose of the model is not to determine the proper way to categorize an entity's controls, but rather to have a basis for analyzing control effectiveness to determine whether controls are capable of achieving their ultimate aim—to reduce to an acceptable level the risk that material misstatements to the financial statements will go undetected.

OVERALL OBJECTIVE OF TESTING ENTITY-LEVEL CONTROLS

The testing of internal control is required to support management's assertion about its effectiveness. The independent auditors will rely, in part, on this testwork reach their conclusions about management's assertion. To be effective, the tests should have

- Clearly stated objectives
- A design that is appropriate to achieve those objectives
- A scope that is comprehensive enough to draw a reliable conclusion

Relationship Between Entity-Level and Application-Level Controls

As described in Chapter 2, the COSO framework describes controls as existing at two different levels, the general, entity-wide level and the specific, application-level. In order to plan and perform tests of entity-level controls, it is important to remember how these controls are fundamentally different from activity-level controls. Consider the following analogy.

Suppose that the citizens of Anytown wish to build a new school. The objective of building the new school is to educate the children of the community. In order to achieve that objective certain elements must be in place: Good teachers must be hired; books, computers, and other resources must be acquired; and so on. All of these elements will have a direct effect on the quality of the child's education. At the end of his or her school years, a child will look back and say "my fifth grade social studies teacher made all the difference for me," or "that book I read in 10th grade will stay with me for the rest of my life."

In order for the teacher to be hired, for the book to be purchased, and for the student to even have the physical space to receive and complete assignments, an important prerequisite must be satisfied. The people of Anytown must raise sufficient funding to build the school, hire the teachers, buy the books, and so on. It is the funding that allows all of the other elements to operate effectively. On their graduation day no one ever says, "I'd like to thank the taxpayers for their continued support of our school," but without sufficient funding, the chances for success are greatly reduced. The school simply does not have the resources to hire enough teachers or buy the books or provide other resources.

Similarly, internal controls operate on two different levels: application-level and entity-level.

Application-level controls are analogous to the teachers and the books. They have a direct effect on the financial statements in that weaknesses in these controls can lead directly to financial statement misstatements. The objective of an application-level control is relatively straightforward—to provide reasonable assurance that material misstatements are prevented or detected in a timely manner. For example, tests of controls related to revenue recognition would be designed to determine whether a material misstatement of revenue could somehow slip undetected through the accounting system and be presented in the financial statements.

In contrast, entity-level controls have an *indirect* effect on the financial statements. They are like the school district funding in our analogy. A weakness in an entity-level control does not necessarily lead to a financial statement misstatement. Entity-level controls *enable* the effective functioning of activity-level controls. Within this context, the objective of an entity-level control is to provide an overall environment in which activity-level controls can operate effectively. Put another way, if an activity-level control has been designed properly but in operation performs poorly, the underlying cause of the poor performance most likely is due to a weakness in entity-level controls.

For example, ABC Company requires monthly bank reconciliations of all its cash accounts. However, at year-end, the company discovers that bank reconciliations have not been performed for the last several months on many of its accounts and that those that have been performed have been done poorly. When investigating the cause of this poor performance, the entity discovers that

- The performance of bank reconciliations was considered a low priority by accounting department personnel.
- The accounting department supervisor was overworked and did not have the time to supervise employees.
- Because of a general lack of supervision, the employees responsible for performing the reconciliations received little feedback on how to perform them properly.

The control procedure was properly designed. The failure of the control was a performance failure. The reasons for the performance failure all had to do with ineffective entity-level controls. The environment in which the control was performed was *not* conducive to effective performance.

Why Test Entity-Level Controls First? To be complete, an evaluation of internal control must include an assessment of both entity- and activity-level controls. There are two basic ways to go about this. The first is an inductive reasoning approach, in which you would test application-level controls first. Based on the information and evidence gathered from this testing, you would then infer the effective or ineffective operation of entity-level controls.

Using the example from the previous section, you would note that bank reconciliations were not prepared properly. You would then probe for the reasons why the control procedure was ineffective, and would (hopefully) learn that the poor performance seemed to be caused by a lack of training and supervision. When testing another activity-level control, you may discover another weakness, and upon further investigation, discover a similar set of causes—lack of training and supervision. Testing of a third activity-level control produces the same result. Putting together all the pieces of the puzzle, you then would be able to draw conclusions and take corrective actions related to the entity-level controls.

This chapter (and the approach presented in this book) presents a deductive reasoning approach to entity-level controls. This chapter recommends testing the effectiveness of internal controls *directly*, as opposed to drawing a conclusion based on inference through the results of activity-level controls. The advantages to testing entity-level controls first relate primarily to

- Efficiency. Understanding the strengths and weaknesses of entity-level controls will allow you to develop more targeted tests of application-level controls. You will be better able to anticipate weaknesses that may be identified in application-level testing, and you will do a better job of following up on application-level control weaknesses.
- Effectiveness. The scope or nature of your application-level tests may not be sufficient to draw conclusions about the effective functioning of *all* entity-level controls. Or you may draw an incorrect conclusions. Direct testing of entity-level controls mitigates this risk.

Design Effectiveness versus Operational Effectiveness

The literature on internal controls typically distinguishes between the design of internal control and its operating effectiveness. Ultimately, management must make an assertion of the *operating effectiveness* of the entity's internal control, not its design.

When testing controls, information and evidence related to operational effectiveness frequently is obtained when gathering information related to the design of a control. Distinguishing between the two—"does this relate to design or performance"—usually is an academic exercise since the assertion about controls relates only to operation. For that reason, these materials do *not* draw a distinction between tests of design and tests of operational effectiveness. The testing approach and techniques described here are designed to provide support about an assertion of operational effectiveness.

TESTING TECHNIQUES

This chapter provides a comprehensive, integrated approach to testing and evaluating entity-level controls. Exhibit 6.5 summarizes the various testing techniques suggested and how these are used to gather evidence to support an assertion for each significant entity-level control objective.

The Nature of Available Evidence

The effect that entity-wide controls have on the financial statements is indirect. It is nonlinear, subjective, and not easily quantified. Supporting an assertion on the effectiveness of entity-wide controls is challenging because the assertion cannot be verified by confirmation, inspection, and observation—that is, the types of tests normally considered by auditors to be the most reliable. Entity-wide controls are *not* transaction oriented, so you will not be able to test their effectiveness by performing transactions-based tests. The techniques described here are the most effective way to gather evidence to support an assertion about entity-wide controls.

Exhibit 6.5   Entity-Level Controls Testing Techniques

	Testing Technique			
Control Objective	Employee Survey	Management Inquiry	Computer General Controls	Document Review
Corporate culture	X	X		X
Entity personnel	X	X		X
General computer controls			X	X
Alignment—objectives and controls		X		X
Risk identification		X		X
Anti-fraud programs		X		X
Top-level financial reporting		X		X
System-wide monitoring		X		X

Survey and Inquiries of Employees

Surveys are an effective way of collecting information that should come directly from people, not documents. In particular, surveys are essential to evaluate whether an entity's culture and personnel policies create an environment that enables the effective functioning of activity-level controls. In other words, a company's written code of conduct or personnel policies, by themselves, will not be sufficient to support an assertion about these entity-level controls. In order to determine whether the policies are operating effectively, you must receive feedback from employees. For most entities, that information will be gathered most efficiently through a survey. (See Exhibit 6.6 for common problems with surveys.)

Included in Appendix 6B is an example survey for gathering and evaluating information from employees regarding the entity's culture and personnel policies.

Who and How Many to Survey. The reliability and validity of the survey results are directly related to who you survey and how many responses you receive. For the purposes of your engagement, it is not anticipated that independent auditors will require the quantified precision of statistical sampling methods to support an assertion about the effectiveness of entity-wide controls. Nonstatistical sampling methods and qualitative analysis of the results should suffice.

However, in order to ensure the most reliable and valid results, you should design the survey in a way that incorporates the main concepts underlying statistical sampling methods, including

- *The more respondents, the more reliable the results.* If it is within the budget for the project, ask for responses from *all* employees.
- *Stratified samples yield better results.* If the entity has several divisions or locations, make sure that your survey includes employees from each. You also should try to obtain results from all the different levels of employee within the organization, from top management on down.

Exhibit 6.6 Common Problems with Surveys

The following are the most common problems with surveys, which will reduce their reliability.

- Questionnaire is too long or hard to read.
- Questions are difficult to answer because
  - Language is unclear.
  - More than one question is being asked.
  - Respondents do not have information available to answer question.
- Choices in a multiple-choice question are incomplete, hard to interpret, or not mutually exclusive.
- Directions or transitions between sections of the survey are hard to follow.

- *To be valid, any sample must be representative of the population.* A simple random sample, in which every employee has an equal chance of being selected for the survey is one technique that can produce a representative sample of the population. In contrast, a block sampling technique (e.g., surveying only those employees whose last name begins with the letter "S") will not produce a representative sample.

- *Think twice before knowingly excluding a group from the population.* Your engagement is limited to testing the effectiveness of internal control over financial reporting. However, it would be a mistake to limit your survey about corporate culture and personnel policies to only those individuals directly involved in the financial reporting process. Operational and administrative personnel can provide valuable insights into the operating effectiveness of several components of the entity's internal control.

Determining whether you have received enough responses to your survey to draw a valid conclusion is a matter of judgment. To help you make that judgment, consider the information gathered from other tests. Does it diverge from the results of the survey or does it tend to corroborate the survey findings? You also should consider addressing the issue with the independent auditors. How many responses would they consider to be sufficient for supporting an assertion about entity-level controls?

When and How Often. Most of the tests you will perform will have to address the issue of timing. Perform the tests too far in advance of the entity's reporting date, and you run the risk that the tests will need to be updated or reperformed. Test too close to the reporting date and you have little or no time to take corrective action if the results identify a weakness.

Surveys can take a long period of time. Individuals need time to respond, and if they don't, you will need time to follow up and obtain more responses. The evaluation of survey results, especially if they include open-ended, non-numeric responses, also can be time consuming.

Additionally, you should consider the nature of the subject matter of the survey, which is the entity's culture and the effectiveness of its personnel policies. Both of these typically change slowly over time. Thus, in most instances, your biggest risk would be in performing your tests too late to take corrective action, *not* in performing them too early and having them change.

If you do perform a survey well in advance of the entity's reporting date, you should consider resurveying later in the reporting period if

- The entity makes significant changes to its policies or takes corrective action for identified weaknesses.
- Other significant events occur that could affect the entity's culture or effectiveness of its personnel policies. For example, unanticipated layoffs can alter employees' perceptions about the entity's culture.
- The entity's system-wide monitoring of control effectiveness is weak.

Pilot Testing. Plan on pilot testing your survey. By pilot testing and making necessary corrections to the survey you will increase response rates and create more reliable and valid results. In their book *How to Conduct Surveys*, Arlene Fink and Jacqueline Kosecoff provide the following suggestions for pilot testing a survey[2]:

- *Pilot test in segments.* For example, you may want to start by testing just the instructions or the wording of a few questions.
- *Test the administrative details.* If the survey is relatively simple, such as a paper-based survey that is filled out and mailed back to you, this test may not be that crucial. However, if the administration of the survey is more complex, such as an online survey, testing the delivery mechanism in advance will be more important.
- *Informal testing can work just fine.* The whole point of pilot testing is to identify weaknesses either in the survey questions or the way it is delivered that can affect the reliability of the survey results. That objective may be accomplished in a relatively informal fashion, for example, by showing the questions to several prospective respondents and asking them how they might respond.
- *Focus on the clarity of the questions and the general format of the survey.* The following may indicate that the survey is unreliable or otherwise needs revision:
  - Failure to answer questions
  - Several answers provided to the same question
  - Writing comments in the margin
- If you expect your survey will result in a range of responses, then be sure that your pilot test includes equal representation from both ends of the range.

Data Analysis and Reporting Results. When planning your survey, give some thought to how you will analyze and interpret the data and report your conclusions to management. For example, a report to management on a survey of employees about the company's culture may read as follows:

> We sent a survey to all of the company's 750 employees asking for their feedback on the company's culture and climate for ethical behavior. Four hundred of those surveys were returned to us. Approximately 60 percent of those who responded were not even aware that the company has a code of conduct, which is posted on the company intranet and reproduced in the employee handbook. Only 15 percent of respondents had read the code. However, of those who read the code, nearly 80 percent agreed with the statement: "The company's code of conduct helps me identify unacceptable business practices."
>
> The response to this survey question, combined with our own reading of the company's code of conduct led us to conclude that, as written, the code could contribute toward creating a control environment that is conducive to the effective operation of activity-level controls. However, in order to be effective, the company should take steps to ensure that more employees are aware of the code's existence and familiar with its contents.

When designing your survey, if you cannot describe how you will analyze the data and report your conclusions, then you should reconsider the survey design.

Writing Your Own Survey Questions. The survey included in Appendix 6B is just an example. You should modify this survey to meet the needs of your specific engagement. Fink and Kosecoff offer the following advice for writing survey questions:

- *Each question should be meaningful to respondents.* If you introduce questions that have no obvious purpose (e.g., demographic information) you will need some transitional text to explain to the respondent why you are asking the question.
- *Use standard English.* Avoid specialized words, such as *entity-level controls*, whose definition is not readily known.
- *Make questions concrete.* Questions should be as close to the respondent's personal experience as possible. For example, the question "Does management conduct itself in an ethical manner?" is abstract. A more concrete question that addresses the same issue would be "Has your supervisor ever asked you to take action that is labeled as unacceptable in the company's code of conduct?"
- *Avoid biased words and phrases.*
- *Each question should have just one thought.* For example, a respondent could be confused by the question "Are the activities of the company's employees and board of directors consistent with the company's ethical values?" What if the respondent believes that the actions of board members are consistent with the ethical values but those of the employees are not? How should he or she respond? To avoid confusion, the question should be split into two questions, one that asks about the board and a second that asks about employees.

Inquiries of Management

Purpose of the Inquiries. The overall purpose of your inquiries is to gather evidence about the effectiveness of entity-level controls. Your primary purpose is *not* to gather information about what the policy is—you can gather that information mostly through reading the relevant documentation (see Chapter 5 for further guidance). Your goal is to determine whether the stated policy is working as intended. To accomplish this objective you will need to consider

- *Who to ask.* You should make inquiries of those individuals who are responsible for the design or implementation of the policy. In many instances several people may be involved in this process. Plan on making inquiries of as many as possible. By gaining multiple perspective you will increase the effectiveness of the procedure.
- *What to ask.* Ask questions that will allow you to evaluate the effectiveness of the policy using the Internal Control Reliability Framework. Appendix 6C includes a list of example questions you may consider. The example control objectives and procedures provided in Appendix 5B also can be used to help you develop additional questions.
- *What to look for.* As an inquiry technique, it often is helpful to ask objective, nonthreatening questions first. For example, you might ask "What process does management follow to . . ." While the literal answer to the question is im-

portant (e.g., "first we . . . then we . . .") you need to evaluate the qualitative, subjective aspects of the response. Use the Internal Control Reliability Model as a guide. For example, based on the way the respondent answers the question "What is the process for . . .", consider whether

- The process seems well-defined, as opposed to ad hoc.
- The respondent understands the process at a level that is appropriate given their responsibilities for implementing or monitoring the control.
- The person's attitude about or evaluation of the process. Does he or she think it works? Is it valuable or more trouble than it's worth?

Other Tips for Improving Effectiveness. Inquiries of management regarding entity-level controls are fundamentally the same as the inquiries you make on other professional assignments. You will rely on the techniques and interpersonal skills you have developed throughout your professional career to conduct the interviews required on this engagement. The previous section highlighted two important considerations when asking management about the effectiveness of entity-level controls.

1. *Ask more than one person.* For inquiries to be a reliable source of evidence about the effectiveness of controls, you should conduct interviews with more than one person. When several different people tell you the same story, you become more confident that the evidence you have gathered is reliable.
2. *Ask empirical questions first.* This strategy will help
   - Put the respondent at ease (people usually are more comfortable describing facts than offering an opinion).
   - Establish a factual basis for asking additional questions.
     Once you establish the facts, you can then probe deeper to understand the respondent's attitudes, opinions or interpretations of those facts.

   Other tips you should consider include

- *Start with open-ended questions.* Try to get the respondent talking so he or she will volunteer information.
- *Carefully choose the interviewer.* The interviewer should have the requisite experience, as well as the stature and gravitas necessary to conduct a meaningful interview. The most junior member of the engagement team should *not* interview the chairman of the board.
- *Don't tip your hand.* Before performing the interview you will have prepared thoroughly, for example by reading the client's documents related to the policy. You also may have interviewed one or more other people about the same subject. It is important that you get an unbiased answer from the person you are interviewing. Avoid prefacing questions with information that could lead to a predetermined answer, such as "Your code of conduct says . . ." or "Other people I have talked to . . ."
- *Nonverbal cues matter.* A study by the Institute of Internal Auditors concluded that only 7 percent of a message communicated in an interview is conveyed

through *what* is said. Thirty-eight percent of the message is conveyed by word emphasis and tone, and 55 percent through nonverbal cues.[3]

- *Debrief with other team members.* Research conducted by the Canadian Institute of Chartered Accountants indicates that the effectiveness of inquiries can be improved when the information about interviews is shared among audit team members. Through the comments and questions received from others, you will be able to identify pertinent information gathered and recognize the importance of things that otherwise might have been overlooked or forgotten.

- *Don't' take too many notes.* During the interview you should focus on making sure that you are gathering all the information you need to make your evaluation. Rather than take extensive notes during the interview, you might consider making short, abbreviated notes during the conversation and then write more immediately after the interview is over.

General Computer Controls

Information technology (IT)-related controls consist of two distinct types, both of which must work effectively to achieve a proper level of control. General controls are defined by COSO as those that apply to many if not all application systems and help ensure their continued, proper operation. Application controls ensure the proper processing of various types of transactions and include both the computerized steps within the application software and the related manual follow-up procedures (e.g., the investigation and resolution of items identified in a computer-generated exception report).

As described in Chapter 2, this book supplements the guidance provided in the COSO report with the guidance provided in the Control Objectives for Information and related Technology (COBIT) report, including guidance on what might be considered general controls.

Preliminary Analysis. Before jumping directly into a detailed assessment of computer general controls, it helps to obtain an understanding of IT-related risks and control objectives at a relatively high level. Some of the questions you should seek to answer include

- Have there been any significant changes to the entity's IT system, including changes to hardware, software, processes, or personnel? If so, what general risks do the changes create? If there have not been any significant changes, what previously existing risks remain? How are risks identified and managed?

- How many different computing platforms or environments exist at the entity? How do multiple systems interface with each other, for example, how is data exchanged and how is this exchange controlled?

- What might impair the reliability of the entity's IT system or otherwise negatively affect the entity's ability to capture, process, and maintain data?

- How could the integrity of the entity's IT system be compromised? What risks exist that might affect the entity's ability to protect its data and systems from unauthorized access, corruption, or loss?
- What risks are posed by the entity's e-commerce activities?

The Computer General Controls Review. Chapter 2 provides a high-level summary of the COBIT framework. Salient points of that summary include the following:

- Underlying the COBIT framework is the notion that an understanding of information technology should focus on *information*, not the technology. Thus, in order to obtain a high-level understanding of IT-related risks, start by obtaining a high-level understanding of the information required to run the business. Chapter 2 provides a summary of the general qualities of information required by management.
- IT processes manage IT resources to produce information that has the necessary qualities. A review of the effectiveness of computer general controls should address the following processes:
  - *Planning and organization*, which covers strategy and tactics directed toward the identification of the way one can best contribute the achievement of stated business objectives.
  - *Acquisition and implementation*, which includes the identification, acquisition (or in-house development), deployment, and integration of IT solutions.
  - *Support*, which includes back-up and business recovery plans and maintaining a suitable physical environment.
  - *Monitoring*, which is the regular assessment of IT processes to assess their continued effectiveness.

Appendix 6D includes a checklist that can help you in designing your tests of computer general controls.

A general computer controls review may require special expertise, the development of which is beyond the scope of this book. You may wish to include an IT specialist on your team to perform the computer general controls tests and evaluate the test results. Chapter 3 describes those conditions that indicate IT expertise is needed on your engagement.

Reading and Assessment of Key Documents

The mere existence of documentation does not provide any evidence as to the effectiveness of the policy documented. To assess effectiveness, you will need to read the document and make a qualitative assessment of the policy.

Chapter 5 provides a description of what you would expect to find in the key documents relating to entity-level controls. Appendix 5B provides examples of the control objectives and policies that should be addressed in these documents. When reading the documentation of entity-wide policies, you should consider this guidance from Chapter 5.

Observation of Processes

For the most part, you will not be able to directly observe the functioning of entity-level controls. However, certain exceptions do exist, and you should be alert for opportunities to observe certain entity-level control policies. These opportunities include the observation of meetings of the board of directors or other senior, policy-making committees (e.g., risk management, disclosure, human resources, ethics, audit), particularly when any of the following matters are being discussed, reviewed, or approved:

- Financial statements, including meetings with the entity's independent auditors
- Internal controls or financial reporting processes
- Internal audit results
- Strategic planning
- Risk management
- Compensation and other personnel policies
- Ethics or other corporate governance matters

When observing meetings your primary objective is to evaluate the effectiveness of the process. Use the Internal Control Reliability Model as a guide for making this evaluation and consider questions such as

- Does the process seem well defined and structured (i.e., have they done this before)?
- Does the group have a relatively well-defined set of criteria for decision making or do the decisions seem ad hoc.
- Are the committee members actively involved in the process? Are they well prepared? Do they have the information necessary to make informed decisions?
- What does the group dynamics reveal about the company's culture?
- When discussing operational matters, does the group consider internal control and financial reporting implications?

To increase the reliability of the evidence gathered from your observations, you should observe several meetings of the same group.

As described in Chapter 5, the entity may use an automated tool to aid in the assessment and reporting of internal control effectiveness. This automated tool may include features that monitor the performance of certain control policies and procedures. The design of the documentation tool should allow you to observe the functions of the entity's monitoring process.

The mere reporting on the timely performance of a control procedure does not constitute effective internal control. As described in Chapter 2, the COSO description of internal control defines monitoring and including all of the following:

- Assessing control design
- Assessing its operating effectiveness (which includes both the timeliness of its performance and whether the procedure was performed properly)
- Taking necessary corrective action

When observing the entity's automated monitoring process, you should consider whether all of the elements described in COSO can be observed.

For example, suppose that Rey is responsible for reconciling the accounts receivable trial balance to the general ledger. The entity has an automated process that monitor's Rey's performance of this control procedure and reports to his supervisor on whether it was performed on a timely basis. If Rey fails to perform the procedure in a timely manner, the system may automatically send him a reminder that his reconciliation is overdue.

You will be able to observe the functioning of this automated process. However, this observation alone is not sufficient for you to draw a conclusion about the effectiveness of monitoring because

- The timely performance of a procedure is only one element of effectiveness. In addition to being timely, the procedure also must be performed *correctly*. To be properly monitored, the entity should have a policy that requires supervisory review of the procedure performed.
- The control policy should be reviewed periodically to determine whether its design remains adequate.
- Appropriate corrective action should be taken. Sending Rey a reminder may not be sufficient. If he is chronically late in performing his task, perhaps he has too many responsibilities, and some of his work should be reassigned. If the reconciliation is not being properly performed, then perhaps he needs additional training.

In order to address these issues, you will need to supplement your observation of the monitoring feature of the entity's automated compliance tool with inquiries of personnel. Appendix 6C provides some example inquiries.

EVALUATING THE EFFECTIVENESS OF ENTITY-LEVEL CONTROLS

Making the Assessment

Your evaluation of the effectiveness of entity-level controls is a process that allows you to

- Determine whether entity-level controls create an overall environment that enables the effective operation of activity-level controls.
- Identify weaknesses in entity-level controls that affect the design of activity-level tests.

Your tests of entity-level controls are directed at specific control objectives, but your evaluation should consider the controls *taken as a whole*, rather than individual control objectives. For example, weaknesses in one control area may be compensated for by the design and operation of strong controls in other areas.

Exhibit 6.2 provides an example of one method used to understand and document an assessment of the overall effectiveness of entity-level controls. The process used to make the evaluation involves

- Using the Internal Control Reliability Model to rate the effectiveness of each control objective
- Combining the individual control objectives into a complete picture of entity-level controls.

How reliable do controls need to be before they are considered effective? Do entity-level controls have to reach the highest level of reliability in order to be effective? The answer to these questions is a matter of judgment that should be made by management with input from its Securities and Exchange Commission (SEC) counsel and the independent auditors. In making that determination, the chief executive officer (CEO) and chief financial officer (CFO) should consider the following:

- *Taken as a whole.* Ultimately, the effectiveness of internal control is assessed for the system as a whole, not for individual components. In designing its system, the company may make trade-offs, leaving opportunity for improvement in certain elements of the system and compensating for this decision through stronger controls elsewhere.
- *Reasonable assurance and materiality.* Internal control can provide only reasonable, not absolute, assurance. The effectiveness of internal control is evaluated within the context of the financial statements and whether any errors that internal control fails to detect or prevent are material.

It would seem unlikely that an initial system of internal control would have the reliability and consistency necessary to provide reasonable assurance that material misstatements are identified and corrected before reaching the financial statements. In a similar vein, it would seem that many entities maintain internal control that would be widely acknowledged as "effective" without having all components of that system operating at an "optimized" level of reliability.

How should you make your final assessment of the effectiveness of controls? The Canadian Institute of Chartered Accountants has done some relevant research in this area, and one of the conclusions reached is worth keeping in mind.

> Evidence is more than a collection of facts. It is the integration of everything the auditor learns. Evidence does not come in a neatly ordered sequence—it is non-linear. It comes piecemeal and must be managed, sorted and synthesized. Some of it is concrete fact that is objectively verifiable. Much of it, however, is [your] impression of what has been seen, heard, or sensed. It includes the attitudes and intentions of people in the entity and its organizational culture and ethical tone. Knowingly or not, [you] take all these factors into account—[you] use them as evidence—when forming conclusions.[4]

Chapter 8 provides additional guidance on evaluating deficiencies and forming a final conclusion about the effectiveness of internal control as a whole.

Responding to Identified Weaknesses

Your testwork may reveal weaknesses in entity-level controls that require one of the following responses:

- Corrective action
- Modifications to planned activity-level controls

Corrective Action. Weaknesses in entity-level controls may be so severe that they require corrective action—to *not* correct the condition would most likely result in a material weakness in the entity's overall internal control.

Exhibit 6.4 summarizes the qualities of reliability that are considered in the Internal Control Reliability Model. The nature of corrective action you take will depend on the source of the control weakness.

- *Documentation*. A lack of documentation can be remediated by creating the necessary documentation. Chapter 5 provides additional guidance on creating documentation.
- *Awareness and understanding*. The awareness and understanding of control-related matters can be improved through comprehensive, formal communications and training programs.
- *Attitude*. Changing attitude is a difficult and time-consuming process. However, some of the actions you take in other areas will change attitude as well as behavior. For example, the introduction of a training program on the company's code of conduct and acceptable behavior will not only help employees understand the code, it also will send the message that the company is serious about ethics, which is a change in attitude. Your engagement to study the effectiveness of controls also can send a message to employees that changes their attitude. Improved communication, training, and coaching also can drive changes in attitude.

- *Procedures*. The most effective way to spur the evolution of an entity's control procedures, from ad hoc and inconsistent to formal and standardized, is through their documentation; the training of personnel; and timely, consistent supervision.
- *Monitoring*. Your engagement and the company's continued compliance with Sarbanes-Oxley Section 404 reporting is the first stage of monitoring, a periodic review. To move to the next level, real-time monitoring, most likely will be required.

Planning Tests of Activity-Level Controls. In response to identified possible control weaknesses, you should modify your planned testing approach of activity-level controls by considering the following:

- The identification and testing of effective compensating controls. For example, employees with significant control responsibilities for financial reporting must have a working knowledge of their responsibilities if the control procedures are to be effective. Suppose that this level of working knowledge does not exist for all employees. It is possible that this weakness may be compensated for by other controls, such as close supervision or redundant control procedures that address the same control objective.
- Expanding the scope of application level control testing. For example, you may wish to
  - Test controls over certain business processes or locations that previously were not considered significant.
  - Modify the nature and extent of the testing of the effectiveness of other significant entity-level aspects of application-level controls.

DOCUMENTING TEST RESULTS

You should document the test procedures you performed and the results of those tests. This documentation is necessary for the independent auditors to conduct their audit, including their requirements to

- Evaluate management's process for assessing the effectiveness of the entity's internal control
- Rely, at least in part, on the tests performed by management as a basis for reducing the scope of their own work

The proposed auditing standard described in Chapter 1 provides only broad guidance on what management should include in the documentation of its tests. In general, you should consider including a description of the following:

- Tests performed and the control they were designed to test
- The time period covered by the tests
- The scope of the testwork, including the consideration of multiple locations or business units, and how that scope was determined
- The results of the tests
- All control deficiencies identified as a result of the tests, a conclusion as to the severity of the deficiencies, and how the existence of these deficiencies was communicated to the board, the independent auditors, and others, as necessary
- Any remedial action taken in response to identified deficiencies, including changes to internal control
- An overall conclusion as to the effectiveness of internal control based on the results of the testwork performed

COORDINATING WITH THE INDEPENDENT AUDITORS

If the entity's independent auditors have developed a framework similar to the Internal Control Reliability Model, you should obtain this framework, understand it, and use it to help guide the design of your tests. Additionally, you should create an ongoing dialogue with the entity's auditors to gain consensus on matters including

- Your overall approach to testing entity-level controls, whether directly or inductively through the performance of activity-level control tests
- The nature and extent of your planned procedures and whether these are considered sufficient to draw a reliable conclusion
- The circumstances under which the planned nature and extent of the procedures should be modified
- The planned timing of your tests and whether this timing will allow you to draw conclusions about the design and operating effectiveness of entity-level controls as of year-end
- The nature and extent of procedures that may be required to update your conclusions about effectiveness from the time your procedures are performed until year-end
- The results of your tests and the tentative and final conclusions reached regarding the effectiveness of entity-level controls
- How the test procedures and results will be documented
- The general type of deviations or conditions that might be considered significant deficiencies or material weaknesses
- The implication that the identification of significant deficiencies or material weaknesses has on other aspects of the engagement

---

APPENDIX 6A

Action Plan:
Testing and Evaluating Entity-Level Controls

The following action plan is intended to help you implement the suggestions contained in this chapter for testing and evaluating entity-level controls.

1. Design Tests

Plan the nature, timing, and extent of tests necessary to draw a conclusion about the operating effectiveness of internal control as of year-end. For example—

- Consider and describe the framework that will be used to measure effectiveness, for example, the Internal Control Reliability Model or a similar framework used by the independent auditors.
- Determine whether you will test entity-level controls directly or indirectly through the testing of activity-level controls.
- Determine the combination of testing techniques that will be used to assess the operating effectiveness of each significant entity-level control. Consider
  - Employee surveys
  - Inquiries
  - Computer general controls review
  - Document review
  - Direct observation

2. Perform and Document Tests

Perform the planned tests. Update as necessary to support a conclusion about operating effectiveness as of year-end. Document the procedures performed and test results.

3. Assess Test Results

Evaluate the effectiveness of entity-level controls based on the results of your testwork. For example

- Determine whether entity-level controls create an overall environment that enables the effective operation of activity-level controls.
- Identify weaknesses in entity-level controls.
- Respond to identified weaknesses in one or both of the following ways:
  1. Take corrective action
  2. Modify planned activity-level controls

4. Coordinate with the Independent Auditors

Establish an ongoing dialogue with the independent auditors that allows you to reach a consensus on

- Your overall approach to testing entity-level controls, whether directly or inductively through the performance of activity-level control tests
- The nature and extent of your planned procedures and whether these are considered sufficient to draw a reliable conclusion
- The circumstances under which the planned nature and extent of the procedures should be modified
- The planned timing of your tests and whether this timing will allow you to draw conclusions about the design and operating effectiveness of entity-level controls "as of" year-end
- The nature and extent of procedures that may be required to update your conclusions about effectiveness from the time your procedures are performed until year-end
- The results of your tests and the tentative and final conclusions reached regarding the effectiveness of entity-level controls
- How the test procedures and results will be documented.
- The general type of deviations or conditions that might be considered significant deficiencies or material weaknesses
- The implication that the identification of significant deficiencies or material weaknesses has on other aspects of the engagement

---

APPENDIX 6B
Survey Tools

This appendix contains several tools that will help you in conducting employee surveys related to the operating effectiveness of entity-wide controls. Included are

- Example Letter to Employees in Advance of Employee Survey
- Example Employee Survey of Corporate Culture and Personnel Policies
- Evaluation of Employee Survey Results

EXAMPLE LETTER TO EMPLOYEES IN ADVANCE OF EMPLOYEE SURVEY

Dear _____,

We are required by law to annually review and report on the policies and procedures we use to manage and control our company. The scope of this review is quite broad and includes evaluating not just individual tasks you perform in your daily work assignments but also the environment in which you perform those assignments.

To help us perform our review we are conducting a survey of all employees to obtain their observations about the way in which our company is managed. Within the next two weeks you will be receiving this survey. We have tried hard to balance our need for comprehensive feedback with everyone's desire to keep the survey as short as possible. We believe we have reached a suitable compromise.

I urge you to complete this survey and return it as soon as possible to _____. Your prompt attention to this matter is important, not only because it will allow us to comply with certain legal requirements, but also because it will help us to continually improve our management practices. All individual responses to the questionnaire will be kept strictly confidential.

/s/ Chief Executive Officer

Notes

- This letter should be sent out a week or two in advance of sending the actual employee survey. The purpose of the letter is to prepare the employees for its arrival and to encourage them to complete it as soon as possible.
- The letter assumes that *all* employees will be receive a survey. If that is not the case, then the letter should explain how the individual employee was selected, for example, "we are sending the survey to 50 percent of all our employees and management. Your name has been selected at random."
- To convey a proper sense of urgency and importance to the completion of the survey, the letter should be signed by a member of senior management, for example, the CEO.

EXAMPLE EMPLOYEE SURVEY OF CORPORATE CULTURE AND PERSONNEL POLICIES

Purpose of the Survey

By law, XYZ Company is required to review and report on the policies and procedures used to manage and control the company. The scope of this review is broad and includes an evaluation of the overall environment in which individual employees perform their assigned responsibilities.

The purpose of this survey is to obtain input from all employees on how the company is managed.

Confidentiality

Individual responses will not be disclosed. All responses will be evaluated as a group and reported to company management in a summarized fashion.

Instructions

Please respond by indicating the degree to which you agree or disagree with the statements presented. When you are done, please mail your completed questionnaire to _____. A self-addressed, stamped envelope has been provided for your convenience.

	Strongly Disagree	Disagree	Neither Agree or Disagree	Agree	Strongly Agree
Ethical Values					
1. I have read the company's code of conduct.	○	○	○	○	○
2. The company's code of conduct helps me identify unacceptable business practices.	○	○	○	○	○
3. If I observe unacceptable behavior on the job and report it to a member of the management team, I believe that the matter will be investigated.	○	○	○	○	○
4. I believe that people who demonstrate a commitment to high ethical standards of behavior will be rewarded (e.g, through compensation or advancement).	○	○	○	○	○
5. I believe that people who act in an unethical manner will be punished (e.g., through diminished compensation, lack of advancement, or termination).	○	○	○	○	○
6. In the last three years, I have been asked by someone senior to me to take action that would be considered unethical.	○	○	○	○	○
7. I know someone at the company who, in the last three years, has been asked by someone senior to them to take action that would be considered unacceptable.	○	○	○	○	○
8. For the most part, company employees act in an ethical manner.	○	○	○	○	○

	Strongly Disagree	Disagree	Neither Agree or Disagree	Agree	Strongly Agree
9. For the most part, company management acts in an ethical manner.	○	○	○	○	○

Personnel Policies

	Strongly Disagree	Disagree	Neither Agree or Disagree	Agree	Strongly Agree
10. My job responsibilities have been communicated to me.	○	○	○	○	○
11. I understand my job responsibilities.	○	○	○	○	○
12. The criteria for assessing my performance have been communicated to me.	○	○	○	○	○
13. The feedback I receive on my performance helps me improve.	○	○	○	○	○
14. The information I need to perform my job is communicated to me					
• Accurately	○	○	○	○	○
• Timely	○	○	○	○	○
• Completely	○	○	○	○	○
15. The training I receive helps me do a better job.	○	○	○	○	○
16. I have been delegated the decision-making authority necessary to effectively perform my job.	○	○	○	○	○
17. For the most part, I have been provided with the following resources necessary to perform my job effectively:					
• Budget/funding	○	○	○	○	○
• Personnel	○	○	○	○	○
• Supervisory guidance	○	○	○	○	○

Company Values

18. Please list the behaviors that are most frequently rewarded (see question 4 for example rewards). Example behaviors might include customer service, profit maximization, innovation, team building, cost reduction, business expansion, etc.

_____

_____

_____

Other

19. Please comment on any other aspect of the company's culture or management policies that contributes to or detracts from your job responsibilities effectively. If a family member or friend were considering employment at ABC Company and asked "What's it like working there?", how would you respond?

_____

_____

_____

Notes

- If you are an outside consultant who has been engaged by the company to conduct the survey, you should print the survey on your letterhead, as this will reinforce the message that responses are confidential and encourage more candid responses.
- All responses should be returned directly to you.
- Questions 4 through 9 make reference to "high ethical standards" and personal ethics, which may introduce an element of unreliability to the survey because what may be unacceptable to one person may be acceptable to another. Alternatively, the questions may be reworded to refer to the company's stated ethical policies or values. However, if you choose to refer to company policies in these questions, you should include these policies as part of the survey. Without easy, immediate access to the company's stated policies, most individuals will not be able to respond to the statement.
- The example behaviors listed in question 18 have been deliberately worded in a way that makes them all seem positive. If negative behaviors are noted in response to this question, then this could indicate the strong presence of negative elements in the entity's control environment. The question leads the respondent to consider only positive characteristics. If the employee makes note of negative characteristics, it is probably because these characteristics have made a strong impression on the respondent.

EVALUATION OF EMPLOYEE SURVEY RESULTS

The example employee survey focuses on two entity-level control objectives: company culture and personnel policies. It is designed to gather information about the effectiveness of each of these controls in three different categories, which are described in more detail in Chapter 6. These categories are—

- Awareness/understanding
- Action
- Attitude

The form in Exhibit 6.7 can be used to summarize the results of the survey. You should complete the form by

- Assigning a numeric value to each of the 5 possible responses. For example, "strongly agree" = 5 and "strongly disagree" = 1.
- Calculating an average value of the response for each question
- Entering that average in the form in the space provided. Note that the form distinguishes the category (awareness, action, attitude) that the question was to address.

Further guidance on how to interpret and respond to the summarized results is provided at the end of the form.

Exhibit 6.7   Form

	Average Response		
Ethical Values	Awareness	Action	Attitude
1. I have read the company's code of conduct.			
2. The company's code of conduct helps me identify unacceptable business practices.			
3. If I observe unacceptable behavior on the job and report it to a member of the management team, I believe that the matter will be investigated.			
4. I believe that people who demonstrate a commitment to high ethical standards of behavior will be rewarded (e.g., through compensation or advancement).			
5. I believe that people who act in an unethical manner will be punished (e.g., through diminished compensation, lack of advancement, or termination).			
6. In the last three years, I have been asked by someone senior to me take action that would be considered unethical.			
7. I know someone at the company who, in the last three years, has been asked by someone senior to them to take action that would be considered unacceptable.			
8. For the most part, company employees act in an ethical manner.			
9. For the most part, company management acts in an ethical manner.			

	Average Response		
Personnel Policies	Awareness	Action	Attitude
10. My job responsibilities have been communicated to me.			
11. I understand my job responsibilities.			
12. The criteria for assessing my performance have been communicated to me.			
13. The feedback I receive on my performance helps me improve.			
14. The information I need to perform my job is communicated to me • Accurately • Timely • Completely			
15. The training I receive helps me do a better job.			
16. I have been delegated the decision-making authority necessary to effectively perform my job.			
17. For the most part, I have been provided with the following resources necessary to perform my job effectively: • Budget/funding • Personnel • Supervisory guidance			

Evaluating Results

For each of the two control objectives, scan the summarized results for each of the three categories

Awareness/Understanding. Low scores in this category indicate that employees lack an awareness or understanding of key control policies. At a minimum, employees should be aware of the existence of company policies and procedures that affect them in the performance of the jobs. Ideally, they would have a working knowledge and detailed understanding of the full implications of those policies.

Corrective Action: A lack of understanding or awareness of important company policies is a symptom of ineffective communications. The company should review its communication efforts to identify ways in which awareness or understanding can be improved, for example:

- Increasing the frequency of communication
- Revising existing documentation to make the policies more clear
- Requiring signed acknowledgement from employees that policies have been read and understood.

Action. Studies sh\ow that much of the information that we receive and process is communicated through action, not through words. The questions that fall into this category gauge the effectiveness of management's actions relating to certain control objectives and whether those actions are consistent with high ethical standards or the companies stated policies and values. Low scores in this area indicate a disconnect between what management says and what it does.

Corrective Action: The entity needs to have its managers act in ways that are consistent with stated policies. If inconsistencies are discovered, then the entity needs to determine whether the problem is caused by the policies or the managers. If the policies are sound, then the behavior of managers needs to be changed.

Additional investigation is required to determine the root cause of the behavior. For example, it may be that managers are simply unaware of how their behavior affects employees, or it could be that they are overburdened with other responsibilities (lack of resources), which causes them to devote less time than is necessary for effective supervision. If the behavior of managers needs to change, the company should consider one or more of the following:

- Formal training
- Informal coaching or mentoring of managers

- Changes to the way the company provides incentives to its employees
- Allocation of additional resources.

Alternatively, the company may determine that management behavior is appropriate, in which case the written policies should be revised.

Attitude. These questions are designed to broadly assess employees' attitudes and perceptions about those elements of their work environment that can affect the performance of application-level controls. Low scores indicate a negative attitude that may adversely affect controls. For example, a widely held perception that management will *not* thoroughly investigate reported instances of wrongdoing may encourage employees in ways that run counter to the company's objectives.

Corrective Action: Additional information should be gathered to obtain a more complete understanding of employee attitudes and the cause of any negative perceptions. Improving attitudes and perceptions may require actions such as

- Changes in the behavior that gives rise to the negative perceptions.
- Improved communications within the entity, for example, an emphasis on candid, interactive communications between management and employees

Implications for the Design of Additional Tests. Low scores in any one area by itself may indicate a material weakness in the system of internal control. For example, employees with significant control responsibilities for financial reporting must have a working knowledge of their responsibilities if the control procedures are to be effective.

However, it is possible that weaknesses identified as a result of the responses to this survey may be compensated for by other controls. For example, close supervision or redundant control procedures that address the same control objective may adequately compensate for a lack of employee understanding of a particular control procedure.

In response to identified possible control weaknesses, you should modify your testing approach by considering

- The identification and testing of compensating controls for effectiveness
- Expanding the scope of application-level control testing. For example, you may wish to
  - Test controls over certain business processes or locations that previously were not considered significant.
  - Modify the nature and extent of the testing of the effectiveness of other significant entity-level of application-level controls.

APPENDIX 6C

Example Inquiries of Management
Regarding Entity-Level Controls

INSTRUCTIONS FOR USE

The following form is designed to be used by an interviewer in face-to-face interviews with members of management. The form consists of example questions, organized according to control objective. At the conclusion of each section you will be asked to document your initial evaluation of the results of the conversation.

Example Questions

Most of example questions are relatively objective and focus on the actions taken by management. They are intended as a way to introduce the subject matter in a relatively nonthreatening way. Follow-up questions should be asked to develop an impression of the respondent's awareness, understanding, and attitude toward the subject. Since these questions will depend primarily on the responses the individual gives to the initial question, the form (Exhibit 6.8) includes only a limited number of follow-up questions. Appendix 5A includes a list of example control objectives and related control policies. These examples can be helpful in formulating potential follow-up questions.

Evaluating Responses

Your interview should be sufficient to allow you to form an initial impression about the effectiveness of the entity-level control policy. The form uses an abbreviated version of the Internal Control Reliability Model introduced in this chapter. Based on your interview, you should evaluate the policy according to the following scale:

- *Initial/Informal.* No awareness or only a limited awareness of the issue and how it affects internal control. Management's actions or process seems ad hoc and not well defined (or no action has even been taken). Attitude indicates a disinclination for change. Sees internal control as separate from the main business operations and someone else's responsibility.

- *Systematic.* Good understanding of the issue and how it contributes to internal control effectiveness. Processes seem to be well defined, and established criteria are used to guide decision making. Individual recognizes that internal controls are integral to the entity achieving its overall objectives. Acknowledges his or her oversight and control responsibilities. Interested in improving internal control.

- *Integrated/Optimized.* The individual's decision-making process routinely considers the internal control and financial reporting implications. Individual is actively involved in implementing and monitoring control effectiveness. Commitment to improvement of internal control is demonstrated through action.

Exhibit 6.8   Example Questions

Corporate Culture	Notes

1. What was the process followed to develop the company's code of conduct?

2. How often is the code reviewed and updated?

3. What was the board's main reason for developing the code?

  a. Has that objective been met?

    Yes   How can you tell?

    No   What have been the major barriers to achieving the objective?

4. If management becomes aware of an allegation of unacceptable behavior, what is the process for investigating the matter?

  a. Do you have any specific examples?
How was the action of management in this matter perceived by the employees?

5. Has the board identified compensation policies or other incentives that may motivate unethical behavior by employees?

    Yes   What are they? How do you monitor these policies for possible unintended consequences?

    No   What criteria are considered when setting incentive policies and programs?

6. Has management become aware of any control deficiencies in the last three years?

  a. How did you become aware?

  b. What action was taken?

7. Do you receive all the information needed to perform your job effectively?

    Yes   Is it reliable? Timely?

    No   What is missing?

8. Does the board periodically discuss the company's culture and "tone at the top" and how these affect the overall effectiveness of controls?

    Yes   What observations has the board made?

    No   What prevents you from doing so?

  a. Do you believe that the company has established standards of behavior that create an effective control environment?

(Continued)

Exhibit 6.8   *(Continued)*

ASSESSMENT:

Policies related to corporate culture seem to be (mark the scale)

Initial/	Systematic	Integrated/
Informal		Optimized

Entity Personnel   Notes

---

1. How did management determine the overall organizational structure for the company?

   a. When was the last time the structure was reviewed for continued relevance and effectiveness?

   b. How do you determine that the structure is effective?

   c. How are internal control and financial reporting matters considered when evaluating the company's organizational structure?

2. Is there a formal process used to determine which responsibilities should be delegated to lower levels?

   a. (Yes or no). How do you ensure that responsibility, authority, and accountability are linked and delegated together as a unit?

3. What is the process for determining the resources that are necessary for employees to perform their responsibilities effectively? Resources include

   • Training

   • Budget/funding

   • Personnel

   • Supervision and feedback

4. Once management decides to pursue a certain strategy, what is the process for determining the human resource needs required to implement the strategy? Consider

   • Number of people needed

   • Required skills

   • Experience level

   • Training

Exhibit 6.8   *(Continued)*

ASSESSMENT:

Policies related to personnel seem to be (mark the scale)

| Initial/ | Systematic | Integrated/ |
| Informal | | Optimized |

Alignment between Objectives and Controls	Notes

1. Describe the company's strategic planning process.

   a. What is the process for soliciting feedback from key managers?

   b. How is this feedback integrated into developing the plan? In its most recent strategic planning effort, what significant issues were raised by the board in their review and approval process? How were these issues resolved?

   c. How are internal control and financial reporting implications considered in the process? In its most recent strategic planning effort, what internal control issues did the company identify? How were these issues resolved?

   d. Does management identify the critical success factors required for the achievement of the strategic plan?

   e. How is progress for the achievement of the plan measured and monitored?

ASSESSMENT:

Policies related to the alignment of strategic objectives with controls seem to be (mark the scale)

| Initial/ | Systematic | Integrated/ |
| Informal | | Optimized |

Risk Identification	Notes

1. Describe the process used to identify the risks reported in the company's most recent Form 10K.

   a. Who is involved in the process?

   b. What criteria are used to determine the risks to report?

2. How does the company decide how to manage identified risk?

(Continued)

Exhibit 6.8 *(Continued)*

3. As part of the strategic planning process, how are risks identified?

4. How is the board of directors involved in the risk management process?

   What concerns and issues have they raised recently about the risks facing the entity?

5. In the past three years, what new risks has the company encountered?

   a. Did management anticipate these risks?

   b. How did the company respond?

ASSESSMENT:

Policies related to risk identification seem to be (mark the scale)

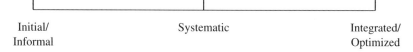

| Initial/ | Systematic | Integrated/ |
| Informal | | Optimized |

Anti-Fraud Programs and Controls	Notes

1. What steps does management take to instill a culture of honesty and high ethics that mitigates the risk of fraud within the entity. For example, consider

   a. Hiring and promotion policies

   b. Training

   c. Investigation and resolution (including disciplinary action) of alleged incidents of fraud

2. In what ways is the entity vulnerable to fraud? Consider

   a. Employee defalcation

   b. Fraudulent financial reporting

3. What is management's process for identifying the risks of fraud in the entity?

4. Does the audit committee get involved in discussions about fraud? If so, what do these discussions entail?

Exhibit 6.8   *(Continued)*

ASSESSMENT:

Policies related to anti-fraud programs and controls seem to be
(mark the scale)

| Initial/ | Systematic | Integrated/ |
| Informal | | Optimized |

Top-Level Financial Reporting Processes   Notes

1. How does the entity comply with the requirement that its board
    of directors has an appropriate level of financial expertise?

    As a whole, do you believe that the board possesses an
    appropriate level of expertise?

2. How does the board stay current on financial reporting matters?

3. What is the process for structuring nonsystematic, nonroutine
    transactions?

    a. What is the source driving these transactions; for example,
        are they necessary to

        • Implement the entity's strategic plan?

        • Achieve forecasted financial results?

    b. At what point in the process does management receive
        input on the accounting treatment of these transactions?

    c. What factors does the board consider when reviewing and
        approving these transactions?

4. What process does the entity follow for making its most
    significant accounting estimates?

    a. How is information relating to the underlying assumptions
        gathered?

    b. How do you know the information is reliable?

    c. What factors are considered when making significant
        assumptions about the estimate?

    d. How are senior management and the board involved in the
        review and approval of significant estimates?

        In the company's most recent financial reporting cycle,
        what were the most significant issues raised by senior
        management or the board regarding the estimates of the
        estimation process?

(Continued)

Exhibit 6.8   *(Continued)*

5. Describe the conversations the board has had with the independent auditors regarding the quality of the entity's accounting principles?

   What actions did the board take as a result of those discussions?

6. What is the process used by management to

   a. Identify emerging accounting issues or other circumstances or events that may require a consideration of accounting policies?

   b. Identify the accounting policies described as "critical" in the entity's 10K?

   c. Choose appropriate accounting policies?

ASSESSMENT:

Policies related to top-level financial reporting processes seem to be (mark the scale)

Initial/ Informal	Systematic	Integrated/ Optimized

System-Wide Monitoring   Notes

1. How does management use the entity's automated compliance tool to monitor the effective operation of internal control? Does the entity's automated tool indicate whether the control was performed in both

   a. A timely manner?

   b. A proper fashion?

2. What steps does management take to

   a. Periodically evaluate the design of internal control policies and procedures?

   b. Understand the underlying causes for identified internal control deficiencies?

   c. Take appropriate corrective action in response to identified deficiencies?

ASSESSMENT:

Policies related to system-wide monitoring seem to be (mark the scale)

Initial/ Informal	Systematic	Integrated/ Optimized

APPENDIX 6D

Guidance for Designing a Computer General Controls Review

The purpose of this matrix (Exhibit 6.9) is to help you design a computer general controls review. This matrix is built on the COBIT framework, which was described in Chapter 2. The contents of the matrix have been adopted from *IT Control Objectives for Sarbanes-Oxley*, published by the Information Systems Audit and Control Association (ISACA) and available as a free download from their Web site at *www.isaca.org*.

Note that the performance of the review and evaluation of results is best performed by an IT specialist.

Exhibit 6.9   Guidance for Designing a Computer General Controls Review

Control Objective	Example Controls
Planning and Organization	
Define a strategic plan.	• IT strategies are aligned with overall business objectives. • Feedback from users is used to monitor quality of planning process. • IT planning committee includes IT personnel, users, and senior management. • IT plans are communicated across the organization. • IT management communicates activities, challenges, and risks with senior management.
Define the information architecture.	• IT management has defined controls relating to the capture, processing, and reporting of information relevant for all financial statement assertions for all significant accounts and disclosures. • Information is classified in accordance with company security and privacy policies. • Security levels for each data classification are defined, implemented, and maintained.

(Continued)

Exhibit 6.9   *(Continued)*

Control Objective	Example Controls
Planning and Organization	
Define the IT organization and relationships.	• IT personnel have adequate knowledge and experience. • Key systems and data are identified. • The roles and responsibilities of IT personnel are defined, documented, communicated, and understood. • Delegation of authority and responsibility to IT personnel is appropriate. • Appropriate segregation of duties is established and maintained. • IT management monitors personnel to ensure that they perform *only* their assigned tasks. • IT management regularly evaluates staff performance. • IT management establishes and communicates policies to protect the entity's information-based assets. • IT management communicates all significant IT events or failures to senior management and the board.
Communicate management aims and direction.	• IT policies and procedures are documented and communicated. • Policies and procedures are periodically reviewed and modified as necessary. • IT management assesses compliance with established policies and procedures, investigates deviations, and takes appropriate corrective action.
Manage human resources.	• When IT personnel change or leave their jobs, controls are in place to ensure continued control effectiveness. • IT management supports a culture of continuous learning. • The IT organization supports the entity's overall culture and code of conduct.
Ensure compliance with external requirements.	• Changes to external reporting requirements are monitored, and changes to IT systems are made, as necessary. • Internal events that affect reporting requirements are identified, considered, and incorporated into IT policies and procedures, as required.

Exhibit 6.9   *(Continued)*

Control Objective	Example Controls
Assess risks.	• The entity's risk assessment process includes the consideration of information-related risks, including technology reliability, information integrity, and IT personnel. • The IT organization maintains a risk assessment process that is aligned with the entity's overall risk assessment process. • The IT organization performs a comprehensive security assessment for all significant systems and locations.
Manage quality.	• All significant IT processes and activities are documented. • Documentation is regularly updated and maintained. • The IT organization has developed a plan to maintain the quality of all IT activities. • Documentation standards are developed, communicated, and reinforced through training. • Data integrity, ownership, and responsibilities have been communicated to data owners, who have acknowledged their responsibilities.
Acquisition and Implementation	

Acquire and maintain application software.	• The IT organization's systems development lifecycle considers
	   – Security
	   – Availability
	   – Processing integrity
	   – Application controls that address all relevant financial statement assertions
	• The IT acquisition process is aligned with the entity's overall strategy.
	• Software is acquired in accordance with the overall IT planning process.
	• Controls exist over the installation of new and modified software.

(Continued)

Exhibit 6.9 (*Continued*)

Control Objective	Example Controls
Acquisition and Implementation (cont'd)	
Acquire and maintain technology infrastructure.	Controls exist to ensure that infrastructure changes such as systems software and network devices are controlled during implementation and maintenance.
Develop and maintain procedures.	• User reference and support manuals are prepared as part of every information system development or modification project. • System documentation is adequate to ensure long-term sustainability of the system.

Install and accredit systems.	• All significant changes in technology are tested.
	• Test procedures include
	  – Unit, system, integration, and user acceptance
	  – Load and stress testing
	  – Interfaces with other systems
	  – Data conversion

Manage changes.	• Formal change management procedures exist for all changes as well as system or supplier maintenance. • The override of established procedures for system changes in emergency situations is identified and controlled. • Users are included in the design, selection, and testing of new or modified software. • Change management standards establish a structured approach to the timely change to systems and applications. • The IT organization monitors systems and applications to determine that they are performing as designed and meet the needs of the users.
Delivery and Support	
Define and manage service levels.	• IT management establishes vendor management policies, which are used to select vendors for outsourced services. IT management defines key performance indicators to manage service level agreements.

Exhibit 6.9   *(Continued)*

Control Objective	Example Controls
Manage third-party service levels.	• The selection process for third-party service providers includes an assessment of capabilities to deliver the required service and the provider's financial viability. • Third-party service contracts include provisions that address the risks, security controls, and procedures for information systems and networks. • The entity's business continuity controls consider risks related to continuity of service from third-party service providers. Escrow contracts exist where appropriate. • Contracts with third-party service providers are executed before any work is initiated. • Third-party service levels are monitored regularly and reported to IT management. • The monitoring of third-party service providers includes a regular review of security, availability, and processing integrity.
Manage performance and capacity.	• Performance and capacity levels of the IT system are monitored. • Appropriate responses are taken when performance and capacity measures are less than optimal. • IT system design and implementation activities include performance and capacity planning.
Ensure continuous service.	• IT management has established a business continuity framework and plan that is aligned with the company's overall business plan. • The continuity plan is tested at least annually, all deficiencies are corrected, and personnel responsible for the plan are adequately trained. • The continuity plan is updated whenever new risks are identified. • Offsite storage and recovery facilities are tested at least annually.

(Continued)

Exhibit 6.9   *(Continued)*

Control Objective	Example Controls
Delivery and Support (cont'd)	
	• Company management has formally assessed the impact of systems failure on the financial reporting and disclosure process. • Management has defined the system recovery procedures necessary to ensure the timely reporting of financial information.
Ensure systems security.	• IT management has developed a security plan, which is regularly updated and maintained. • All users are authenticated to the system as a means to ensure the validity of transactions. • Control policies and procedures are established to maintain the effectiveness of authentication and access mechanisms. • Control policies and procedures exist relating to requesting, establishing, issuing, suspending, and closing user accounts • Where appropriate, controls exist to ensure that transactions cannot be denied by either party and that the origin of receipt, proof of submission, and receipt of transactions cannot be repudiated • Where appropriate, controls such as firewalls exist to prevent unauthorized access to the network. • IT management regularly performs security assessments, which are used to update the IT security plan. • The IT security administrator monitors and logs security activity, and identifies and reports all security violations
Educate and train users.	• The entity identifies and documents the training needs of all personnel using IT services. • Education and training programs include ethical conduct, system security practices, confidentiality standards, integrity standards, and security responsibilities

Exhibit 6.9   *(Continued)*

Control Objective	Example Controls
Manage the configuration.	• Only authorized software is permitted to be used by employees. • System infrastructure is properly configured to prevent unauthorized access. • Application software and data storage systems are properly configured to provision access based on an individual's demonstrated need. • Procedures have been established across the entire organization to protect the IT systems from computer viruses. • Software and network infrastructure are periodically tested to ensure that it is properly configured.
Manage problems and incidents.	• All operational events that are not part of the standard operation are recorded, analyzed, and resolved in a timely manner. • Emergency program changes are approved, tested, documented, and monitored • The problem management system allows for the tracing from incident to underlying cause.
Manage data.	• Data processing controls address the completeness and accuracy of transaction processing, authorization, and validity. • Data input is checked for accuracy and validity. • Errors are identified, reported, and resolved in a consistent and authorized manner. • IT management has established policies and procedures for the handling, distribution, and retention of data and reporting output. • Sensitive information is protected during its storage and transmission. • The company has established retention periods and storage terms for data, programs, reports messages, and documents.

(Continued)

Exhibit 6.9 *(Continued)*

Control Objective	Example Controls
Delivery and Support (cont'd)	
	• Data retention policies comply with all applicable laws and regulations. • The contents of a media library containing sensitive data are physically protected and periodically accounted for. • Data and programs are backed up. • The restoration process and the quality of backup media are tested periodically. • Changes to data structures are authorized, made in accordance with design specifications, and implemented in a timely manner. • Changes to data structures are evaluated to their effect on the financial reporting process.
Manage facilities.	• Physical access to facilities is restricted and controlled. • Physical facilities are equipped with adequate environmental controls.
Manage operations.	• Management has established and documented standard procedures for IT operations. • Processing continuity is maintained during operator shift changes. • Metrics are used to manage the daily activities of the IT department. • Sufficient system event data is retained to enable the reconstruction, review, and examination of the time sequences of processing.
Monitoring	
Monitor the processes.	• IT management measures IT activities against well-defined benchmarks. • Processes exist to identify IT weaknesses and take appropriate remedial action.
Assess internal control adequacy.	• IT controls are monitored regularly, and deficiencies are reported to senior management.
Obtain independent assurance.	• The IT organization uses independent reviews to provide assurance over significant IT services and activities.

Notes

1. This model has been adapted from the "capabilities maturity model" for software development, which was developed by the computer software community with stewardship and resources provided by the Software Engineering Institute. The model provides a basis for judging the capabilities of a software development process, and it also identifies key practices that are required to further the maturity of this process.

    Since its introduction, the maturity model approach has been adopted by COBIT as a way to assess the effectiveness of IT-related controls. More recently, several public accounting firms have recommended this type of approach to their clients as a means to assess overall internal control effectiveness. It is anticipated that a capabilities maturity model approach ultimately will gain wide acceptance within the independent auditor community as a means for evaluating management's assertion about the effectiveness of its internal control.

2. Arlene Fink and Jacqueline Kosecoff, *How to Conduct Surveys: A Step-by-Step Guide* (Thousand Oaks, CA: Sage Publications, 1998).

3. J.W. Harmeyer, S.P. Golden, and G.E. Summers, *Conducting Internal Audit Interviews* (Altamonte Springs: Institute of Internal Auditors Research Foundation, 1994). Cited in *Audit Enquiry: Seeking More Reliable Evidence from Audit Enquiry*, a research report published by the Canadian Institute of Chartered Accountants, Toronto, Ontario, 2000.

5. *Audit Enquiry: Seeking More Reliable Evidence from Audit Enquiry*, a research report published by the Canadian Institute of Chartered Accountants, Toronto, Ontario, 2000, page 6.

Chapter 7

Testing and Evaluating Activity-Level Controls

Chapter Summary

Evaluate effectiveness of design of activity-level controls.

Design tests of operating effectiveness.

Provide guidance on the effective performance of various types of tests.

Evaluate the results of tests.

INTRODUCTION

The objective of your tests of activity-level controls is the same as your objective for testing entity-level controls. As described in Chapter 6, the testing of internal controls is necessary in order to support management's assertion about their effectiveness. To be effective, the tests should have

- Clearly stated objectives
- A design that is appropriate to achieve those objectives
- A scope that is comprehensive enough to draw a reliable conclusion

ASSESSING THE EFFECTIVENESS OF DESIGN

Activity-level controls are effective when they can provide reasonable assurance that material financial statement errors will be prevented or detected in a timely fashion. Assessing design effectiveness will require you to review and evaluate the documentation described in Chapter 5 to determine whether the system as described is capable of providing that level of assurance. To make your assessment, you should consider

- The general types of errors that could occur
- The points in the processing stream where errors may be introduced

Once you understand what could go wrong and where, you then look to see whether the system, as designed, adequately addresses these potential errors and error points.

Financial Statement Assertions and Controls

The auditing literature uses a framework based on financial statement "assertions" to understand and identify potential misstatements. This same framework can be used to define activity-level control objectives.

Assertions are the representations of management that are embodied in the entity's financial statements. These assertions may be either explicit or implicit. For example, the balance sheet line item that reads "Cash.........$xx,xxx" is an explicit assertion that the company's cash accounts at the balance sheet date totaled the stated amount. *Implicit* assertions include the following:

- The company has the right to spend the cash.
- The stated amount includes *all* the company's cash accounts.
- The accounts included in the total are valid company accounts that exist at bona fide financial institutions.

The auditing literature describes the following financial statement assertions:

- Existence (of assets or liabilities) or occurrence (of transactions)
- Valuation or measurement of the amounts reported in the financial statements
- Completeness of the financial statements
- Rights (to reported assets) and obligations (for reported liabilities)
- Presentation and disclosure of the amounts and captions in the financial statements

In an effectively designed system, activlty-level control objectives (and the related controls) will exist to ensure that each financial statement assertion is free of material misstatement. Exhibit 7.1 summarizes the link between financial statement assertions and control objectives.

The COSO report describes example control objectives and related activities for the business process activities in the entity's value chain (see Chapter 2 for an in-depth discussion of the value chain). Those COSO examples have been included in Appendix 7C.

Information-Processing Streams

Chapter 5 describes the fundamental characteristics of an information-processing stream. Within this stream, errors can be introduced at the following points:

- The system boundary, where events or transactions are initially identified, authorized and captured
- The update and maintenance of databases, master files, or other electronic storage systems that are accessed by one or more applications.

Exhibit 7.1   Linking Financial Statement Assertions to Control Objectives

Assertion	Description	Control Objectives
Existence	Reported assets and liabilities exist at the reporting date	• Only properly authorized assets and liabilities are recorded. • Assets are safeguarded and protected from unauthorized use or disposition. • Accountability for assets is maintained.
Occurrence	Reported transactions or events took place during the reporting period.	• Proper cutoff between accounting periods • Fictitious, unauthorized, or duplicate transactions are detected and prevented from being recorded.
Valuation or Measurement	Assets, liabilities, transactions, and events are recorded at their proper amount.	• Assets and liabilities are initially recorded at the appropriate amount. • Recoverability of assets and valuation of liabilities are assessed periodically. • Transactions are recorded at correct amounts.
Completeness	The financial statements include *all* the assets and liabilities of the entity and the effect of its transactions during the reporting period.	• All authorized, valid transactions are reported in the financial statements. • Proper cutoff between accounting periods.
Rights and Obligations	The entity has the rights to use reported assets and is obligated to settle reported liabilities.	• Entity has legal title to assets. • Proper authorization for the assignment of rights or encumbrance of assets • Only the obligations of the entity are reported or disclosed.
Presentation and Disclosure	Items are properly classified, described, and disclosed in the financial statements.	• Financial statements are fairly presented in accordance with GAAP. • Disclosure is adequate and not misleading.

- The processing points in the stream, where information is manipulated or processed, for example:
  - Matched with other data
  - Combined with other data
  - Used as part of a calculation
  - Posted to the general ledger, subsidiary ledger, or other accounting records

Errors can be introduced whenever information is changed or otherwise processed, so your testwork should focus on the identification of these points in the information stream.

OPERATING EFFECTIVENESS

Test Design Considerations

Your tests of application-level controls should allow you to gather sufficient evidential matter to support your conclusion about the effectiveness of internal control. To be "sufficient" the evidence should be persuasive or convincing. A preponderance of the evidence gathered should support your conclusion. The evidence does not have to be incontrovertible to support your conclusion. You do not have to prove your point beyond a shadow of a doubt.

Your tests of operating effectiveness should be designed to determine

- How the control procedure was performed
- The consistency with which it was applied
- By whom it was applied

Nature, Timing, and Extent of Tests

Nature: You will need to decide on the types of tests you will perform. For example, will you conduct inquiries, observe controls being performed, or reperform certain control procedures? The nature of the tests you perform depends on the type of control procedure being tested and whether its performance is documented.

Typically, you will perform a combination of one or more controls in order to gather evidence about their effective operations. It would be unlikely that one test will give you all the evidence needed to support your conclusion. For example, suppose you observe the operation of a control procedure such as an edit check on the electronic input of information. You observe the control to be functioning properly, but how do you know that the control was in place and operating effectively throughout the reporting period? Your observation will have to be supplemented with other procedures, such as inquiry.

When determining the nature of the tests you will perform to support your conclusion, consider that your opinion most likely will be formed by the congruence and consistency of the evidence you gather from *several* sources and types of tests.

Timing: The Sarbanes-Oxley Act mandates you to report on the effectiveness of internal control as of a point in time, namely, year-end. As a practical matter, you most likely will perform many of your tests in advance of the reporting date. When you do, you must consider the need to perform additional tests to establish the effectiveness of the control procedure from the time the tests were performed until year-end. For example, if you tested the effectiveness of bank reconciliations as of June 30 and the reporting date was December 31, you will need to consider performing tests to cover the period from July 1 through December 31. These tests may *not* require you to repeat the detailed tests performed at June 30 for the subsequent six-month period. If you establish the effectiveness of the control procedure at June 30 you may be able to support a conclusion about the effectiveness of the control at the reporting date indirectly through the consideration of entity-level controls and other procedures such as

- The effectiveness of personnel-related controls such as the training and supervision of personnel who perform control procedures. For example, are the people performing the bank reconciliations adequately supervised, and was their work reviewed during the second half of the year?
- The effectiveness of risk identification and management controls, including change management. For example, would management be able to identify changes in the entity's business or its circumstances that would affect the continued effectiveness of bank reconciliations as a control procedure?
- The effectiveness of the monitoring component of the entity's internal control.
- Inquiries of personnel to determine what changes, if any, occurred during the period that would affect the performance of controls.
- Repeating the procedures performed earlier in the year, focusing primarily on elements of the control procedure that have changed during the period. For example, if the entity added new bank accounts or new personnel performing certain bank reconciliations, you would focus your tests on those accounts and individuals.

Computer Application Controls. As described in Chapter 6, the COSO report describes two different levels of computer controls—general and application specific. Application controls are the structure, policies, and procedures that apply to separate, individual business process application systems. They include both the automated control procedures (i.e., those routines contained within the computer program) and the policies and procedures associated with user activities, such as the manual follow-up required to investigate potential errors identified during processing.

As with all other control procedures, computer application controls should be designed to achieve specified control objectives, which in turn are driven by the risks to achieving certain business objectives. In general, the objectives of a computer application are to ensure that

- Data remains complete, accurate, and valid during its input, update, and storage.
- Output files and reports are distributed and made available only to authorized users

   Specific application-level controls should address the risks to achieving these objectives. Exhibit 7.2 provides examples of computer application control objectives and related controls.

   The way in which computer control objectives are met will depend on the types of technologies used by the entity. For example, the specific control procedures used to control access to an online, real-time database will be different than those procedures related to access of a "flat file" stored on a disk.

   An IT controls specialist most likely will be needed to understand the risks involved in various technologies and the related activity-level controls.

Exhibit 7.2   Example Computer Application Control Objectives and Controls

Control Objective	Control Activity
Authorization	
All application users are appropriately identified and authenticated.	• Passwords and personal identification numbers • "Nonrepudiation" that prevents senders and receivers of information from denying that they sent or received the information • Emerging technologies such as digital certificates or smart cards
Access to the application and related data files is restricted to authorized users for authorized purposes.	• Logical access control system restricts access to the application and data to authorized users. • Firewalls protect application and data from unauthorized use. • Terminals automatically disconnect from the system when not used after a specified period of time. • Computer equipment is located in physically secure locations.
All data are authorized before entering the application.	• Critical input information is tested against predefined criteria. All exceptions are reviewed by an individual with the proper authority to approve them. • Paper-based information is reviewed and approved prior to input.

(Continued)

Exhibit 7.2   *(Continued)*

Control Objective	Control Activity
Completeness	
All authorized data enters and is processed by the application.	• Transactions are numbered prior to entry; sequence is checked periodically. • Control totals, hash totals, and record counts ensure that all data is processed. • Transaction data are matched with data in a master or suspense file. Unmatched items from both the transaction data and master or suspense files are reported for investigation.
Accuracy	
Data entry design features contribute to data accuracy.	• Preformatted screens and menu-driven input • Electronic input of information
Data validation and editing are performed to identify erroneous data.	• Automated validation and edit checks
Erroneous data are captured, reported, investigated, and corrected	• Suspense files capture and control errors. • Suspense files are regularly reviewed and items are appropriately resolved.
Confidentiality	
Access to application output is restricted to authorized users.	• Access to confidential information is limited to authorized individuals consistent with the entity's confidentiality policies. • Data encryption technologies protect the transmission of user authentication, verification, and confidential information.

Considering the Results of Entity-Level Tests. As described in Chapter 6, entity-level controls affect the operational effectiveness of activity-level controls. For example, the entity may have thorough, well-designed controls to ensure a proper sales cut-off at year-end (activity-level control), but if they do a poor job of communicating and monitoring the performance of the people responsible for performing the procedure (an entity-level control), then ultimately the control will lack full effectiveness. When designing your activity-level tests, your conclusions about the effectiveness of entity-level controls should be used in two ways. First, plan your activity-level tests to gather first-hand information about the effectiveness of entity-level controls. Use this information to (hopefully) corroborate your earlier assessment of entity-level control effectiveness.

For example, when making inquiries of an individual about the control procedures he or she performs, consider expanding your inquiries to include questions about entity-level controls. Examples of inquiries that go beyond understanding activity-level control procedures include

- If changes to your procedures were required, how would they be communicated?
- What kind of on-the-job or formal classroom training do you receive? Do you find it helpful?
- How closely is your work supervised?
- If any problems or errors that you can't fix are identified, do you ever get the impression that they are either ignored or "made to go away" without being adequately addressed?

To help you devise a questioning strategy or formulate individual questions, you may find it helpful to refer to the Employee Summary of Corporate Culture and Personnel Policies, included in Appendix 6B. By asking these or similar questions in an interview setting, you have the opportunity to ask follow-up questions that will allow you to obtain a more in-depth understanding of the operating entity-level controls. Thus, activity-level control testing provides you with an excellent opportunity to confirm your initial assessment of entity-level control effectiveness.

The second way in which entity-level controls affect the design of activity-level controls is in the scope of your testwork. As described in Chapter 6, weaknesses in entity-level controls should lead you to expand the scope of your activity-level testing. Conversely, strengths in entity-level controls may allow you to reduce the scope of activity-level tests.

For example, consider two companies, both in the same industry. Revenue is a significant activity, and the 10Ks for both entities identify revenue recognition as a critical accounting policy. However, their entity-level controls have significant differences, as indicated in Exhibit 7.3.

In the case of company A, you would want to expand the scope of your activity-level testwork for processing revenue transactions. For example, if your tests included transaction testing, you would increase your sample size. Inquiries might be made of more individuals or people you otherwise would not consider interviewing. You may even expand your procedures to include divisions or locations you otherwise would not consider. For company B the opposite is true.

Additionally, the relative strength of entity-level controls should be considered when you plan the timing of your procedures. With company B, where entity-level controls are strong, you may be able to test the activity-level controls well in advance of the reporting date and place reliance on entity-level controls to draw a conclusion about operating effectiveness at the reporting date. With company A, you probably will have to adopt a different strategy, for example, testing the controls closer to the reporting date or reperforming a limited number of activity-level tests near the reporting date.

Exhibit 7.3   Example Entity-Level Controls

Company A	Company B
• Management and employee incentives are based exclusively on profitability. • The company has a highly competitive "up-or-out" culture. • Communication and training of employees generally is poor. • Oversight and supervision are lax.	• Incentives based on profitability plus "balanced scorecard" financial and nonfinancial metrics such as customer satisfaction and product quality. • Culture built on product innovation and customer service • Formal training methods for communicating policies and acceptable behavior • Effective oversight and supervision

Shared Activities. Some activities in a company are performed centrally and affect several different financial account balances. For example, cash disbursements affect not only cash balances but also accounts payable and payroll. The most common types of shared activities include

- Cash receipts
- Cash disbursements
- Payroll
- Data processing

When designing your activity-level tests, you should be sure to coordinate your tests of shared activities with your tests of individual processing streams. For example, you should plan on testing cash disbursements only once, not several times for each different processing stream that includes cash disbursements.

Types of Tests

Inquiry and Focus Groups. Formal inquiries of entity personnel—either individually or as part of a focus group—can be a reliable source of evidence about the operating effectiveness of application-level controls. Inquiries can serve two main purposes:

1. To confirm your understanding of the design of the control (what should happen)
2. To identify exceptions to the entity's stated control procedures (what *really* happens)

Confirming Control Design: Chapter 5 describes a process for documenting the design of activity-level controls. Typically, this process consists primarily of a review of documentation (such as policies and procedures manuals) and limited inquiries of high-level individuals or those in the accounting department. To confirm this understanding of the processing stream and control procedures, you should expand your inquiries to include operating personnel and those responsible for performing the control. To help you conduct your discussion, it often is helpful to use a flowchart of the information-processing stream, as described in Chapter 5, as a guide.

When conducting your inquiries, consider the following:

- Focus first on what *should* happen and whether the employees' understanding of the control procedure is consistent with your understanding. This strategy accomplishes two important objectives:

  1. It provides you with a baseline understanding of the procedure that everyone can agree on. It helps to start with everyone "on the same page." You can then discuss exceptions to the norm later.

  2. If the employees' understanding of what should happen varies significantly from what is documented, that may indicate a weakness in entity-level controls. For example, you may determine that a weakness in the entity's hiring or training policies is the cause of the lack of understanding of what should happen. This weakness may have implications for the operating effectiveness of other application-level controls.

     Differences between the documentation and the employee's understanding of the procedures also may indicate that the implementation or use of the entity's automated documentation tool was poorly planned or executed. For example, documentation of a new control may have been created without informing operating personnel of the change.

- Ask open-ended questions. Open-ended questions get people talking and allow them to *volunteer information*. The results of your inquiries are more reliable when individuals volunteer information that is consistent with your own understanding rather than simply confirming that understanding with a direct statement.

- Focus on how the procedure is applied and documented. As described earlier, operating effectiveness is determined by how the procedure was applied, the consistency with which it was applied, and by whom (e.g., whether the person performing the control has other, conflicting duties). The last two elements will be the subject of your inquiries to identify exceptions to the stated policy. Questions about what somebody does or how he or she documents control performance (e.g., by initialing a source document) typically are less threatening than questions related to consistency ("under what circumstances do you *not* follow the required procedure?") or possible incompatible functions.

- Interviewers should share their findings and observations with each other. Research indicates that the effectiveness of inquiries as an evidence-gathering technique improves when engagement team members debrief the results.

- Ask "what could go wrong?" Interviewees will easily understand a line of questioning that starts with

  "Tell me what could go wrong in processing this information."

followed by

"What do you do to make sure those errors don't occur?"

Toward that end, consider using the financial statement assertions model to frame your questions. As described previously, one way to organize your understanding of activity-level controls is to link them to financial statement assertions. You can use these assertions to formulate questions. For example, "What procedures do you perform to make sure that you capture all the transactions?" is related to the completeness assertion.

- Consider the difference between processes and controls. Chapter 5 draws a distinction between processes and controls. A process changes or manipulates the information in the stream. Processes introduce the possibility of error. Controls detect errors or prevent them from occurring during the processing of information. Your inquiries should confirm your understanding of *both* the steps involved in processing the information and the related controls.

  The duties of an individual employee may include the processing of information (e.g., the manual input of data into the computer system or the preparation of source documents), control procedures (e.g., the performance of a reconciliation or the follow-up on items identified in an exception report), or both. In making your inquiries, you should remain cognizant of the distinction between processes and controls and the responsibilities of the individual being interviewed.

Appendix 7B provides example questions you might use to gather evidence relating to the design effectiveness of internal control.

Identify Exceptions: In every entity, there will be differences between the company's stated procedures and what individuals actually do in the course of everyday work. The existence of differences is normal. In testing the effectiveness of application-level controls, you should anticipate that these differences will exist, and you should plan your procedures to identify them and assess how they affect the effectiveness of activity-level controls. Differences between what *should* happen and what *really* happens can arise from

- The existence of transactions that were not contemplated in the design of the system
- Different application of the procedure according division, location, or differences between the people
- Changes in personnel or in their assigned responsibilities during the period under review
- Practical, field-level "work-arounds" as a way to satisfy other objectives, such as bypassing a control to better respond to customer needs.

Once you and the interviewee reach a common understanding of the company's stated procedures, you should be prepared to discuss the circumstances that result in a variation from these procedures. When making these inquiries, consider the following:

- *Don't make value judgments.* In any organization, the information that flows through a processing stream will follow the path of least resistance. Controls that are seen as barriers to the processing of legitimate transactions that meet the company's overall objectives may be bypassed. The employee may not be at fault. More importantly, if you adopt a judgmental attitude toward the interviewee, he or she will be less inclined to participate productively in the information-gathering process, and your interview will lose effectiveness.
- *Separate information gathering from evaluation.* Remember that this phase of your inquiries is a two-step process: (1) identify the exceptions to the stated policy, and (2) assess the effect that these have on operating effectiveness. Keep these two objectives separate. Be careful that you don't perform your evaluation prematurely, before you gather all the necessary information. When performing your inquiries, remember that your only objective is to gather information—you will perform your evaluation once you have completed your inquiries.
- *Use hypothetical or indirect questions to probe sensitive areas.* Many interviewees will feel uncomfortable describing to you how they circumvent company policies or how they have incompatible duties that could leave the company vulnerable to fraud. To gather this type of information, use indirect questioning techniques that do not confront the employee directly or otherwise put him or her on the defensive. For example, you might preface your questions with qualifying statements, such as
  - "If a situation arose in which . . ."
  - "Suppose that . . ."
  - "If someone wanted to . . ."
- *Ask them directly about their opinion of control effectiveness.* The overall objective of your inquiry is to gather information to assess the effectiveness of controls. The opinions of those who perform the control procedures on a daily basis are important. Ask them to share those opinions. Do they think the controls are effective? Why or why not?

Qualifications of Employees: As described earlier, assessing the operating effectiveness of control activities requires you to consider who performs such activities. Your inquiries should determine whether the interviewee is qualified to perform the required procedures. To be "qualified" the individual should have the necessary skills, training, and experience, and should have no incompatible functions.

Appendix 7B provides example inquiries that can help you assess the operating effectiveness of internal control procedures.

Focus Groups: As a supplement to, or perhaps instead of, interviewing people individually, you may wish to facilitate a group discussion about the entity's activity-level control activities and their effectiveness. The purpose of the group discussion would be the same as a discussion with individuals: to confirm your understanding of control design and to gather information about operating effectiveness. However, the advantages of conducting a group discussion include the following:

- *See the whole process.* You may be able to convene a group of individuals who represent every step in the processing stream, from the initiation of the transaction through to its posting in the general ledger. A group discussion that includes these members will help you to understand more quickly how the entire process fits together.

- *Foster communication and understanding.* In conducting your group discussion, you will bring together people in the company who may not interact together on a regular basis, and you will engage them in a discussion about operating procedures and controls. By participating in this process, employees will gain a greater understanding of their responsibilities and how these fit into the larger picture. This improved understanding among employees will allow your project to provide value to the company that goes beyond mere compliance.

To conduct a group discussion, follow these steps:

1. Review the documentation of the processing stream and determine who should be invited to participate. Groups of five to ten people usually work the best—everyone can make a meaningful contribution to the conversation without things getting out of hand. Try to make sure that someone is present who has experience with every process, control, document, or electronic file described in your documentation of the processing stream.

2. Prepare a flowchart of the process on a large piece of paper. Use stickies to document processes and control points. Your group discussion will be highly interactive, and the participants will have the opportunity to change your original flowchart to provide a more accurate description of what really happens in the process. Therefore, you should prepare your flowchart in a way that allows the group to work with it easily. Low tech, high touch works the best.

3. Assemble the group and explain
   - The purpose of the discussion, as described previously
   - The process, in which you will facilitate a discussion of how the process really works and the participants will be free to describe what happens by modifying the flowchart
   - How long the discussion will take. Usually, one to two hours is the longest that a group discussion of this nature can remain productive. If you need more time, it is better to have more sessions rather than have longer sessions.

4. Post the flowchart on the wall and walk the participants through your understanding of the process.

5. Using the questioning strategies and example questions provided in Appendix 7B, facilitate a discussion among the participants. As described earlier,

  – First, reach an understanding about what should happen
  – Next, identify those instances in which exceptions exist (what really happens)
  Throughout the discussion, encourage the participants to change the flowchart as necessary so that it reflects what they have said.

Here are some tips for facilitating your group discussion:

- Keep people focused on the flow of information, not on the flow of documents.
- Have the boundaries of the processing stream well defined. Make sure that people understand that you are concerned only about information that flows into the financial statements. Also, when discussing how information is prepared, your discussion should be limited to what the company does *internally*, not on how third parties may prepare information that the company uses. (You will, however, discuss how the company *reviews or otherwise controls* the information provided from external sources.)
- Participants will probably disagree on certain matters. That is normal, and you should set an expectation that differences of opinion are acceptable. In facilitating the discussion, try to probe and gain a better understanding for the source of these differences.
- Whenever possible, try to *quantify* what you learn about the process. For example, you might ask questions that begin with "How often do you encounter . . . ?" or "About what percentage of transactions . . . ?"
- Try to build consensus. Before drawing any conclusions about the process and related controls, make sure that you have a consensus among the group members. You should not draw conclusions if significant differences exist among members of the group. At some level, you should seek agreement on these issues.

Tests of Transactions. Some control procedures allow you to select a sample of transactions that were recorded during the period and

- Examine the documentation indicating that the control procedure was performed.
- Reperform the procedure to determine that the control was performed properly.

  For example, the process for recording inventory purchases may require

- Physically matching a paper-based warehouse receiving report with an approved purchase order
- Determining that the purchase order was properly approved, as indicated by a signature
- Determining that the vendor is an approved vendor
- Observing evidence (e.g., checkmarks, initials) that warehouse personnel counted the goods received

To test the effectiveness of this control procedure you could

- Examine documentation that the control was performed, including
  - Documents were matched
  - Purchase order was signed
  - Receiving report was marked

- Determine that the control was performed properly, including
  - Purchase order and receiving report are for the same transaction.
  - Vendor is an approved vendor.
  - Signer of the purchase order has the authority to approve the transaction.

Computer application controls also may lend themselves to similar testing techniques. For example, suppose that purchased goods are accompanied with a bar code that identifies the goods received and their quantities. The bar code is scanned, and the information is matched electronically to purchase order files and approved vendor master files. Unmatched transactions are placed in a suspense file for subsequent follow-up. (As indicated previously, the computer application control consists of *both* the programmed elements of the control and the manual follow-up of identified errors). To test the effectiveness of this control, you could

- Prepare a file of test transactions and run through the system to determine that all errors are identified.
- Review the resolution of the suspense account items performed throughout the period to determine that they were resolved properly.

When performing tests of transactions, you will have to address issues related to scope—how many items to test. Suggestions for considering the scope of tests were provided earlier in this chapter.

Before performing your tests of transactions you also should define what you will consider a control procedure error. In instances in which the evidence of performing the procedure is documented (e.g., an initial or signature), the lack of documentation (a missing signature) should be considered an error in the operation of the control. That is, in order for a documented control to be considered properly performed, *both* of the following must be true:

- The documentation indicates that the control procedure was performed.
- Your reperformance of the procedure indicates it was performed properly.

Reconciliations. Reconciliations are a common control procedure, for example, bank reconciliations or the reconciliation of the general ledger account total to a subsidiary ledger. In some instances, a well-designed reconciliation can provide an effective control over the majority of a processing stream. Testing the effectiveness of a reconciliation is similar to tests of transactions:

- Review documentation that the test was performed on a timely basis throughout the period.
- Reperform the test to determine that all reconciling items were identified properly.
- Investigate the resolution of significant reconciling items.

Observation. You may be able to observe the application of some control procedures, such as computer input controls like edit checks. A physical inventory count also lends itself to observation as a means of assessing effectiveness. For a control performed only occasionally, such as a physical count, it may be possible to observe the control each time it is performed. For controls that are performed continuously for large volumes of transactions, you will need to supplement your observations with other tests such as

- Inquiry
- Tests of entity-level controls

EVALUATING TEST RESULTS

The results of your tests of activity-level controls should support your conclusion about their operating effectiveness. If your tests revealed no deviations or deficiencies in the performance of control procedures, then you should be able to conclude that the control is operating effectively (assuming that the scope of your testwork, as discussed earlier in this chapter, was sufficient).

When your testwork reveals deficiencies in either the design or operating effectiveness of a control procedure, you will need to exercise your judgment in order to reach a conclusion about control effectiveness. Chapter 8 provides guidance on the factors you should consider when making this judgment. (See the sections titled "The Nature of Internal Control Deficiencies" and "Making Judgments about the Severity of Internal Control Deficiencies.")

Ultimately, you should consider that you are making a conclusion about the effectiveness of internal control *as a whole*. When you evaluate activity-level controls, you should consider the effectiveness of the entire information processing stream, not individual control procedures in isolation.

DOCUMENTATION OF TEST PROCEDURES AND RESULTS

As described in Chapter 6, you will need to document the test procedures you performed and the results of those tests. Chapter 6 provides guidance on what should be included in the documentation related to tests of entity-level controls, and that guidance is applicable for tests of activity-level controls as well.

COORDINATING WITH THE INDEPENDENT AUDITORS

Determining the nature, timing, and extent of your tests is a significant decision that will affect the ability of the independent auditors to attest to management's assertion. If the independent auditors determine that your tests were not sufficient to support your evaluation of the effectiveness of controls, then additional testwork will be required. The scope of additional tests may be significant, and the performance of these tests could delay the preparation of the required report.

For these reasons, it is important that you review your planned procedures with the independent auditors before conducting a significant portion of the tests. Describe how these procedures build on your assessment of entity-level controls. Consider discussing how the testing strategy relates to the various financial statement assertions. Periodically, as the tests are performed and results received and evaluated, you also should consider discussing the progress of the tests with the auditors to confirm that the original plan is still sufficient for their purposes.

For example, you should establish an ongoing dialogue with the independent auditors to establish consensus on matters such as the following:

- The nature and extent of your planned procedures and whether these are considered sufficient to draw a reliable conclusion
- The circumstances under which the planned nature and extent of the procedures should be modified
- The planned timing of your tests and whether this timing will allow you to draw conclusions about the design and operating effectiveness of activity-level controls as of year-end
- The nature and extent of procedures that may be required to update your conclusions about effectiveness from the time your procedures are performed until year-end
- The results of your tests and the tentative and final conclusions reached regarding the effectiveness of activity-level controls
- How the test procedures and results will be documented
- The general type of deviations or conditions that might be considered significant deficiencies or material weaknesses
- The corrective actions and possible reporting implications required to respond to the identification of significant deficiencies or material weaknesses

APPENDIX 7A
Action Plan:
Documentation

The following action plan is intended to help you implement the suggestions contained in this chapter for testing and evaluating activity-level controls.

1. Design Tests

Plan the nature, timing and extent of tests necessary to draw a conclusion about the operating effectiveness of internal control as of year-end. For example:

- Consider the nature of possible errors that may occur in the information processing stream.
  - Consider using the financial statement assertions framework to help you identify potential errors
- Consider the control activities that are expected to exist based on your review of
  - The entity's internal control documentation
  - The example control activities provided by COSO or others
- Consider the results of entity-level tests
- Determine the combination of testing techniques that will be used to assess the operating effectiveness of each significant entity-level control. Consider
  - Computer application controls
  - Inquiries and focus groups
  - Tests of transactions
  - Tests of reconciliations
  - Direct observation

2. Perform and Document Tests

Perform the planned tests. Update as necessary to support a conclusion about operating effectiveness as of year-end. Document the procedures performed and the test results.

3. Assess Test Results

Evaluate the effectiveness of activity-level controls based on the results of your testwork. For example:

- Determine whether activity-level controls are functioning at a level that will prevent or detect material financial statement misstatements in a timely manner.

- Identify weaknesses in activity-level controls.
- Respond to identified weaknesses by taking corrective action.

4. Coordinate with the Independent Auditors

Establish an ongoing dialogue with the independent auditors that allows you to reach a consensus on the following:

- The nature and extent of your planned procedures and whether these are considered sufficient to draw a reliable conclusion
- The circumstances under which the planned nature and extent of the procedures should be modified
- The planned timing of your tests and whether this timing will allow you to draw conclusions about the design and operating effectiveness of activity-level controls as of year-end
- The nature and extent of procedures that may be required to update your conclusions about effectiveness from the time your procedures are performed until year-end
- The results of your tests and the tentative and final conclusions reached regarding the effectiveness of activity-level controls
- How the test procedures and results will be documented
- The general type of deviations or conditions that might be considered significant deficiencies or material weaknesses
- The corrective actions and possible reporting implications required to respond to the identification of significant deficiencies or material weaknesses

---

APPENDIX 7B

Example Inquiries

Exhibit 7.4   Example Inquiries

Design Effectiveness

- What documents or electronic files are necessary for you to perform your job? From whom do you receive the document? How do you access the electronic information? (Process)
- In what ways do you add to, combine, manipulate, or change the data you receive? (Process)
- What happens to a file or document when you're finished with it? (Process)
- When you discover errors, how do they get corrected? (Process)
- What checks do you perform on the information you use to make sure it's accurate? (Accuracy control)
- How do you know that you receive all the transactions you should receive? How do you make sure that you process everything you receive and that some transactions don't get accidentally dropped from the process? (Completeness control)

Exhibit 7.4 *(Continued)*

- When you're processing the information, what steps do you take to make sure that no errors are introduced into the system? What controls are built into the system itself? (Completeness, accuracy controls)
- What signatures or other types of documentation are required before you process a transaction? How do you know that the transactions presented to you for processing are valid? (Existence, authorization control)

Operating Effectiveness

Your inquiries of operating effectiveness should be directed toward gathering information about two broad areas: the consistency with which the control procedure was applied and the qualifications of the person who performed the control. You also should consider asking employees for their opinion about the operating effectiveness of controls.

CONSISTENCY

- What kinds of situations do you encounter for which company policies or procedures do not exist? How often do you encounter these situations?
  - If you encountered a situation or transaction for which no written policy existed, what would you do? How likely is it that you would encounter such a situation? What would it be? (Indirect)
- In what ways are written policies and procedures inefficient or otherwise "don't make sense"? How do you work around these policies? How often do you have to do this?
  - If you were in charge of designing policies and procedures, what changes would you make to improve their efficiency? (Indirect)
- Although it might not be written, when is it "okay" to not follow written policies exactly? How do you know it's "okay"?
- Do you think that others in the company with the same job functions as yours perform the job in the same way? If differences exist, what are they? What causes these differences?
- Have you performed the procedures every day since the last annual evaluation of internal control effectiveness? Who took your place when you were not available to perform the procedures?
- Have there been any changes to the procedures since the last annual evaluation of internal control effectiveness?

QUALIFICATIONS OF PERSONNEL

- Do you feel adequately trained to perform your duties?
  - If you could design the training for your position, what topics would you be sure to include? How did you learn these things? How long did it take you to learn them? What else would you like to be trained in that would help you do your job better?
- Incompatible responsibilities exist when one individual is in a position where they must both process data (for example, prepare invoices, or post the general ledger) AND check their own work for errors AND no one checks their work. Have you observed situations like that in your department?
  - Suppose that someone was inclined to deliberately create an error in the reporting process, for example, by introducing a fictitious or unauthorized transaction. How would they do it without getting caught? (Indirect)
  - Which company assets are most vulnerable to employee theft? How could these assets "disappear" without someone finding out? (Indirect)

ASSESSMENT OF EFFECTIVENESS

- Overall, how effective is your system at preventing or detecting and correcting errors? Consider the reliability of your system. If you had to give it a letter grade, what grade would you give it? What recommendations would you make to improve the system?
  - Suppose that you leave the company, and shortly after you leave, you learn that there was a major error in the company's financial statements relating to your division/location. What is that error? Why was it never detected? (Indirect)

APPENDIX 7C
Example Control Activities[1]

This appendix provides example internal control activities, linked to control objectives and the risks of achieving those objectives. These examples, which have been reproduced from the COSO report, have been included to provide you with a possible benchmark for assessing the entity's existing controls. These examples are organized according to the following business process activities, as described in Chapter 2:

- Inbound activities
- Operations
- Outbound activities
- Marketing and sales
- Service
- Procurement
- Firm infrastructure

INBOUND ACTIVITIES   (See Exhibit 7.5.)

OPERATIONS   (See Exhibit 7.6.)

OUTBOUND ACTIVITIES   (See Exhibit 7.7.)

MARKETING AND SALES   (See Exhibit 7.8.)

SERVICE   (See Exhibit 7.9.)

PROCUREMENT   (See Exhibit 7.10.)

FIRM INFRASTRUCTURE   (See Exhibit 7.11.)

Note

1. Copyright © 1992 by the American Institute of Certified Public Accountants, Inc. Reprinted with permission.

Exhibit 7.5 Inbound Activities

Objectives	Risks	Control Activities
Manage Logistics		
1. Ensure that materials received and related information are processed and promptly made available to production, stores, or other departments.	• Plans and schedules are not communicated to inbound activities or do not clearly identify when or where materials are needed.	• Specify on plans and schedules what materials are needed and when they are needed. • Communicate all plans and schedules to inbound activities. • Summarize material requirements and submit them to receiving periodically. • Maintain material routing procedures for received items. • Provide inbound activities with nonroutine material routing instructions. • Monitor production problems related to unavailable materials and parts (performance indicator). • Consider implementing just-in-time or a similar inventory and production management philosophy.
	• Information on materials received is not entered into the information system accurately or on a timely basis.	• Maintain procedures for promptly updating inventory records • Match dates on receiving information and inventory information and follow up as appropriate. • Periodically verify that prenumbered receiving documents have been entered in the information system.
2. Ensure purchase orders not filled on a timely basis are investigated.	• Purchase orders are lost or not forwarded to inbound activities. • Due date information is not available.	• Purchase orders are prenumbered and missing documents are investigated. • Maintain open purchase order information in a manner that facilitates identification of purchase orders remaining unfilled past the due date.
3. Completely and accurately document goods received and goods returned.	• Lost receiving reports or lost shipping records	• Prenumber documents and investigate missing documents.

(Continued)

227

Exhibit 7.5 (*Continued*)

Objectives	Risks	Control Activities
Receive		
4. Accept only items that were properly ordered.	• Purchase order information is not made available to inbound activities.	• Compare materials received, including verification of quantities received, to properly approved purchase orders. Do not accept materials not properly ordered. • Monitor instances of invoices presented for payment when materials were accepted without a valid purchase order (performance indicator).
5. Accept only materials that meet purchase order specifications.	• Purchase order specifications are unclear.	• Maintain current lists of specifications to be used in inspecting and testing goods. • Verify specifications with purchasing or other appropriate personnel. • Monitor production problems related to substandard materials (performance indicator).
6. Ensure that all materials transferred from the receiving activity to other activities are recorded.	• Transfer procedures do not require preparation of supporting documentation. • Transfer documentation may be lost.	• Require appropriate documentation of materials transferred from receiving to other business activities. • Prenumber documents and investigate missing documents. • Periodically count materials on hand and reconcile with perpetual records; investigate any differences (performance indicator).
7. Safeguard goods received.	• Inadequate physical security over goods received	• Maintain physical security over goods received. • Segregate custodial and record-keeping functions.
8. Ensure that vendor, inventory, and purchase order information is accurately updated to reflect receipts.	• Receiving information may be lost.	• Prenumber receiving documents and investigate missing documents. • Periodically identify and investigate open purchase orders. • Periodically count inventory and reconcile with perpetual inventory records; investigate differences (performance indicator).

#	Objective	Risks	Controls
9.	Return rejected items promptly.	• Receiving information may be entered inaccurately in the information system, or may not be timely.	• Periodically verify accuracy of vendor, inventory and open purchase order information. • Periodically ensure information is being entered into the information system on a timely basis.
10.	Completely and accurately document all transfers to and from storage.	• Inadequate or untimely inspection of items received • Incomplete or inaccurate information regarding materials transferred to/from storage • Transfer documents may be lost.	• Maintain appropriate procedures for inspecting items received. • Transfer documentation accompanies all transfers; stores or other activities personnel verify materials and quantities received. • Prenumber transfer documents and investigate missing documents. • Periodically count materials and reconcile with perpetual records. Investigate differences (performance indicator).
11.	Appropriately requisition all goods to be transferred to operations.	• Inadequate transfer or requisition procedures	• Transfer materials only on the basis of a properly approved requisition.
12.	Properly transfer all materials requisitioned.	• Requisitions may be lost. • Materials not requisitioned are transferred.	• Prenumber requisitions and investigate missing documents. • Verify that material received complies with approved requisition.
13.	Maintain safe working conditions and storage of hazardous materials.	• Inadequate safety considerations	• Maintain relevant policies consistent with Occupational Safety and Health Administration (OSHA) and other pertinent laws and regulations, approved by technical and legal personnel, and monitor compliance. • Follow up on reported safety concerns. • Maintain appropriate procedures for handling and storing hazardous materials.

Exhibit 7.6   Operations

Objectives	Risks	Control Activities
Manage and Schedule Operations		
1. Schedule operations to minimize inventory and to ensure sufficient availability of completed products in a timely manner.	• Poor communication with marketing regarding sales forecasts.	• Use standard documents to prepare and communicate sales forecasts. • Ensure that production personnel receive all sales forecasts. • Compare production schedules to sales forecasts to ensure that scheduled timing and production quantities are appropriate.
	• Several products compete for concurrent production.	• Determine production priorities based on established criteria or management judgment. • Evaluate adequacy of production capacity. • Approve all production schedules.
	• Insufficient or excess raw materials due to poor communication with procurement, or inaccurate or untimely material requirement forecasts	• Use formalized communication channels to inform procurement of material requirements, including quantities and dates materials are required. • Compare material requirement forecasts with production schedule and product bills of materials; consider effect of lead times required to obtain materials. • Establish and adhere to accurate and realistic production schedules. • Consider the costs/benefits of establishing a just-in-time system or similar production and inventory management philosophy. • Monitor instances of insufficient or excessive raw materials inventory (performance indicator).
2. Minimize production downtime.	• Poorly maintained, misused or obsolete equipment	• Maintain equipment in accordance with an established preventative maintenance program. • Periodically evaluate production equipment in light of repairs and maintenance cost, capacity, breakdowns, obsolescence and other factors. Consider the costs/ benefits of acquiring new equipment. • Train employees in the proper use of equipment. • Monitor instances of production downtime due to equipment failure (performance indicator).

Perform Operations

Objective	Risks	Controls
3. Produce product in appropriate quantities and in accordance with specifications and production schedules. 4. Comply with OSHA laws and regulations.	• Inadequate skilled labor • Natural or other disasters • Quantities to be produced are not communicated clearly. • Inappropriate or unclear specifications • Excessive work steps/operations • Pressure to meet production deadlines • Lack of awareness of laws and regulations	• Train existing employees to perform various tasks. • Maintain and update contingency and natural disaster plans. • Periodically test such plans. • Use standardized documents to prepare and communicate production plans and directives. • Use standardized documents to communicate product specifications. • Consider methods to simplify production. • Upper management supports, in statements and actions, safety considerations. • Enforce disciplinary action on employees who violate safety procedures. • Monitor safety violations (performance indicator). • Conduct periodic training sessions. • Post laws, regulations and company policy in conspicuous locations.

Assure Quality

Objective	Risks	Controls
5. Product is produced in accordance with quality control standards.	• Production processes do not include procedures designed to ensure quality production. • Product is difficult to produce. • Inadequate product testing • Quality problems are not discovered or appropriately reported during the production process.	• Integrate quality assurance procedures into production processes. • Standardize production processes to the extent practicable. • Design product with appropriate consideration given to potential production difficulties. • Test sufficient quantities of each production run to ensure compliance with quality control standards. • Monitor defect rates (performance indicator). • Test products using personnel independent of production processes. • Monitor customer quality-related returns and complaints (performance indicator).

Exhibit 7.7 Outbound Activities

Objectives	Risks	Control Activities
Process Orders		
1. Process orders only for customers who are authorized for credit.	• Incomplete, untimely, or inaccurate credit information	• Credit authorization systems that provide accurate and timely customer information regarding approved credit limits, current balances due, age of receivable balance, and other pertinent information
2. Process orders accurately and expeditiously.	• Inaccurate or untimely pricing and inventory information	• Use current pricing and inventory information.
	• Untimely processing of order information	• Prenumber order forms and periodically follow up on those not processed in a reasonable time frame.
	• Customer order information may be unclear, inaccurate, or incomplete.	• Verify customer order information with appropriate marketing/sales personnel; contact customer if necessary.
3. Process only valid customer orders.	• Customer orders may not be authorized.	• Verify appropriate marketing/sales personnel approved customer order.
4. Process all approved orders.	• Order documentation is lost.	• Prenumber order forms; investigate missing documents.
Store Product		
5. Protect products from damage.	• Employee carelessness	• Monitor damage caused by employee carelessness (performance indicator).
	• Handling and storage procedures, including storage containers, facilities and maintenance, are inappropriate for the nature of the products.	• Store products in containers and facilities designed with consideration for product features and legal and regulatory requirements.
	• Employees are not familiar with handling and storage requirements or procedures.	• Create appropriate maintenance procedures and schedules for the nature of the storage facility.
		• Communicate handling and storage policies and procedures clearly to store's employees.
		• Monitor compliance with handling and storage policies and procedures (performance indicator).

#	Objective	Risk	Controls
6.	Store products to facilitate timely order processing.	• Improper organization of storage facility • Insufficient storage capacity	• Design and maintain efficient warehouse layout to facilitate order fulfillment. • Minimize product inventory while enabling timely order fulfillment. • Identify the appropriate number and location of warehouses.
7.	Materials are handled and stored in compliance with applicable laws and regulations.	• Employees may not be aware of applicable laws and regulations. • Inappropriate handling and storage policies and procedures	• Legal counsel, or other qualified personnel, provide information regarding applicable laws and regulations. • Periodic training regarding legal and regulatory requirements. • Review of handling and storage procedures by legal counsel or other qualified personnel. • Monitor accidents or problems due to inappropriate handling or storage policies or procedures (performance indicator).
8.	Maintain complete and accurate records of product stored and available for shipment.	• Product moved into or out of storage may not be documented or recorded. • Product may be moved into or out of storage without proper authorization.	• Product transfer documents are required for movements of product into or out of storage. Such documents are prenumbered, and missing documents are investigated. • Physical security measures to prevent unauthorized addition to or removal of product from storage. • Periodically count product in storage and reconcile to perpetual records. Investigate differences between physical count and accounting records.

Ship Product

#	Objective	Risk	Controls
9.	Obtain proper products and quantities from storage.	• Improper products or improper quantities are retrieved from storage. • Product is unavailable in sufficient quantity.	• Compare products and quantities retrieved from storage with the customer order and/or product requisition. • Maintain perpetual product inventory records. Notify operations or other appropriate personnel when inventory drops below a predetermined level.

(Continued)

Exhibit 7.7 (*Continued*)

Objectives	Risks	Control Activities
10. Ensure product is packed properly to minimize damage.	• Packing materials, containers, or procedures are inappropriate for the nature of the product or method of shipment.	• Use packing materials, containers, or procedures that were designed giving consideration to the nature of the product and method of shipment.
11. Ship only those products that are authorized for shipment.	• Incomplete or inaccurate information from order processing • Unordered or unauthorized products are included in customer shipment.	• Compare documents authorizing product shipment with customer order. • Compare products to customer order prior to shipment. • Monitor customer returns or billing disputes relating to products delivered but not ordered (performance indicator).
12. Deliver products in the most efficient manner.	• Disruption of normal shipping channels • Inaccurate or incomplete shipping documents • Use of inefficient shipping methods	• Identify alternative shipping arrangements. • Review shipping documents for completeness and compare to customer order for accuracy before shipment. • Periodically review shipping alternatives and identify the most efficient alternative.
13. All shipments are accurately documented, and such documentation is forwarded to accounts receivable on a timely basis.	• Incorrect information is entered on shipping documentation. • Shipping documents are lost.	• Compare shipping document information with customer order information before shipment. • Independent verification of shipping document information before shipment • Prenumber shipping documents and investigate missing documents.
14. Ensure timely shipment of customer order.	• Order or shipping documentation may be lost.	• Prenumber order and shipping documents; investigate missing documents.

Exhibit 7.8 Marketing and Sales

Objectives	Risks	Control Activities
Manage Marketing Activities		
1. Design marketing strategies giving consideration to competitive, regulatory, business environment, or other factors that may influence the entity's marketing activities, and potential changes in those factors.	• Inadequate information regarding factors that may influence the entity's marketing strategy	• Retain marketing personnel experienced in the entity's industry. • Promote active membership in industry, trade, or professional associations. • Monitor legal and regulatory initiatives that may affect the entity • Conduct market research, and monitor and analyze economic, customer, and industry trends.
2. Identify potential and existing customers, and develop marketing strategies to influence those parties to purchase the entity's products or services.	• Inaccurate, untimely, or unavailable information regarding pricing, products, actual or potential customers, advertising, and promotion	• Conduct market research. • Evaluate pricing strategies vis-à-vis competitors' products and pricing. • Evaluate the effectiveness of advertising and promotion (performance indicator). • Communication of product capabilities, enhancements, or new products from technology development personnel • Identify and evaluate alternative distribution arrangements.
3. Maintain delivery capabilities for delivery of products to customers on a timely basis at the least distribution cost.	• Limited number of appropriate distributors • Poor performance of distributors	• Communicate appropriate customer information to distributors to ensure timely delivery. • Monitor distributors' performance in the context of the entity's overall marketing strategy
4. Address market needs for product, including introduction of new products and continuance, changes to, or discontinuance of existing products.	• Lack of or inaccurate information regarding competitive products or potential new products • Products become obsolete. • Lack of product demand	• Conduct market research, including existence of competitive products, products under development and customer preferences. • Promote active membership in industry, trade, or professional associations. • Conduct market research, focusing on competitors' technical innovations and customers' acceptance of or preference for such innovations. • Monitor the trend of product sales by the entity and the industry. • Evaluate advertising and promotion effectiveness. • Conduct market research.

(Continued)

Exhibit 7.8 (*Continued*)

Objectives	Risks	Control Activities
Manage Marketing Activities (cont'd)		
	• Lack of information regarding profit margins and/or sales prices	• Communicate information needs to accounting, management information systems, and other appropriate personnel. • Monitor profit margins and sales prices for signs of competitive price pressures.
Manage Sales Activities		
5. Implement marketing strategies effectively.	• Sales personnel are unaware of marketing strategies. • Sales personnel disregard marketing strategies.	• Communicate marketing strategies to sales personnel. • Establish sales quotas, commissions and other compensation or other performance criteria in such a manner that failure to implement marketing strategies results in substandard performance evaluations and compensation, and positive implementation of strategies results in increased compensation and recognition.
6. Meet or exceed sales targets in an efficient manner.	• Sales personnel are unaware of potential customers. • Salespeople lack knowledge about product features or benefits. • Incomplete or inaccurate customer information	• Communication of market research results from marketing to sales personnel. • Provide product awareness training. • Retain qualified and experienced sales staff. • Maintain customer information system, including name, address, phone number, contact, size, locations, history of previous orders, plans to expand or change the business, or other information that could be useful in marketing the entity's products or services. • Periodically verify the accuracy of customer information.
	• Salespeople perform poorly.	• Retain qualified and experienced salespeople. • Organize sales force and align territories in the most efficient manner.
7. Forward all sales orders to outbound activities and service in a timely manner.	• Sales orders are lost.	• Prenumber sales orders and investigate missing documents.

Exhibit 7.9 Service

Objectives	Risks	Control Activities
Provide Customer Service		
1. Handle customer inquiries expeditiously and efficiently.	• Inadequate information systems • Untrained staff	• Maintain accurate and timely product and customer information. • Provide staff with initial and periodic product and customer service training. • Customer service representatives present favorable image to customers and are knowledgeable about products.
2. Satisfy customer service needs so as to further sales and marketing objectives.	• Poor organization of customer service department • Lack of awareness of sales and marketing objectives	• Organize customer service department in the most efficient manner (e.g., along product lines, geographical lines, etc.). • Customer service representatives understand the objectives common to marketing sales and customer service.
Install		
3. Make authorized installations correctly, efficiently, and on a timely basis.	• Untrained staff	• Provide installers with initial and periodic training regarding installation techniques and product features. • Monitor customer complaints regarding product installation (performance indicator).
	• Product unavailability	• Coordinate scheduled installations with operations' production schedule and shipping's delivery schedule.
	• Inaccurate or unavailable customer information	• Compare installation authorization documents with customer orders to verify information accuracy and review such documents for completeness. • Prenumber installation authorization documents and investigate missing documents.
	• Unavailability of service personnel	• Schedule installations and staff utilization to minimize costs.

(Continued)

Exhibit 7.9 (*Continued*)

Objectives	Risks	Control Activities
Provide Warranty Service		
4. Warranty policies are consistent with marketing and financial strategies.	• Inaccurate market information	• Make certain that market information developed by marketing is considered when establishing warranties.
5. Investigate and respond to requests for service on a timely basis and in accordance with warranties.	• Insufficient staff	• Forecast staffing-level requirements. • Monitor adequacy of staffing, overtime, and workloads.
	• Uncommunicated changes in warranty policies	• Communicate changes in product warranty policies to appropriate personnel.
Provide Post-Warranty Service		
6. Customer service representatives use up-to-date pricing and other product information.	• Unavailable or inaccurate information	• Update pricing information on order processing systems on a daily basis. • Provide customer representatives access to order-processing systems.
7. Investigate and respond to requests for services in the most efficient manner and on a timely basis.	• Insufficient number of customer service representatives or service personnel	• Maintain proper staffing levels and organize the customer service department in the most efficient manner.
	• Improperly trained service personnel	• Properly train staff.

Exhibit 7.10 Procurement

Objectives	Risks	Control Activities
Select Vendors		

1. Identify and purchase from vendors capable of meeting the entity's needs.	• Inadequate vendor screening, including periodic requalification of existing vendors, relating to vendors' abilities to meet
	
	  – Technical specifications
	  – Quantity requirements
	  – Price
	  – Delivery dates/lead time
	  – Service
		• Investigate and periodically update vendor capabilities regarding production quality and capacity, price (including volume or cash discounts and payment terms), order lead-time requirements, current and former customer satisfaction, financial condition, management stability, possible legal restrictions on providing the materials required and pending litigation.
		• Periodically update vendor information based on vendor performance in meeting terms and specifications of contracts or purchase orders (e.g., timely delivery of acceptable items, correction of errors or problems, and service).
		• Appropriate review of purchase orders.
		• Monitor production problems related to out-of-stock materials and to material specifications (performance indicator).
		• Monitor frequency of returned purchases (performance indicator).
		• Develop data on alternative vendors and periodically reevaluate vendor selection decisions.
		• Specify procedures for notification by vendors of potential performance problems and for appropriate investigation and follow-through.

2. Purchase items only from legally qualified vendors and in conformity with applicable laws, regulations, and contracts.	• Unavailable or inaccurate information about fraudulent acts or other improper activities of vendors	• Maintain updated vendor information. • Review and approve purchase orders. • Institute and monitor code of conduct. • Consider ways to simplify vendor investigation procedures.

(Continued)

Exhibit 7.10 *(Continued)*

Objectives	Risks	Control Activities
Select Vendors (cont'd)		
3. Ensure adequate supply of materials.	• Poor communication of operations' or other activities' needs • Vendors' inability to provide needed quantities due to other higher-priority orders or an interruption in their own supplies	• Timely communication to procurement of operations' or other activities' needs • Utilize forward contracts. • Identify alternate vendors. • Utilize long-term needs analysis.
Purchase		
4. Order items that meet appropriate specifications.	• Inappropriate production specifications	• Review existing and revised specifications by technical personnel. • Monitor and analyze production problems related to material specifications (performance indicator); examples of performance indicators include comparing current-period data on production stoppages and slowdowns, rush orders, spoilage, and material price and quantity variances to prior-period data, peer or industry data, budgets, or other pre-established goals. • Communicate production specifications to procurement personnel. • Appropriate review and approval of contracts and purchase orders.
5. Pay appropriate prices.	• Out-of-date or incomplete price information	• Obtain competitive bids for each acquisition periodically. • Consider volume purchases by determining total usage of similar materials; combine orders to obtain volume discount. • Appropriate review of purchase orders. • Monitor material price variances (performance indicator). • Use hedging or forward contracts.

6. Order appropriate quantities at appropriate times.	• Unavailable or inaccurate information on inventory levels or production needs	• Maintain accurate perpetual inventory records. • Match periodic production schedules to inventory information and order lead-time requirements. • Appropriate review of purchase orders. • Use forecasts. • Consider implementing just-in-time or a similar inventory and production management philosophy.
7. Update vendor information completely and accurately to reflect open purchase orders.	• Information in issued purchase orders is not clearly or completely communicated.	• Route copies of purchase orders to appropriate personnel.
8. Receive items ordered on a timely basis.	• Purchase orders are not entered into the system on a timely basis. • Unavailable or inaccurate information on items ordered but not received.	• Prenumber purchase orders and periodically verify their entry into the system. Investigate unusual time delays in entering data. • Specify shipment mode and delivery date on purchase orders. • Prenumber and account for purchase orders. • Match receiving information with purchase order information and promptly follow through on outstanding orders. • Monitor vendor performance in terms of timely delivery; follow up in cases of poorly performing vendors.
9. Record authorized purchase orders completely and accurately.	• Purchase orders may be lost.	• Prenumber and account for purchase orders.
10. Prevent unauthorized use of purchase orders.	• Inadequate policies and procedures to prevent unauthorized use.	• Prenumber and account for purchase orders. • Maintain physical security of purchase orders. • Approve purchase orders. • Notify vendors of company personnel authorized to approve purchase orders.

Exhibit 7.11 Firm Infrastructure

Objectives	Risks	Control Activities
Process Accounts Payable		
1. Accurately record invoices on a timely basis for accepted purchases that have been authorized and only for such purchases.	• Missing documents or information	• Prenumber and account for purchase orders and receiving reports. • Match invoice, receiving, and purchase order information and follow up on missing or inconsistent information. • Follow up on unmatched open purchase orders, receiving reports and invoices and resolve missing, duplicate or unmatched items, by individuals independent of purchasing and receiving functions.
	• Inaccurate input of data	• Use of control totals or one-for-one checking
	• Invalid accounts payable fraudulently created for unauthorized or nonexistent purchases	• Restrict ability to modify data. • Reconcile vendor statements to accounts payable items.
2. Identify available discounts.	• Missing or untimely receipt of documents	• Investigate unmatched information before due date. • Maintain accounts payable ledger by discount date.
3. Accurately record returns and allowances for all authorized credits, and only for such credits.	• Missing documents or information	• Prenumber and account for shipping orders for returned goods. • Match shipping orders for returned goods with vendors' credit memos. • Follow up on unmatched shipping orders for returned goods and related receiving reports and invoices and resolve missing, duplicate or unmatched items, by individuals independent of accounts payable function. • Review vendor correspondence authorizing returns and allowances.
	• Inaccurate input of data	• Reconcile accounts payable records with vendor statements. • Use of control totals or one-for-one checking.
4. Ensure completeness and accuracy of accounts payable.	• Unauthorized input for nonexistent returns	• Reconcile accounts payable subsidiary ledger with purchase and cash disbursement transactions.
	• Unauthorized additions to accounts payable	• Resolve differences between the accounts payable subsidiary ledger and the accounts payable control account.
5. Safeguard accounts payable records.	• Unauthorized access to accounts payable records and stored data	• Restrict access to accounts payable and files used in processing payables. • Restrict access to mechanical check signers and signature plates.

Process Accounts Receivable

1. All goods shipped are accurately billed in the proper period.	• Missing documents or incorrect information	• Use standard shipping or contract terms.
		• Communicate nonstandard shipping or contract terms to accounts receivable.
	• Improper cutoff of shipments at the end of a period	• Verify shipping or contract terms before invoice processing.
		• Identify shipments as being before or after period-end by means of a shipping log and prenumbered shipping documents.
		• Reconcile goods shipped to goods billed.
2. Accurately record invoices for all authorized shipments, and only for such shipments.	• Missing documents or incorrect information	• Prenumber and account for shipping documents and sales invoices.
		• Match orders, shipping documents, invoices, and customer information, and follow through on missing or inconsistent information.
		• Mail customer statements periodically and investigate and resolve disputes or inquiries, by individuals independent of the invoicing function.
		• Monitor number of customer complaints regarding improper invoices or statements (performance indicator).
3. Accurately record all authorized sales returns and allowances and only such returns and allowances.	• Missing documents or incorrect information	• Authorize credit memos by individuals independent of accounts receivable function.
		• Prenumber and account for credit memos and receiving documents.
		• Match credit memos and receiving documents and resolve unmatched items by individuals independent of the accounts receivable function.
	• Inaccurate input of data	• Mail customer statements periodically and investigate and resolve disputes or inquiries, by individuals independent of the invoicing function.
4. Ensure continued completeness and accuracy of accounts receivable.	• Unauthorized input for nonexistent returns, allowances, and write-offs	• Review correspondence authorizing returns and allowances.
		• Reconcile accounts receivable subsidiary ledger with the sale and cash receipts transactions.
		• Resolve differences between the accounts receivable subsidiary ledger and the accounts receivable control account.
5. Safeguard accounts receivable records.	• Unauthorized access to accounts receivable records and stored data	• Restrict access to accounts receivable files and data used in processing receivables.

(Continued)

Exhibit 7.11 (*Continued*)

Objectives	Risks	Control Activities
Process Funds		
1. Accurately forecast cash balances to maximize short-term investmen income and to avoid cash shortfalls.	• Inaccurate, untimely, or unavailable information regarding cash inflows and outflows	• Information systems identify all sources of cash and dates cash is due or expected to be collected. • Information systems identify all cash requirements and dates cash is needed. • Identify all internal sources of information. • Compare information used to prepare cash forecasts with supporting records or underlying documents to verify information is internally consistent.
2. Ensure necessary financing is available in the event of a cash shortfall.	• Lack of awareness regarding financing alternatives • Failure to establish or maintain appropriate relationships with financing sources	• Retain financial personnel experienced in obtaining financing for similar entities. • Identify professional advisors who can assist in locating alternative sources of financing and consult those advisors as appropriate. • Establish relationships with financing sources before financing is needed. • Maintain proper and current relationships to facilitate access to cash as the need arises.
3. Optimize return on temporary cash investments.	• Lack of knowledge regarding investment alternatives	• Retain financial personnel experienced in short-term investments. • Use professional investment advisors.
4. Accelerate cash collections.	• Handling cash receipts internally can delay deposit of such receipts. • Customers delay remittance. • Excessive accounts receivable collection problems	• Consider lock-box arrangements. • Factor accounts receivable. • Honor bank credit cards. • Offer discounts for timely remittance. • Establish and enforce collection policies. • Monitor accounts receivable for overdue balances; implement collection procedures on a timely basis. • Establish and enforce a credit policy that reflects an appropriate balance between risk of credit loss and sales volume.

5. Record cash receipts on accounts receivable completely and accurately.	• Cash received is diverted, lost, or otherwise not reported accurately to accounts receivable.	• Assign opening of mail to an individual with no responsibility for or access to files or documents pertaining to accounts receivable or cash accounts; compare listed receipts to credits to accounts receivable and bank deposits.
		• Consider use of lock-box or other arrangements to accelerate deposits.
		• Consider ability to have customers transfer funds electronically to the entity's bank account, and notify the entity of payment through electronic data interchange.
	• Receipts are for amounts different than invoiced amounts or are not identifiable.	• Send periodic statements to customers and investigate customer-noted differences (performance indicator).
		• Reconcile general ledger with accounts receivable subsidiary records; investigate differences.
		• Contact payor to determine reasons for payment, or payment different than amounts invoiced.
6. Manage timing of cash disbursements.	• Inaccurate, untimely, or unavailable information regarding payment due dates.	• Information system identifies all cash requirements and dates cash is needed.
		• Use accounts payable aging analysis.
	• Bills are paid before due dates.	• Delay check preparation or signature until the due date.
		• Release check at the latest possible time and at the end of a day or week, if possible.
	• Checks clear the bank quickly.	• Consider check-clearing time when selecting a bank.
7. Minimize cash disbursements.	• Information system does not identify available discounts and related required payment dates.	• Information system identifies payment dates related to available discounts.
8. Disburse cash only for authorized purchases.	• Fictitious documentation is created.	• Examine supporting documents, payments approved by individuals independent of procurement, receiving and accounts payable.
	• Reuse of supporting documents	• Cancel supporting documents to prevent resubmission for payment.

(Continued)

245

Exhibit 7.11 (*Continued*)

Objectives	Risks	Control Activities
Process Funds (cont'd)		
9. Remit disbursements to vendors and others, such as for dividends, debt service, and tax or other payments, in a timely and accurate manner.	• Inaccurate, untimely, or unavailable information regarding amounts or due dates of payments.	• Detailed comparison of actual versus budgeted disbursements • Compare payment amounts and recipients with source documents; verify accuracy of supporting documents. • Establish a "tickler file" to identify payment due dates. • Modify information systems as necessary to provide payment information.
10. Record cash disbursements completely and accurately.	• Missing documents or information	• Match disbursement records against accounts payable/open invoice files. • Prenumber and account for checks. • Reconcile bank statements to cash accounts and investigate long-outstanding checks by individuals independent of accounts payable and cash disbursement functions.
11. Safeguard cash and the related accounting records.	• Inadequate physical security over cash and documents that can be used to transfer cash	• Segregate custodial and record-keeping functions. • Reconcile bank accounts by individuals without responsibility for cash receipts, disbursements or custody. • Receive and prelist cash by individuals independent of recording cash receipts. • Restrictively endorse checks on receipt. • Deposits receipts intact daily. • Restrict access to accounts receivable files and files used in processing cash receipts. • Mail checks by individuals independent of recording accounts payable. • Authorized check signers are independent of cash receipts functions. • Physically protect mechanical check signers and signature plates. • Restrict access to accounts payable files and files used in processing cash disbursements.
Process Fixed Assets		
1. Completely and accurately record fixed asset transfers,	• Acquisition documentation may be lost or otherwise not communicated	• Prenumber individual capital expenditure authorizations and investigate missing documents.

acquisitions, dispositions, and related depreciation. to proper personnel.	• Route copy of purchase orders for capital expenditures to personnel who process fixed assets; investigate purchase orders not matched with receiving documentation after anticipated receipt date.
• Acquired assets may not be adequately described.	• Reconcile fixed asset additions with capital expenditure authorizations. • Inquire of purchasing or other personnel to clarify asset description or function. • Establish clear definitions for asset categories.
• Asset disposals or transfers may not be communicated to proper personnel.	• Dispose of or transfer fixed assets only with proper authorization, a copy of which is provided to appropriate personnel. • Prenumber fixed asset disposal and transfer authorization forms and investigate missing documents. • Count fixed assets periodically, reconcile count with fixed asset records and investigate differences.
• Incorrect depreciation lives or methods may be used.	• Establish policies regarding depreciation lives and methods, communicate them to appropriate personnel, and periodically review them to ensure continued appropriateness. • Review depreciation detail for accuracy and compliance with policies and procedures.
2. Safeguard fixed assets from loss through theft. • Inadequate physical security over fixed assets	• Restrict access to facilities during non-working hours. • Affix an identification plate and number to office furniture and fixtures, equipment, and other portable fixed assets. • Develop, implement, and communicate safeguarding policies
Analyze and Reconcile 1. Compare operating results with pre-established standards, such as budgets or prior-period results. Identify variances, trends, or unusual	
• Pre-established standards are not determined.	• Periodically establish operating standards, such as quarterly or annual budgets.

(Continued)

Exhibit 7.11 *(Continued)*

Objectives	Risks	Control Activities
Analyze and Reconcile (cont'd) changes and their causes.	• Lack of or inaccurate information needed to compare actual results with pre-established standards.	• Specify information needed to identify and explain variances, trends or unusual changes. • Design information systems to communicate necessary information to appropriate people on a timely basis.
Process Benefits and Retiree Information 1. Ensure that all eligible individuals, and only such individuals, are included in benefit programs.	• Program eligibility requirements are not clearly communicated to appropriate personnel. • Inaccurate employee information is provided to benefits personnel. • Eligible employees are improperly excluded from participation. • Nonexistent employees are entered as program participants or beneficiaries.	• Train and update appropriate personnel regarding plan eligibility requirements and amendments thereto. • Compare information to employee personnel file or otherwise verify its accuracy. • Limit access to employee database • Periodically match participant list to employee and/or retiree list and to documentation of employees' elections not to participate. • Periodically compare participant list to employee and/or retiree list. • Approval by an authorized official of all additions to participant database. • Verify existence and status of participant.
2. Accurately calculate benefits due to each participant.	• Plan benefit provisions are unclear or complex. • Errors are made in calculating benefits. • Inaccurate information	• Ensure plan documents describe benefit provisions clearly and include sample calculations. • Amend plan as necessary to clarify benefit computations. • Consult legal, actuarial or other professionals as needed to clarify benefit provisions. • Standardize forms or programs for calculating benefits. • Review benefit calculations. • Limit access to information and data used in calculating benefits.
3. Summarize and track benefit information.	• Lost or misplaced information	• Approve all changes to data bases used to calculate benefits. • Reconcile various related reports. • Use logs or other devices to ensure completeness of processing.

4. Comply with applicable laws and regulations.

- Personnel are unaware of applicable laws and regulations.

- Train human resource or other personnel on applicable laws and regulations.
- Review and approve all plan documents and policies by legal counsel experienced in employee and retiree benefit programs.

5. Generate and distribute benefits reports in an accurate and timely manner.

- Lack of adequate systems

- Ensure that report-generation systems process information accurately and satisfy reporting deadlines.

- Lack of understanding of reporting requirements

- Implement and monitor training programs.

Process Payroll

1. Pay employees in accordance with wage contracts and other established policies.

- System is not designed to reflect payment schedule included in collective bargaining agreements or individual agreements with employees.

- Implement payment schedule that reflects wage contracts and agreed-upon payment schedules.

2. Calculate and record payroll accurately and completely for all services actually performed and approved, and only for such services.

- Pay rates or deductions are not properly authorized or are inaccurate.

- Review and approve initial pay and any subsequent additions or changes.
- Periodically verify payroll database information.
- Review and approve initial deductions/benefit elections.
- Use standard forms for making changes to payroll information.
- Review and approve all nonstandard items such as sick, vacation, and bonus pay.
- Review payroll register and checks for reasonableness.
- Security controls that limit access to payroll data base

- Hours are not authorized or are inaccurate.

- Review and approve time records for unusual or nonstandard hours and for overtime.
- Use standardized policies and procedures when hiring employees.

- Time cards or other source information is submitted for nonexistent employees.

- Security procedures relating to additions and deletions of employees to or from the database

(Continued)

249

Exhibit 7.11 *(Continued)*

Objectives	Risks	Control Activities
Process Payroll (cont'd)		
	• Lack or loss of information or documents	• Maintain logs or other documentation supporting or tracking changes to payroll database.
		• Where practical, require valid identification and employee signature to receive paycheck.
		• Prohibit payment of wages in cash, except in prescribed circumstances.
		• Use direct deposit systems.
		• Verify that source documents such as time cards are received for all employees.
		• Maintain back-up records of employees' time in case source documents are lost.
		• Reconcile the employee subsidiary ledger to the general ledger control accounts; investigate any differences.
		• Compare total hours and number of employees input with the totals in the payroll register.
3. Restrict access to payroll data information to only those individuals who need such information to discharge duties.	• Unauthorized personnel may gain access to payroll information.	• Access to information stored on electronic media is restricted by frequently changed passwords.
		• Payroll-processing systems and written information are subject to physical security.
4. Provide payroll information to relevant personnel to satisfy management information needs.	• Management information needs with respect to payroll are not defined.	• Identify how payroll information can satisfy other management objectives and link information sources.
Process Product Costs		
1. Develop standard costs of producing products, including costs at each stage of the production process.	• Inadequate or inaccurate information	• Identify information necessary to develop standard product costs; ensure information systems accurately provide such information on a timely basis.
		• Periodically evaluate the production process and estimate the costs associated with each stage of the process.

2. Record actual costs incurred completely and accurately.	• Inability to identify the stage of production	• Clearly define and organize each stage of production; appropriately document such stages.
		• Establish systems to routinely identify stage of completion; periodically verify that system is functioning properly.
	• Inaccurate, untimely, or unavailable information regarding actual costs incurred	• Prenumber and account for the numerical sequence of requisitions of materials and component parts issued to and returned from production; investigate missing or duplicate (unmatched) items by people independent of the materials handling function.
		• Reconcile records of labor and overhead charges to payrolls and overhead cost incurred; investigate differences.
		• Prenumber and account for the numerical sequence of production reports or other records of finished production and transfers within work-in-process; reconcile those reports to quantities recorded; investigate missing documents and differences.
		• Review and approve monthly summarizing entries.
		• Maintain perpetual inventory records.
		• Periodically balance the raw materials, work-in-process, and finished goods records.
		• Periodically count raw materials, work-in-process, and finished goods inventories and compare with the perpetual records; investigate differences
		• Reconcile the perpetual records to the general ledger control accounts, and approve adjustments, by personnel other than those responsible for maintaining related perpetual records or for safeguarding inventories.
3. Determine variances from standard costs and their effect on inventory and cost of sales.	• Variances are computed or recorded inaccurately.	• Compute variances for each appropriate product; verify completeness by comparison to product list or other appropriate document.
		• Verify variance accuracy by recomputation or other appropriate methods.
		• Review general ledger or other records to ensure variances are recorded accurately.

Chapter 8

Reporting

Chapter Summary

Describe and explain the requirements for management's quarterly and annual reports on internal control.

Guidance for reporting significant deficiencies and material weaknesses in internal control

Reporting when internal control deficiencies have been corrected during the period

Management reporting on internal control in annual reports to shareholders

---

ANNUAL AND QUARTERLY REPORTING REQUIREMENTS

Chapter 1 summarizes the Securities and Exchange Commission (SEC) rules regarding management's internal control reporting requirements on both a quarterly and an annual basis. The chapter also summarizes the corresponding certifications regarding internal control that the entity's chief executive officer (CEO) and chief financial officer (CFO) are required to provide.

As described in Chapter 1, under the SEC rules, the company's 10K must include[1]

- *Management's annual report on internal control over financial reporting.* Provide a report on the company's internal control over financial reporting that contains:

  1. A statement of management's responsibilities for establishing and maintaining adequate internal control over financial reporting,

  2. A statement identifying the framework used by management to evaluate the effectiveness of the company's internal control over financial reporting

  3. Management's assessment of the effectiveness of the company's internal control over financial reporting as of the end of the most recent fiscal year, including a statement as to whether internal control over financial reporting is effective. This discussion must include disclosure of any material weakness in the company's internal control over financial reporting identified by management. Management is not permitted to conclude that the registrant's internal control over financial reporting is effective if there are one or more material weaknesses in the company's internal control over financial reporting.

  4. A statement that the registered public accounting firm that audited the financial statements included in the annual report has issued an attestation report on management's assessment of the registrant's internal control over financial reporting

- *Attestation report of the registered public accounting firm.* Provide the registered public accounting firm's attestation report on management's assessment of the company's internal control over financial reporting
- *Changes in internal control over financial reporting.* Disclose any change in the company's internal control over financial reporting that has materially affected, or is reasonably likely to materially affect, the company's internal control over financial reporting.

The company's annual report filed with the SEC also should include management's fourth-quarter report on the effectiveness of the entity's disclosure controls and procedures, as described in Chapter 1.

Exhibit 8.1 provides an example report that complies with the SEC reporting requirements. Note that this example includes a paragraph that describes the inherent limitations of internal control systems. This paragraph is *not* required by the SEC rules but has been included for illustrative purposes.

Key provisions of these annual reporting requirements that merit further discussion include

- *Management's statement of effectiveness.* Under guidance provided by the SEC, management must state whether internal control is functioning effectively. Negative assurance, in which management states that "nothing has come to its attention that would lead it to believe that internal control was not functioning effectively" is not acceptable.[2]

Exhibit 8.1   Example Management's Report on Internal Control over Financial Reporting

---

The management of XYZ is responsible for establishing and maintaining adequate internal control over financial reporting. This internal control system has been designed to provide reasonable assurance to the company's management and board of directors regarding the preparation and fair presentation of the company's published financial statements.

All internal control systems, no matter how well designed, have inherent limitations. Therefore, even those systems determined to be effective can provide only reasonable assurance with respect to financial statement preparation and presentation.[a]

The management of XYZ has assessed the effectiveness of the company's internal control over financial reporting as of December 31, 20XX. To make this assessment, we used the criteria for effective internal control over financial reporting described in *Internal Control—Integrated Framework*, issued by the Committee of Sponsoring Organizations of the Treadway Commission. Based on our assessment, we believe that, as of December 31, 20XX, the Company's internal control over financial reporting met those criteria.

Our independent auditors have issued an attestation report on our assessment of the company's internal control over financial reporting. You can find this report on page xx.

---

[a]This statement regarding the inherent limitation of internal control is *not* required by the SEC rules. It has been included in this example report solely for illustrative purposes.

- *Material weakness in internal control*. Management is required to disclose any material weakness in the company's internal control. Further, the existence of one or more material weaknesses precludes management from concluding that its internal control is effective.
- *"As of" reporting*. Management assesses the effectiveness of internal control *as of* the end of the fiscal year, rather than throughout the reporting period. This reporting requirement has significant implications for the reporting of material weaknesses that were identified and corrected during the period.

Material Weaknesses and Significant Deficiencies

The Nature of Internal Control Deficiencies. Deficiencies in internal control can arise in one of the following two ways:

1. *Design deficiency*. A design deficiency exists when either
   - A control necessary to achieve a control objective does not exist, or
   - A control policy or procedure exists but it is not designed in a way that will ensure that the control objective is met even if the procedure operates as designed.
2. *Operating deficiency*. An operating deficiency exists when a properly designed control either
   - Is not operating as designed, or
   - The person performing the procedure does not possess the necessary authority or qualifications to perform the control effectively.

   Internal control deficiencies adversely affect the entity's ability to

- Record
- Process
- Summarize
- Report

data consistent with management's assertions in the financial statements.

As indicated in Exhibit 8.2, internal control deficiencies range from inconsequential to material weakness. Note that the three levels of deficiency are placed in a continuum. If a deficiency is not inconsequential, then it is, at a minimum, significant.

Exhibit 8.2 Internal Control Deficiencies

At issue is where one should "draw the line," that is, at what point is a deficiency no longer inconsequential, and when does a significant deficiency become a material weakness?

The SEC has stated that the term *material weakness* has the same meaning as the definition under generally accepted auditing standards. The auditing literature defines material weakness in Statement of Accounting Standards (SAS) No. 60, *Communication of Internal Control Related Matters Noted in an Audit* (AU Section 325). The terms *reportable condition* (as used in the auditing literature) and *significant deficiency* (which the SEC uses in its rules) are synonymous.

The accepted definitions for the two key terms are as follows:[3]

1. *Significant deficiency.* An internal control deficiency in a significant control or an aggregation of such deficiencies that could result in a misstatement of the financial statements that is more than inconsequential.

2. *Material weakness.* A significant deficiency or *an aggregation of significant deficiencies* that preclude the entity's internal control from providing reasonable assurance that material misstatements in the financial statements will be prevented or detected on a timely basis by employees in the normal course of performing their assigned functions. The inability to provide such reasonable assurance results from one or more significant deficiencies in which the design or operation of one or more of the internal control components does not reduce to a relatively low level the risk that misstatements caused by errors or fraud in amounts that would be material in relation to the financial statements may occur and not be detected within a timely period by employees in the normal course of performing their assigned functions.

Note that these definitions of internal control deficiencies are stated within the typical audit constraints of reasonable assurance and financial statement materiality.

Making Judgments about the Severity of Internal Control Deficiencies.
Determining whether an internal control deficiency is more than inconsequential is, at its core, a risk assessment process in which management should consider

- *Likelihood*, that is, the chance that the deficiency could result in a financial statement misstatement. When assessing likelihood, consider
  - The susceptibility of the related assets or liability to loss or fraud
  - The subjectivity, complexity, or extent of judgment required to determine the amount involved
  - The nature of the accounts, processes or disclosures. For example, suspense accounts and related party transactions involve greater risk.
  - The relative importance of the control and whether the overall control objective is achieved by other control activities or a combination of control activities
  - If the deficiency is an operating deficiency, the frequency of the operating failure rate. For example, numerous or repeated failures in the operation of a

control would be more likely to be considered a significant deficiency than failures that are considered isolated occurrences.

- Whether the control is automated and therefore could be expected to perform consistently over time.

• *Significance*, that is, the magnitude of potential misstatements resulting from the deficiency. When assessing significance, consider

  - The nature of the account balance or total of transactions affected by the deficiency and the financial statement assertions involved

  - Whether the deficiency relates to an entity-level or activity-level control. Because entity-level controls can affect many account balances, classes of transactions, or financial statement assertions, weaknesses in entity-level controls that seem relatively insignificant by themselves could result in material financial statement misstatements.

  - The volume of activity in the account balance or class of transactions exposed to the deficiency that has occurred in the current period, or that is expected in future periods

When evaluating the significance or magnitude of a potential misstatement, keep in mind that the significance of the misstatement depends on the *potential* for misstatement, not on whether a misstatement actually has occurred.

Considering the Results of the Independent Audit. When assessing the relative significance of an entity's internal control deficiencies, it is helpful to consider the results of the entity's most recent independent audit. A material misstatement detected by the independent auditor's procedures that was not first identified by the entity itself normally is indicative of the existence of a material weakness in internal control. However, the converse is not necessarily true. The absence of a material misstatement does not, in and of itself, allow management to conclude that no material weaknesses exist in the entity's internal control.

Example Internal Control Deficiencies. Exhibit 8.3 provides examples of possible significant internal control deficiencies.[4]

Required Disclosure of Material Weaknesses. As described in Chapter 1 and summarized at the beginning of this chapter, management's annual report on internal control is required to disclose any material weakness in internal control. Except for the requirement that the entity disclose any change to internal control that has materially affected or is reasonably likely to materially affect the entity's internal control, the rules do not prescribe any format or other requirements for the disclosure. However, in practice, it is common for the disclosure to include

• The fact that management has identified a material weakness in its internal control over financial reporting

• A definition of or reference to the definition of *material weakness*

• The actions taken by management to correct the deficiency

Exhibit 8.3 Examples of Significant Deficiencies in Internal Control

Deficiencies in internal control design	• Inadequate overall internal control design • Absence of appropriate segregation of duties consistent with appropriate control objectives • Absence of appropriate reviews and approvals of transactions, accounting entries, or systems output • Inadequate procedures for appropriately assessing and applying accounting principles • Inadequate provisions for the safeguarding of assets • Absence of other controls considered appropriate for the type and level of transaction activity • Evidence that a system fails to provide complete and accurate output that is consistent with objectives and current needs because of design flaws
Failures in the operation of internal control	• Evidence of failure of identified controls in preventing or detecting misstatements of accounting information • Evidence that a system fails to provide complete and accurate output consistent with the entity's control objectives because of the misapplication of controls • Evidence of failure to safeguard assets from loss, damage, or misappropriation • Evidence of intentional override of internal control by those in authority to the detriment of the overall objectives of the system • Evidence of failure to perform tasks that are part of internal control, such as reconciliations not prepared or not timely prepared • Evidence of willful wrongdoing by employees or management • Evidence of manipulation, falsification, or alteration of accounting records or supporting documents. • Evidence of intentional misapplication of accounting principles • Evidence of misrepresentation by client personnel to the auditor • Evidence that employees or management lack the qualifications and training to fulfill their assigned functions
Others	• Absence of a sufficient level of control consciousness within the organization • Failure to follow up and correct previously identified internal control deficiencies • Evidence of significant or extensive undisclosed related-party transactions • Evidence of undue bias or lack of objectivity by those responsible for accounting decisions

Appendix 8B includes several examples of the disclosure of a material weakness. Exhibit 8.4 provides an example of how management's required report on internal control could be modified to report a material weakness.

"Drawing the Line"—Proposed PCAOB Guidance

As described in Chapter 1, at the time these materials were being finalized, the PCAOB had issued a proposed auditing standard on internal control reporting. That proposed standard would provide additional guidance on determining whether an exception noted during testing is an internal control deficiency and, if so, whether the deficiency is "significant" or rises to the level of "material weakness."

First, the proposed standard recognizes that you may identify "exceptions" in your testwork, for example a control procedure was performed improperly. The auditor's first consideration is whether the exception is an isolated incident or indicative of an internal control deficiency. In making this determination, the proposed standard states that

> When [you] identify exceptions to the company's prescribed control procedures, [you] should determine, using professional skepticism, the effect of the exception on the nature

Exhibit 8.4 Example Management's Report on Internal Control Over Financial Reporting

---

(Introductory paragraph. See Exhibit 8.1)

(Optional inherent limitations paragraph. See Exhibit 8.1)

A material weakness in internal control is a significant deficiency or an aggregation of significant deficiencies that preclude the entity's internal control from providing reasonable assurance that material misstatements in the financial statements will be prevented or detected on a timely basis by employees in the normal course of performing their assigned functions. A significant deficiency is an internal control deficiency in a significant control or an aggregation of such deficiencies that could result in a misstatement of the financial statements that is more than inconsequential.

The management of XYZ has assessed the effectiveness of the company's internal control over financial reporting as of December 31, 20XX, and this assessment identified the following material weakness in the company's internal control over financial reporting

(Describe material weakness)

To make our assessment of internal control over financial reporting, we used the criteria described in *Internal Control—Integrated Framework*, issued by the Committee of Sponsoring Organizations of the Treadway Commission. Except for the effect of the material weakness described in the preceding paragraph, we believe that, as of December 31, 20XX, the company's internal control over financial reporting met those criteria.

Our independent auditors have issued an attestation report on our assessment of the company's internal control over financial reporting. You can find this report on page xx.

---

and extent of additional testing that may be appropriate or necessary and on the operating effectiveness of the control being tested. A conclusion that an identified exception does not represent an internal control deficiency is appropriate only if evidence beyond what [you] had initially planned and beyond inquiry supports that conclusion.

If you determine that an internal control deficiency exists, your next step is to decide whether the deficiency is "significant." To make this decision, the proposed standard provides the following guidance.

When evaluating the significance of a deficiency in internal control over financial reporting, [you] also should determine the level of detail and degree of assurance that would satisfy prudent officials in the conduct of their own affairs that they have reasonable assurance that transactions are recorded as necessary to permit the preparation of financial statements in conformity with generally accepted accounting principles. If [you] determine that the deficiency would prevent prudent officials in the conduct of their own affairs from concluding that they have reasonable assurance, then [you] should consider the deficiency to be at least a significant deficiency. Having determined in this manner that a deficiency represents a significant deficiency, [you] must further evaluate the deficiency to determine whether individually, or in combination with other deficiencies, the deficiency is a material weakness.

The proposed standard goes on to state that certain deficiencies are, at a minimum, significant deficiencies in internal control. These de facto significant deficiencies are deficiencies in the following areas:

- Controls over the selection and application of accounting policies that are in conformity with generally accepted accounting principles
- Antifraud programs and controls
- Controls over nonroutine and nonsystematic transactions
- Controls over the period-end financial reporting process, including controls over procedures used to enter transaction totals into the general ledger; initiate, record, and process journal entries into the general ledger; and record recurring and nonrecurring adjustments to the financial statements

Additionally, the proposed standard states that certain circumstances should be regarded as at least a significant deficiency and a strong indicator that a material weakness exists. These circumstances are

- Restatement of previously issued financial statements to reflect the correction of a misstatement
- Identification by the auditor of a material misstatement in financial statements in the current period that was not initially identified by the company's internal control over financial reporting (This is still a strong indicator of a material weakness even if management subsequently corrects the misstatement.)
- Oversight of the company's external financial reporting and internal control over financial reporting by the company's audit committee is ineffective (Paragraphs

56 through 59 of the proposed standard present factors to evaluate when determining whether the audit committee is ineffective.)

- For larger, more complex entities, the internal audit function or the risk assessment function is ineffective.
- For complex entities in highly regulated industries, an ineffective regulatory compliance function
- Identification of fraud of any magnitude on the part of senior management
- Significant deficiencies that have been communicated to management and the audit committee remain uncorrected after some reasonable period of time.

Finally, as indicated in Chapter 5, inadequate documentation of the design of controls is an internal control deficiency that should be evaluated in the same manner as any other deficiency.

"As Of" Reporting Implications

As described in Chapter 1, the SEC rules require management to report on the effectiveness of internal control *as of* a point in time, rather than during a given period. This distinction is important for several reasons, including

- *Extent of testing.* Reporting on controls at a point in time will require testing of controls that is considerably *less* extensive than the testing required for reporting on the effectiveness of controls over a period of time. Testing strategies and the extent of tests is covered in more detail in Chapters 6 and 7.
- *Correction of deficiencies.* Point-in-time reporting is more conducive to the identification and correction of deficiencies. This is because the correction of a deficiency early in the reporting period may allow management to conclude that internal control is functioning effectively *at the end of the period.* For example, suppose the company identified a material weakness during the first quarter of its fiscal year, and it took immediate corrective action. That corrective action would require disclosure in the entity's first quarter 10Q, since it would be a change in internal control that would have a material effect on internal control. Going forward, assuming that the corrective actions were successful, the company may be able to conclude that controls are effective at subsequent reporting dates.

Correction of Deficiencies. For management to conclude that an identified control deficiency has been remediated successfully, the corrected control must be in place and operating effectively for a period of time that is sufficient to draw a reliable conclusion about its effectiveness. Determining what constitutes a "sufficient period of time" will require management to exercise its judgment. Matters to be considered when making this determination include

- *Nature of the control objective.* The nature of the control objective being addressed should be considered. For example, some control objectives are transaction oriented, narrowly focused, and have a direct effect on the financial statements. A bank reconciliation and the matching of vendor invoices to an approved vendor list are examples of controls that meet these types of objectives. Other control objectives are control environment oriented, affect the entity broadly, and have only an indirect effect on the financial statements. Management's "tone at the top" and the entity's hiring and training practices are examples of these types of controls.

  In general, because of their indirect effect on the financial statements and their ability to influence the effectiveness of other controls, corrections to environmental-oriented controls should be in place and operating effectively for a much *longer* period of time than corrections to controls that are more transactions based. That is, it will take you longer to determine whether a change in management's attitude is having its desired affect on internal control performance than it will to determine whether a new reconciliation procedure is being performed properly.

- *Nature of the correction.* Some corrections may be programmed into the entity's information-processing system. For example, to correct a control deficiency the entity may reprogram its system to generate an exception report. Assuming the entity has effective computer general controls, a computer application should perform the same task consistently for an indefinite period of time. Thus, the reprogrammed application may be operational for a relatively short period of time before you can draw a reliable conclusion about its effectiveness.

  In contrast, suppose that a *person* is required to investigate and properly resolve the items identified on an exception report. Unlike a computer application, the performance of an individual will vary. For this reason, a correction that depends on people (rather than a computer system) should be operating effectively for a relatively long period of time before a reliable conclusion is reached.

- *Frequency of the corrected control procedure.* Some control procedures are performed frequently, for example, the authentication of credit card information for all online customers who purchase goods. Other procedures are performed less frequently, for example, account reconciliations. When control procedures are performed frequently, less time is needed for you to have enough sample transactions to draw a reliable conclusion. For a credit card authorization, the control procedure may be performed thousands of times in just a few days. However, if an account reconciliation is performed only once a month, the control may need to be in place for several months before you would have enough evidence to assess its effectiveness.

Ultimately, taking steps to correct a control deficiency and then waiting a certain amount of time is not sufficient for management to conclude that the deficiency no longer exists. New controls must be tested, and the evidence from these tests must be sufficient to enable management to reach a conclusion about their effectiveness.

EXPANDED REPORTING ON MANAGEMENT'S RESPONSIBILITIES FOR INTERNAL CONTROL

Although not required, many companies include management reports relating to internal control in their annual reports to shareholders. Typically, these reports are located in close proximity to the company's financial statements. These optional reports to shareholders are *not* usually designed to comply with the SEC reporting requirements.

COSO has provided guidelines on the preparation of these optional internal control reports to shareholders. These guidelines attempt to achieve a balance between two competing needs: conformity and flexibility. On one hand, consistency in reporting between entities enhances communication between the entity and its shareholders. On the other hand, "boilerplate" language may not be meaningful—management needs the flexibility to emphasize certain matters or to communicate in a certain style.

With this in mind, COSO recommends that a report to shareholders on internal control should include

- *The category of controls being addressed.* Typically, management limits its reporting to internal control over financial reporting and will not address operational or compliance-related controls.
- *A statement about the inherent limitations of internal control systems.* It is helpful to remind readers of the limitations of internal control, although some judgment is required to determine the extent of this discussion.
- *A statement about the existence of mechanisms for system monitoring and responding to identified control deficiencies.* Shareholders desire some information that will help them assess whether and for how long an entity's internal control will continue to be effective. For this reason, statements about monitoring and the correction of identified deficiencies are useful.
- *A frame of reference for reporting*—that is, identification of the criteria against which the internal control system is measured.
- *A conclusion on the effectiveness of internal control.* A statement that management is responsible for establishing effective internal control usually is not sufficient unless management draws a conclusion as to whether those responsibilities have been met.
- The date as of which the conclusion of effectiveness is made
- The names of the report signers

Exhibit 8.5 is an illustrative report provided by COSO.

In addition to the internal control matters recommended by COSO, some companies choose to include the following in their internal control reports to shareholders:

- *Statement of responsibility.* It is relatively common for management to describe its responsibilities relating to the design and maintenance of effective internal control.

Exhibit 8.5   Example Report on Internal Control in an Annual Report to Shareholders[a, b, c]

Internal Control System

XYZ Company maintains a system of internal control over financial reporting, which is designed to provide reasonable assurance to the company's management and board of directors regarding the preparation of reliable published financial statements. The system contains self-monitoring mechanisms, and actions are taken to correct deficiencies as they are identified. Even an effective internal control system, no matter how well designed, has inherent limitations—including the possibility of the circumvention or overriding of controls—and therefore can provide only reasonable assurance with respect to financial statement preparation. Further, because of changes in conditions, internal control system effectiveness may vary over time.

The Company assessed its internal control system as of December 31, 20XX, in relation to criteria for effective internal control over financial reporting described in *Internal Control—Integrated Framework* issued by the Committee of Sponsoring Organizations of the Treadway Commission. Based on this assessment, the company believes that, as of December 31, 20XX, its system of internal control over financial reporting met those criteria.

XYZ Company

by _____
   Signature (CEO)

by _____
   Signature (CFO/Chief Accounting Officer)

Date

---

[a]*Internal Control—Integrated Framework*, by the Committee of Sponsoring Organizations of the Treadway Commission, published by the AICPA, 1994, p. 139.
[b]The COSO report notes that "the wording of this illustrative report is provided as a guide, which may be particularly useful to managements with little or no experience with reporting on internal control. The illustrative report's wording is not intended as an absolute standard—managements may modify or expand on its contents."
[c]This example report is an optional report on internal control that the company may include in its annual report to shareholders. It is not intended to comply with the SEC's required internal control report.

- *Audit committee*. Statements about the audit committee usually include a description of the committee's role and its duties.
- *Communication of written policies*. The company may wish to describe its processes for documenting its internal control policies and procedures, and communicating these policies to employees.
- *Organizational relationships*. These comments focus on the delegation of responsibility and establishment of appropriate reporting relationships within the system of internal control.

- *Personnel.* In some circumstances, the company may choose to highlight its personnel policies, such as hiring, retention, training, or compensation, and how these policies contribute to effective internal control.
- *Code of conduct.* Discussions of the entity's code of conduct may include one or more of the following:
  - A brief description of major elements of the code
  - How the code is communicated
  - How compliance with the code is monitored and enforced

- *Internal audit.* Usually, these statements are limited to a simple description of the role that internal audit plays in the overall system of internal control.

Appendix 8C contains several examples of these optional reports on internal control included in the company's annual report to shareholders.

Responsibility for Financial Reporting

Management may wish to report on matters other than internal control to its shareholders. These matters may include

- Management's responsibility for preparing the financial statements
- The use of estimates and judgments in the preparation of the financial statements
- The responsibility of the independent auditors

When the company elects to include this information in its report, it should do so in a way that is separate from the discussion and conclusions on internal control. It is not necessary for the company to have two reports—rather, it can combine a report on financial reporting with a discussion of internal control, as long as the combined report is clear. For example, this might be achieved by separate headings that identify the two elements of the combined report.

Exhibit 8.6 is an illustrative report of management's responsibility for financial reporting.

COORDINATING WITH THE INDEPENDENT AUDITORS AND LEGAL COUNSEL

Independent Auditors

You should consult with your independent auditors during the drafting of your report(s) on internal control over financial reporting. During this time you should reach consensus on the following matters:

Exhibit 8.6 Example Report on Management's Responsibility for Financial Reporting in an Annual Report to Shareholders[a]

Financial Statements

XYZ Company is responsible for the preparation, integrity and fair presentation of its published financial statements. The financial statements, presented on pages xx to yy, have been prepared in accordance with generally accepted accounting principles and, as such, include amounts based on judgments and estimates made by management. The company also prepared the other information included in the annual report and is responsible for its accuracy and consistency with the financial statements.

The financial statements have been audited by the independent accounting firm, ABC & Co., which was given unrestricted access to all financial records and related data, including minutes of all meetings of stockholders, the board of directors and committees of the board. The company believes that all representations made to the independent auditors during their audit were valid and appropriate. ABC & Co.'s audit report is presented on page xx.

[a]*Internal Control—Integrated Framework*, p. 140.

- Contents of the report(s), including
  - Completeness and whether the contents satisfy the SEC reporting requirements
  - Possible deletion of material that is not required
- Report language
- Definition of "significant deficiency" and "material weakness" provided by the most current auditing standards.
- Disclosure of material weaknesses that exist at the reporting date
- The nonreporting of material weaknesses that existed and were reported at an interim period but have subsequently been remediated

Legal Counsel

In addition to the independent auditors, the entity's SEC counsel also should be involved in the drafting process to ensure that the resulting report(s) meet the reporting requirements without exposing the entity or the individuals signing the reports to unnecessary legal risk.

APPENDIX 8A

Action Plan:
Reporting

The following action plan is intended to help you implement the suggestions contained in this chapter for reporting on internal control effectiveness.

1. Identification of Report(s)

Identify all reports that management will prepare on internal control. For example

- Management's Report on Internal Control Over Financial Reporting (**required by SEC Regulation S-K, Item 308**).
- Report to Shareholders on Internal Control (**optional**)
- Report to Shareholders on Responsibility for Financial Reporting (**optional**)

2. Prepare Required Report

Prepare Management's Report on Internal Control Over Financial Reporting, which is required by the SEC.

- Determine the contents of the report, including
  - Required elements:
    - Statement of management's responsibility for establishing and maintaining adequate internal control
    - Statement identifying the framework used to evaluate internal control
    - Management's assessment of the effectiveness of internal control as of the end of the fiscal year
    - Statement that the independent auditors have issued an attestation report on management's assessment of internal control
  - Optional elements:
    - Statement of the inherent limitations of internal control
    - Other, as necessary
- Draft report after considering
  - SEC rules
  - Guidance provided in the COSO Report
  - Feedback from independent auditors
  - Feedback from SEC counsel
  - Published reports from other entities

3. Prepare Optional Report(s)

Prepare other reports on internal control.

- Determine the contents of the report, including
  - COSO-recommended elements:
    - Category of controls being addressed
    - Statement of inherent limitations of internal control

- ○ Statement about the existence of mechanisms for system monitoring and responding to identified control deficiencies
- ○ Identification of the criteria against which internal control is measured
- ○ Date as of which the conclusion of effectiveness is made
- ○ Names of the report signers
- – Other possible elements:
  - ○ Statement of management's responsibilities relating to internal control
  - ○ Statements about the audit committee's role and its duties
  - ○ Description of the documentation of internal control policies and procedures
  - ○ Comments on the delegation of responsibility and reporting relationships within the system of internal control
  - ○ Description of personnel policies relevant to internal control
  - ○ Description of the entity's code of conduct
  - ○ Statements about internal audit's role and its duties
- • Draft report after considering
  - – The entity's previously published reports on internal control, if any
  - – Guidance provided in the COSO Report
  - – Feedback from independent auditors
  - – Feedback from SEC counsel
  - – Published reports from other entities

APPENDIX 8B

Example Disclosures of a Material Weakness

THE SOUTH FINANCIAL GROUP
ANNUAL 10-K
MARCH 20, 2003

During the past year, TSFG noted one matter involving internal controls that is considered to be a material weakness under standards established by American Institute of Certified Public Accountants (AICPA). Accrued interest payable related to repurchase agreements was not being reconciled to the correct investment sub-ledger system report, which resulted in an overstatement of interest expense for the nine months ended September 30, 2002, of $2.4 million. TSFG corrected the over-accrual of interest expense in the fourth quarter 2002 and restated the prior three quarters of 2002. TSFG has reviewed its procedures in this area and is now using the correct system reports to reconcile the accrued interest. In addition, TSFG has implemented procedures to verify the integrity of system data when upgrades and other changes are made to the investment subledger system.

CUTTER & BUCK
QUARTERLY 10-Q
JULY 3, 2003

The following item was noted as a Risk Factor in Item 2 of Management's Discussion and Analysis (MD&A):

Our auditors have indicated that they believe there was a material weakness in our internal controls and procedures. Following our decision to restate our financial results, our independent auditors issued a letter to us indicating that they believed there was a material weakness, as defined in authoritative auditing literature, in our internal accounting controls. The material weakness related to lack of compliance with or circumvention of our procedures and controls by employees and management at various levels. In an effort to address these concerns, we brought in new managers, including a new Chief Financial Officer and have begun educating both employees and management about complying with procedures and controls and setting the "tone at the top" to mitigate the risk that the events underlying the financial restatement will recur. There can be no assurance, however, that these efforts will be adequate to prevent future occurrences of the type giving rise to the restatement. If we fail to adequately address concerns regarding our internal controls and procedures, our business may be materially harmed.

Subsequent to this disclosure, the entity included an expanded discussion of the matter in Item 4 of its MD&A. Included in that discussion was the following:

We operated without a CFO from August 8, 2002, to November 15, 2002. During that time, our current CEO served as our principal accounting officer in addition to acting in her official capacity as CEO. Our current CEO was appointed in late April 2002. Throughout the majority of her tenure, we have been undertaking the restructuring of our operations and the restatement of certain of our historical financial results, and responding to the resulting shareholder lawsuits, SEC investigation, NASDAQ investigation, and NASDAQ delisting proceedings.

Our current CFO was appointed to that position on November 15, 2002, and has had only a short time to affect our current controls and procedures. While he has assisted in our most recent evaluation efforts, his evaluation of our controls and procedures has relied heavily on the reports of others within the Company.

As stated above, management, including the CEO and CFO, evaluated the effectiveness of the registrant's Disclosure Controls as of the Evaluation Date. That evaluation included inquiring of senior managers whether the quarterly reports are correct and complete. It also included an independent accounting firm's performing their initial review of our internal controls. This review was based on employees' reports of their processes. The review has indicated some areas for improvement, and we are planning follow-up activities as well as continuing the accounting firm's review.

In previous quarters, our evaluation emphasized our investigation into accounting irregularities and errors leading to the restatement of certain of our historical financial statements. With the assistance of our legal advisors, special legal counsel, and the accountants for the special legal counsel, we conducted an investigation for any errors in our financial statements, which would in turn lead to identifying data errors, control problems, or acts of fraud and to confirming that appropriate corrective action, including process improvements, was being undertaken. Our independent auditors also performed numerous tests to satisfy themselves on the same issues.

Conclusions. As reported in Note 1 to our financial statements, we recently restated our financial results for the fiscal years ended April 30, 2000 and 2001, and for the quarters ended July 31, 2001, October 31, 2001, and January 31, 2002, as a result of accounting irregularities stemming from a failure of our internal controls and procedures. During the course of our restatement, our independent auditors indicated to us that they believe there was a material weakness in our Internal Controls, as evidenced by the ability of our former management to override our Internal Controls.

Even before this communication by our independent auditors, we started to institute corrective measures to ensure that all of our managers and employees follow our policies and procedures. These measures included bringing in new managers, implementing new procedures for transaction reporting, establishing a confidential reporting procedure by which employees can report concerns directly to the CEO or the audit committee, and holding management and employee meetings at which expectations of integrity were explicitly discussed.

After the extensive investigative work of our staff, our auditors, our counsel, independent counsel, and the independent counsel's accountants, as of the Evaluation Date we had not found irregularities other than those previously disclosed. This lack of additional indications of irregularities is a principal factor in our belief that for the quarter and up to the Evaluation Date, our Internal Controls are adequate to permit the preparation of our financial statements in conformity with generally accepted accounting principles. Based on the same factors, the CEO and CFO believe that our Disclosure Controls are effective to ensure that material information is made known to management, including the CEO and CFO, particularly during the period in which this quarterly report is being prepared. However, we see areas where additional controls would provide welcome additional assurance. We intend to continue to assess our controls and to improve them. We do not yet have formal written controls and procedures in place for all of our internal operations. We engaged a firm of accountants to assist us in the documentation of our controls and procedures. This work is the first phase of establishing our internal audit function. Our intent is that the Disclosure Controls and Internal Controls will be maintained as dynamic systems that change and improve as conditions and resources warrant. We will periodically reevaluate our controls so that our conclusions concerning controls' effectiveness can be reported in our Quarterly reports on Form 10Q and Annual Report on Form 10K.

CUMMINS INC.
ANNUAL FORM 10K
AUGUST 4, 2003

We maintain a system of internal controls and procedures and disclosure controls and procedures designed to provide reasonable assurance as to the reliability of our Consolidated Financial Statements and other disclosures included in this report. Our Board of Directors, operating through its Audit Committee, which is composed entirely of independent outside directors, provides oversight to our financial reporting process.

During the course of their audit of our Consolidated Financial Statements for the year ended December 31, 2002, our independent auditors, PricewaterhouseCoopers LLP (PwC) advised management and the Audit Committee of the Board of Directors that they had identified certain deficiencies in internal control. The deficiencies are considered to be a material weakness as defined under standards established by the American Institute of Certified Public Accountants. The weakness relates to the failure of the Company's control processes to identify material accounts payable reconciliation issues at two manufacturing locations.

In response to these issues, senior management and the Audit Committee directed the Company to dedicate resources and take additional steps to strengthen its control processes and procedures to ensure that these internal control deficiencies do not result in a material misstatement of our Consolidated Financial Statements. Specifically, we have implemented the following corrective actions as well as additional procedures:

- Instituted standard policies, procedures, and controls regarding the completion of balance sheet reconciliations and timely resolution of reconciliation discrepancies on a global basis
- Expanded and enhanced our review and certification process for our annual and quarterly reports that are filed with the SEC
- Implemented additional controls and procedures to ensure global compliance with U.S. GAAP
- Instituted post-implementation reviews on all new systems implementations
- Improved the capability of our global finance organization, including additional skills training and providing additional resources in certain areas.

We will continue to evaluate the effectiveness of our internal controls and procedures on an ongoing basis and implement actions to enhance our resources and training in the area of financial reporting and disclosure responsibilities and to review such actions with the Audit Committee and PwC. We have discussed our corrective actions and plans with the Audit Committee and PwC and as of the date of this report, we believe the actions outlined have corrected the deficiencies in internal controls that are considered to be a material weakness. PwC is unable to assess the effectiveness of our actions until they have completed their audit for the fiscal year ended December 31, 2003.

NEOFORMA, INC.
QUARTERLY 10Q
DECEMBER 31, 2002

Note that this disclosure was made in the company's December 31, 2002 10Q. Subsequent to this filing, based on the corrective action taken by management as described in the disclosure, management concluded that the material weakness no longer existed, and later filings made no mention of it.

(a) Evaluation of disclosure controls and procedures. Our senior management team, led by our chief executive officer and chief financial officer, after evaluating the effectiveness of our disclosure controls and procedures (as defined in Exchange Act Rules 13a-14(c) and 15d-14(c)) within 90 days of the filing date of this report, has concluded that there were deficiencies in the design and operation of our internal controls which adversely affected our ability to record, process, summarize, and report financial data. One such deficiency is considered to be a material weakness under standards as established by the American Institute of Certified Public Accountants. The material weakness was related to our inability to review for impairment of long-lived assets whenever events or changes in circumstances indicate that the carrying amount of an asset may not be recoverable or that such an asset may be obsolete.

(b) Changes in Internal Controls. As a result of the conclusions discussed above, under the direction of the Audit Committee and the Board of Directors, we have taken corrective action and made certain changes to strengthen our internal controls and procedures to ensure that information required to be disclosed in the reports that we file or submit under the Securities Exchange Act of 1934 is recorded, processed, summarized and accurately reported, within the time periods specified in the SEC's rules and forms. Specifically, we have expanded the scope of periodic discussions between our finance department and our other operational departments, and expanded our formal reporting procedures, to ensure that all long-lived assets are periodically reviewed for obsolescence.

Additionally, to improve the overall effectiveness of our disclosure controls and procedures, we have (i) established a Disclosure Committee, constituted with finance, investor relations, operational and legal personnel, with a mandate to assist our chief executive officer and chief financial officer in overseeing the accuracy and timeliness of our disclosure controls and procedures; (ii) established a policy of financial and operational certifications for key company contributors, finance team members, human resources team members, and sales employees that will assist senior management; and (iii) formalized a corporate compliance policy that is expected to be distributed within a short period, and pursuant to which a series of educational seminars will also be held for all employees, describing the legal and ethical standards we expect all our employees to uphold.

APPENDIX 8C

Example Reports on Management's Responsibilities
for Reporting and Internal Control

GREAT WEST LIFE ASSURANCE COMPANY
ANNUAL FORM 40F
JULY 2, 2003

Management's Responsibility

The consolidated financial statements are the responsibility of management and are prepared in accordance with generally accepted accounting principles. The financial information contained elsewhere in the annual report is consistent with that in the consolidated financial statements. The financial statements necessarily include amounts that are based on management's best estimate due to dependency on subsequent events. These estimates are based on careful judgments and have been properly reflected in the financial statements. In the opinion of management, the accounting practices utilized are appropriate in the circumstances and the financial statements fairly reflect the financial position and results of operations of the Company within reasonable limits of materiality.

In carrying out its responsibilities, management maintains appropriate systems of internal and administrative controls designed to provide reasonable assurance that the financial information produced is relevant and reliable.

The consolidated financial statements were approved by the Board of Directors, which has overall responsibility for their contents. The Board of Directors is assisted with this responsibility by its Audit Committee, which consists entirely of Directors not involved in the daily operations of the Company. The function of the Audit Committee is to

- Review the quarterly and annual financial statements and recommend them for approval to the Board of Directors.
- Review the systems of internal control and security.
- Recommend the appointment of the external auditors and their fee arrangements to the Board of Directors.
- Review other audit, accounting, financial and security matters as required.

In carrying out the above responsibilities, this Committee meets regularly with management, and with both the Company's external and internal auditors to approve the scope and timing of their respective audits, to review their findings and to satisfy itself that their responsibilities have been properly discharged. The Committee is readily accessible to the external and internal auditors.

The Board of Directors of The Great West Life Assurance Company, pursuant to Section 165(2)(i) of the Insurance Companies Act (Canada), appoints the Actuary who is:

- Responsible for ensuring that the assumptions and methods used in the valuation of policy liabilities are in accordance with accepted actuarial practice, applicable legislation, and associated regulations or directives
- Required to provide an opinion regarding the appropriateness of the policy liabilities at the balance sheet date to meet all policyholder obligations of the Company. Examination of supporting data for accuracy and completeness, and analysis of Company assets for their ability to support the amount of policy liabilities, are important elements of the work required to form this opinion.
- Required each year to analyze the financial condition of the Company and prepare a report for the Board of Directors. The analysis tests the capital adequacy of the Company until December 31, 2003, under adverse economic and business conditions.

Deloitte & Touche LLP Chartered Accountants, as the Company's appointed external auditors, have audited the consolidated financial statements. The Auditors' Report to the Shareholders is presented following the financial statements. Their opinion is based upon an examination conducted in accordance with generally accepted auditing standards, performing such tests and other procedures as they consider necessary in order to obtain reasonable assurance that the consolidated financial statements are free of material misstatement and present fairly the financial position and results of operations of the Company in accordance with generally accepted accounting principles.

SYMONS INTERNATIONAL
ANNUAL 10-K
JUNE 3, 2003

Management's Responsibility

Management recognizes its responsibility for conducting the Company's affairs in the best interests of all its shareholders. The consolidated financial statements and related information in this Annual Report are the responsibility of management. The consolidated financial statements have been prepared in accordance with generally accepted accounting principles, which involve the use of judgment and estimates in applying the accounting principles selected. Other financial information in this Annual Report is consistent with that in the consolidated financial statements.

The Company maintains a system of internal controls, which is designed to provide reasonable assurance that accounting records are reliable and to safeguard the Company's assets. The independent accounting firm of BDO Seidman, LLP has audited and reported on the Company's consolidated financial statements for 2002, 2001, and 2000. Their opinion is based upon audits conducted by them in accordance with generally accepted auditing standards to obtain assurance that the consolidated financial statements are free of material misstatements.

The Board of Directors, two members of which include outside directors, meets with the independent external auditors and management representatives to review the internal accounting controls, the consolidated financial statements and other financial reporting matters. In addition to having unrestricted access to the books and records of the Company, the independent external auditors also have unrestricted access to the Board of Directors.

KIMBERLY-CLARK ANNUAL REPORT FEBRUARY 18, 2003

The management of Kimberly-Clark Corporation is responsible for conducting all aspects of the business, including the preparation of the consolidated financial statements in this annual report. The consolidated financial statements have been prepared using generally accepted accounting principles considered appropriate in the circumstances to present fairly the Corporation's consolidated financial position, results of operations and cash flows on a consistent basis. Management also has prepared the other information in this annual report and is responsible for its accuracy and consistency with the consolidated financial statements.

As can be expected in a complex and dynamic business environment, some financial statement amounts are based on management's estimates and judgments. Even though estimates and judgments are used, measures have been taken to provide reasonable assurance of the integrity and reliability of the financial information contained in this annual report. These measures include an effective control-oriented environment in which the internal audit function plays an important role, an Audit Committee of the board of directors that oversees the financial reporting process, and independent audits.

One characteristic of a control-oriented environment is a system of internal control over financial reporting and over safeguarding of assets against unauthorized acquisition, use or disposition, designed to provide reasonable assurance to management and the board of directors regarding preparation of reliable published financial statements and such asset safeguarding. The system is supported with written policies and procedures, contains self-monitoring mechanisms and is audited by the internal audit function. Appropriate actions are taken by management to correct deficiencies as they are identified. All internal control systems have inherent limitations, including the possibility of circumvention and overriding of controls, and, therefore, can provide only reasonable assurance as to financial statement preparation and such asset safeguarding.

The Corporation also has adopted a code of conduct that, among other things, contains policies for conducting business affairs in a lawful and ethical manner everyplace in which it does business, for avoiding potential conflicts of interest and for preserving confidentiality of information and business ideas. Internal controls have been implemented to provide reasonable assurance that the code of conduct is followed.

The consolidated financial statements have been audited by the independent accounting firm, Deloitte & Touche LLP. During their audits, independent auditors were given unrestricted access to all financial records and related data, including minutes of all meetings of stockholders and the board of directors and all committees of the board. Management believes that all representations made to the independent auditors during their audits were valid and appropriate.

During the audits conducted by both the independent auditors and the internal audit function, management received recommendations to strengthen or modify internal controls in response to developments and changes. Management has adopted, or is in the process of adopting, all recommendations that are cost effective.

The Corporation has assessed its internal control system as of December 31, 2002, in relation to criteria for effective internal control over financial reporting described in "Internal Control—Integrated Framework" issued by the Committee of Sponsoring Organizations of the Treadway Commission.

Based on this assessment, management believes that, as of December 31, 2002, its system of internal control over the preparation of its published interim and annual consolidated financial statements and over safeguarding of assets against unauthorized acquisition, use, or disposition met those criteria.

AMERICAN GENERAL FINANCE INC.
QUARTERLY 10Q
JULY 30, 2003

Report Of Management's Responsibility

The Company's management is responsible for the integrity and fair presentation of our condensed consolidated financial statements and all other financial information presented in this report. We prepared our condensed consolidated financial statements using accounting principles generally accepted in the United States (GAAP). We made estimates and assumptions that affect amounts recorded in the financial statements and disclosures of contingent assets and liabilities.

The Company's management is responsible for establishing and maintaining an internal control structure and procedures for financial reporting. These systems are designed to provide reasonable assurance that assets are safeguarded from loss or unauthorized use, that transactions are recorded according to GAAP under management's direction, and that financial records are reliable to prepare financial statements. We support the internal control structure with careful selection, training and development of qualified personnel. The Company's employees are subject to AIG's Code of Conduct designed to assure that all employees perform their duties with honesty and integrity. We do not allow loans to executive officers. The systems include a documented organizational structure and policies and procedures that we communicate throughout the Company. Our internal auditors report directly to AIG to strengthen independence. They continually monitor the operation of our internal controls and report their findings to the Company's management and AIG's internal audit department. We take prompt action to correct control deficiencies and address opportunities for improving the system. The Company's management assesses the adequacy of our internal control structure quarterly. Based on these assessments, management has concluded that the internal control structure and the procedures for financial reporting have functioned effectively and that the condensed consolidated financial statements fairly present our consolidated financial position and the results of our operations for the periods presented.

PEPSICO, INC.

Management's Responsibility for Financial Statements

To Our Shareholders:

Management is responsible for the reliability of the consolidated financial statements and related notes. The financial statements were prepared in conformity with generally accepted accounting principles and include amounts based upon our estimates and assumptions, as required. The financial statements have been audited by our independent auditors, KPMG LLP, who were given free access to all financial records and related data, including minutes of the meetings of the Board of Directors and Committees of the Board. We believe that our representations to the independent auditors are valid and appropriate.

Management maintains a system of internal controls designed to provide reasonable assurance as to the reliability of the financial statements, as well as to safeguard assets from unauthorized use or disposition. The system is supported by formal policies and procedures, including an active Code of Conduct program intended to ensure employees adhere to the highest standards of personal and professional integrity. Our internal audit function monitors and reports on the adequacy of and compliance with the internal control system, and appropriate actions are taken to address significant control deficiencies and other opportunities for improving the system as they are identified. The Audit Committee of the Board of Directors consists solely of directors who are not salaried employees and who are, in the opinion of the Board of Directors, free from any relationship that would interfere with the exercise of independent judgment as a committee member.

The Committee meets during the year with representatives of management, including internal auditors and the independent auditors to review our financial reporting process and our controls to safeguard assets. Both our independent auditors and internal auditors have free access to the Audit Committee.

Although no cost-effective internal control system will preclude all errors and irregularities, we believe our controls as of December 28, 2002, provide reasonable assurance that the financial statements are reliable and that our assets are reasonably safeguarded.

Notes

1. See Regulation S-K, Item 308 (17 CFR §229.308).
2. See footnote 62 to the SEC's final rule "Management's Reports on Internal Control Over Financial Reporting and Certification of Disclosure in Exchange Act Periodic Reports (release numbers 33-8238 and 34-47986).
3. As described in Chapter 1, at the time these materials were being finalized, the PCAOB had issued a proposed auditing standard on internal control reporting. That proposed standard would supercede SAS No. 60 and change the definitions of "significant deficiency" and "material weakness" listed here. The proposed standard would change these definitions to the following:

    A *significant deficiency* is an internal control deficiency that adversely affects the company's ability to initiate, record, process, or report external financial data reliably in accordance with generally accepted accounting principles. A significant deficiency could be a single deficiency, or a combination of deficiencies, that results in more than a remote likelihood that a misstatement of the annual or interim financial statements that is more than inconsequential in amount will not be prevented or detected.

    A *material weakness* is a significant deficiency that, by itself, or in combination with other significant deficiencies, results in more than a remote likelihood that a material misstatement of the annual or interim financial statements will not be prevented or detected.

    At the time these materials were prepared, it was uncertain whether the final auditing standard would retain the definitions presented here or change them as indicated. When planning and performing your project to assess and report on internal control, you should review the final auditing standard and consult with the entity's external auditors to determine the final definition of these terms.
4. These example deficiencies are provided in the auditing literature. See *AICPA Professional Standards*, AU Sec 325.21.

Index